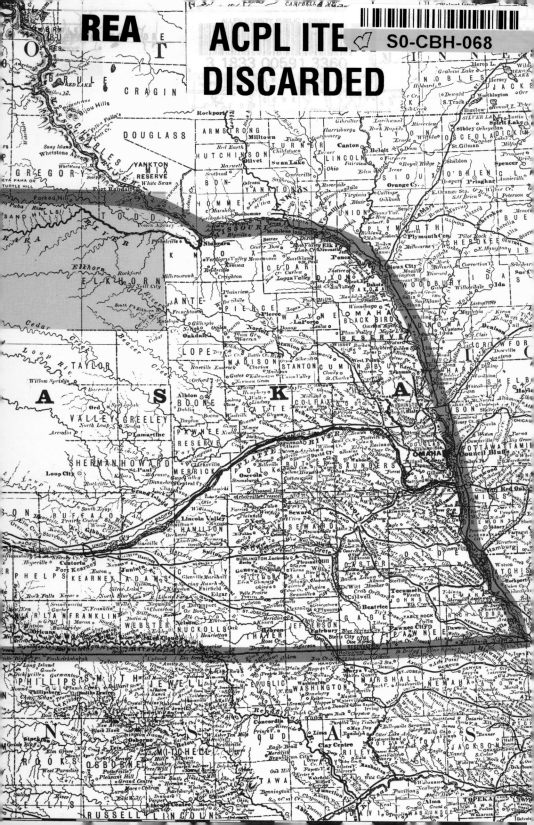

4-1874

On January 13, 1877, a freighting out-fit worker killed a soldier in a Sidney, Nebraska dancehall brawl. The civilian was James Riley, alias Doc Middleton. That is a fact. Middleton escaped the Sidney lawmen and quickly became the most colorful outlaw in Nebraska, with a Robin Hood reputation; part of the state was even called "Doc Middleton country." That is a fact. Other facts about Middleton have been hard to come by.

He was probably born in February 1851, in Bastrop County, Texas; maybe legitimate, maybe illegitimate. He definitely died in December 1913, in Douglas, Wyoming. During the intervening sixty-two years, Middleton was wanted for murder, chased for horse thefts, loved by the people, betrayed, tracked by detectives, in and out of prison, on both sides of the law, a respectable businessman, and married three times. As a wanted man, Middleton concealed his past at every turn, burned telltale letters, threw out red herring tales, and lived under a dozen aliases. Writers have listed his birthplace in six different states.

After fifteen years of stubborn research, Harold Hutton has brought to life the real Doc Middleton: his Texas origins, his cattle driving days, his horse thief rule along the Niobrara, his family life, his ride in the great 900-mile Chadron-Chicago horse race of 1893, and scores of other experiences. Even the facts make Middleton a legendary figure; Hutton has captured the elusive Doc in a fascinating but factual portrait of genuine breadth and depth. Not only does Hutton set his definitive biography against a social history of the times, but he also draws upon sources—for example, a long interview by Hutton with Middleton's elderly brother-in-law—which give a fruitful personal flavor to the work.

DOC MIDDLETON

Life and Legends
of the Notorious Plains Outlaw

HAROLD HUTTON

SAGE BOOKS

THE SWALLOW PRESS INC.
CHICAGO

First Edition
  First Printing

Sage Books are published by
The Swallow Press Incorporated
1139 South Wabash Avenue
Chicago, Illinois 60605

ISBN 0-8040-0532-X
Library of Congress Catalog Card Number 67-14260

There were only a few of us then to the north of the North Platte River, all cattle ranchmen, and no nearer settlement than Cheyenne, our supply town, two hundred miles to the southwest. For three years we had no county organisation. Every man was a law unto himself. In the extreme northwest corner of Nebraska we were nominally attached for all legal and taxable purposes to the next organised county on the east, Holt, whose county seat, O'Neil, lay nearly three hundred miles away. But, in merry frontier practice, Indians and road agents were so industrious that for the first three years of our occupation no tax assessor or other county or state official ever appeared as a reminder that, technically, we dwelt within the pale of the law. Such a state of society naturally appealed to and attracted predatory reds and whites. Thus the one thing perhaps a trifle more insecure than human life was property.

Edgar Beecher Bronson

There are about fifty men engaged in this nefarious business of horse and cattle stealing, who have headquarters on Turtle Creek [the Keya Paha]. They are freebooters—bandits, like those of Italy and Spain. No United States marshal dares to penetrate that nest, although they can have, if they wish, the whole United States army to back them.

Adoniram J. Leach

A great many efforts have been made to capture Doc Middleton, but as yet he is still at large. He has had many escapes and adventures and is regarded as the luckiest outlaw who ever infested the western frontier.

Cheyenne Daily Leader, April 8, 1879

Contents

Illustrations

Maps

1

Up to Nebraska

One of the few early references to Doc Middleton pegs him as a hand on a cattle drive. Captain James H. Cook, author of *Fifty Years on the Old Frontier,* recalled:

In the year 1876, I helped drive a herd of Texas steers, numbering about twenty-five hundred, from a point on the Nueces River, Texas, a short distance above the town of Corpus Christi, to what was then known as the Whetstone Bottom on the Missouri River, Dakota. These cattle had been purchased by men who had contracted with the United States Interior Department to supply a number of Indian Agencies with beef. The herd, being all strong cattle, made good time and led the drive made that season from southern Texas. It was the first great herd of Texas cattle to be driven through western Nebraska into Dakota.

Our experience in getting as far as the North Platte River in western Nebraska was that common to those who drove the trail in those days — high water, stormy weather, stampedes of both cattle and saddle horses, hunger at times, also great thirst, as well as a few other discomforts, all of which aided the cowboy in rounding out his full measure of whichever he might choose to call it, misery or joy. . . .

Among the men who in the days of which I write participated in the gay life of Ogalalla, were some who became notorious characters of the West. One of these men went by the name of Doc Middleton on the ranges of the North. In Texas he was called by another name. . . . It was in the spring and summer of the year of 1876 that he and his brother, or half-brother, worked with the same trail herd that I did, from Texas as far north as the Arkansas River. At that point he left us, but his brother and I, who became friends, stayed with the herd until delivered to Mr. Bosler, who had contracts with the U.S. Government to supply beef to some of the Indian Agencies.

During the two months in which I saw Doc Middleton quite frequently when bringing cattle up the trail, I failed to see that he was what I called a first class cow hand, that is, one whose first thought was the safety of a cow or herd, and last, the comfort and safety of himself. His brother Joe was the opposite; no nights were too dark, or no rivers too wide for him to tackle, when the safety of a cow or herd were at stake. I met Doc Middleton on numerous occasions after the time when I worked with him on the trail. He preferred gambling and other forms of recreation to trail driving or ranch work. He did work for the Powers outfit near the place now called Bridgeport on the North Platte River for a time.[1]

Then in the fall of 1876 Doc signed on with a freighting outfit. The Black Hills gold rush was booming and business was brisk getting supplies into the new settlements. In 1876, for example, there were 25,000 people in Deadwood Gulch. Sidney, a transshipping spot for the Black Hills, now becomes a focal point in the Doc Middleton saga. Let us allow S. D. Butcher to give us the account of that fateful January 13th night in 1877. But first a brief story behind the story. Although the Sidney fracas quickly became well-known Nebraska lore—it was talked about and

written about extensively—when Butcher was compiling his
Pioneer History of Custer County, he wanted a first-hand telling
from Doc himself. Butcher visited Doc and succeeded in engaging
him in a rather lengthy conversation. After a time Middleton
became suspicious, so it is said, drew his six-shooter, jabbed it
into Butcher's ribs, and exclaimed: "If you print a word of this
I'll be down and blow your goddamn head off!"[2] Butcher printed
it all right, and in such a thinly disguised fashion it is surprising
he kept his head. For "Dick Milton" read "Doc Middleton":

> In 1876, during the Black Hills excitement, he worked for
> a big freighting outfit, Pratt & Ferris. He was night herder.
> It was his duty to take the mules or oxen belonging to the
> outfit at night to some convenient feeding ground near the
> trail, herd them during the night and have them ready for
> a start in the morning. He slept in the wagons during the day
> as they traveled along.
>
> Roving bands of Indians infested the plains at this early
> day and they resented the encroachment of the white man,
> following wagon trains and watching for a chance to pillage
> and murder. This made the duty of night herder extremely
> dangerous, and it took a man of iron nerve to serve in that
> capacity. The wages were high. Milton performed his work
> faithfully and to the entire satisfaction of his employers.
> It is on one of the return trips of this freighting outfit, at
> Sidney, Nebraska, that the career of this man, as an outlaw,
> begins. [Butcher did not know of Doc Middleton's prior
> record.] And, as far as we know, what transpired at this
> time and place laid the foundation for his many wild and
> daring deeds of outlawry.
>
> At that time Sidney was an important station on the
> overland trail. It was an outfitting station for Black Hills
> freighters, a favorite resort for gamblers, desperadoes and
> the shifting and heterogeneous population of the border.
> It was also a military post. Among the many saloons and
> gambling houses that ran wide open in this lively frontier
> city, one of the most popular was Joe Lane's dance hall,

known in the early days as the Saratoga house.

On the night upon which the Pratt & Ferris freighting outfit struck the town, as mentioned above, this resort was filled to overflowing with a mixed crowd of freighters, mule skinners and others who had just come in for loads of freight for the Black Hills, watching for opportunities to flirt with the feminine portion of the crowd. This diversion was a great change from the monotony of their lives, traveling for days and weeks at a snail's pace over the long, dusty trail, sleeping in wagons at night with a Winchester for a pillow and expecting to be awakened at any moment by the blood-curdling war whoop of a band of savages.

On this occasion they were determined to throw care to the winds for one night and have a good time. The place was full of gamblers, cowboys and bad men galore, seemingly from all parts of the earth. Some were gathered in groups in front of the bar drinking, others were singing snatches of ribald songs, while still others were watching the dancers who were whirling around in the giddy waltz. It was soldiers' night, and no one was allowed to participate in the dance unless he wore the uniform of blue. The hours glided by and the crowd became more mellow and the dance wilder. White-aproned waiters were kept busy rushing to and fro with drinks that were called for with increasing frequency by soldiers who were anxious to show their gallantry to their fair companions, even to the extent of blowing in their entire month's pay in a single night. The crowd around the bar grew more boisterous as the hours passed by, and drunken men wrangled and boasted of deeds that would bring the blush of shame to even their cheeks in their soberer moments.

Milton and a friend were standing near a soldier and his fair companion. The soldier wore the straps of a sergeant [he was a private]. As the dance stopped for a moment the girl turned to Milton and, shaking her blonde curls saucily, taunted him about being out of luck in not wearing a uniform that he might join in the dance. The sergeant was greatly displeased with this familiarity upon the part of his companion with a common herder of mules and oxen, and at the next pause in the dance he tried to force a fight with the young man, who tried to avoid any trouble. We have it from an eye witness that what followed was entirely the fault of the hot-headed sergeant, who forced the fight which ended his career.

In a moment everything was confusion and uproar in the place and the two men were locked in a fierce struggle. The music ceased and a stampede was made for that part of the room in which the fight was going on. It was a mob of drunken and liquor-crazed men and women. Milton was getting the best of his antagonist when the other soldiers in the room took a hand in the fight and kicked and beat the herder unmercifully. The sharp report of a revolver was heard in the melee and the sergeant fell back into the arms of one of his friends.

In none of the many and varying accounts of this affair was Middleton ever blamed. According to several accounts, the other soldiers took a hand and clubbed Middleton over the head with bottles. Doc himself claimed that his antagonist said to him, "I run this place and I'm going to run you."[3] To continue with Butcher's story:

The lights were suddenly extinguished, leaving the great hall in total darkness and pandemonium indescribable. The trampling and fighting of the mob to reach the open air can be better imagined than described, and we leave the reader to imagine the scene that followed. The poor herder escaped in the darkness and confusion. A price was set upon his head. Friends offered to furnish money to defend him if he would stand a trial. . . . [He] escaped to the wilds of northern Nebraska, which was at that time, to a great extent, unorganized territory, where bad men roamed at will knowing no law but the six-shooter and the bowie knife. Whenever he tried to work the bloodhounds of the law would get on his track and he was compelled to move on. At last he gathered a band of daring outlaws around him and it is said did a wholesale business in running off whole herds of ponies belonging to the Indians, and becoming a terror to law-abiding citizens.[4]

The Sidney newspapers covering the shooting affair are missing, but the following appeared in the *Cheyenne Daily Leader* of January 16, 1877, entitled "A Frontier Episode":

In a row between a lot of soldiers and teamsters at Sidney, Nebraska, Sunday night, Private James Keith [sic] of Co. C, 5th Cavalry, was shot and instantly killed. After the shooting of Keith, about twenty soldiers procured arms from the barracks, returned to town, stopping in front of the place where Keith was killed and fired several volleys through the doors and windows of the building, fortunately injuring no one. The firing was stopped by the arrival of a patrol. The body of Keith was taken in charge by the commanding officer of Sidney Barracks.

Later, John Y. Nelson, police chief at Sidney when the shooting took place, related:

At the Dancing Hall in Sidney, a citizen killed a soldier, and afterwards became one of the most noted desperadoes in the country. I was in the place at the time, and, seeing the fight, tried to stop it; the soldier was dead, however, before I could give any practical assistance.

The citizen's name was Doc Middleton, and I could not blame him in any way for what he had done. The soldiers were always bullying the people in the most outrageous manner, and taking every opportunity of insulting them.

This particular soldier had knocked Middleton down three times for no reason whatever, and then the latter shot him.

It so happened that Middleton, who was a quiet, peaceable

fellow and a freighter, was a friend of mine, and I told him
to skip out of the town as quickly as he could, giving him
the chance of doing so whilst I went to pick up the soldier.
Of course, by the time I had fumbled the latter about and
pronounced him dead, Doc had got clean away, and I had
to make a terrible fuss with those present for having allowed
him to escape.[5]

Army records show that James Keefe, Private, Co. D., "died
of disease" on January 13, 1877 at Sidney Barracks, Nebraska,
"as a result of accidental gunshot."

After the shooting, Middleton walked out to the first stage stop
north of Sidney, and was waiting at the station when the stage
arrived the next day, it having come out over the same route he
had taken. The seats were all taken and he had to ride outside
with the driver. The weather was bitterly cold and he was in-
sufficiently clad, but he was loaned a buffalo robe by one of the
North brothers until the stage reached Fort Robinson, where he
got off.[6] This was the last that was positively known of Middleton's
whereabouts for several months.

On April 7, 1877, a grand jury for the 5th Judicial District of
the State of Nebraska within and for Cheyenne County brought
in an indictment against "Dock Middleton" for murder in the
second degree.[7]

2

From Texas

Who was this Doc Middleton? Where was he from? What explains his many assumed names? When I began my research into the Doc Middleton story, I found his background obscured in deadends and contradictions. No extensive treatment of Doc's life has been written, but the brief accounts which have been published list his birthplace, for example, in six different states. I determined to track down every particle of information available and put together as authentic a biography of Doc Middleton as possible.

In order to clear away the obscurity of Doc's beginnings, we must people the Texas stage with a few actors.[1] On October 27, 1834, James Riley arrived in Texas from Illinois with a wife and five children. Five months later, Riley received from the Mexican government a land grant of one square league (4,428 acres) in Leon County. One of the Riley children was a son, James B., known throughout his life as J. B.; he had been born in Illinois in 1826.

Shortly after the Rileys came to Texas, William Middleton, also from Illinois, settled near them in Leon County. There were indications that they were related; for instance, he was referred

8

to as "Uncle Bill" by the Riley children.

Joel Cherry and his family arrived from Tennessee in 1841. He received a land grant from Texas—now an independent republic—of 640 acres in Titus County. Among the Cherrys' seven children were Rebecca, born about 1826, and Nancy, born in 1832. About two years after the Cherrys settled in Texas, Rebecca married a John G. Shepherd. She was probably seventeen years old at the time; he was twenty-one years her senior. Between 1844 and 1847, three children were born to the Shepherds. In early 1846 Nancy Cherry, not quite fourteen years old, was apparently seduced by John G. Shepherd, her older sister's husband; on November 15, 1846 Nancy gave birth to a son, whom she named John. Two years later Nancy gave birth to a daughter, Margaret; there is no record of her being married and there is no record of who the father was.

About 1850 the Shepherd and Cherry families moved to Bastrop, Texas. Living nearby was J. B. Riley, gunsmith, now twenty-four years old. On February 9, 1851 Nancy Cherry gave birth to her third child, a son she named James M. Family descendents say the "M" was for Middleton. About this time there was a man named Middleton hanged at Bastrop.[2] The following year, on the 5th of July, 1852, Nancy Cherry and J. B. Riley were married at Lockhart in Caldwell County. J. B. Riley took Nancy's three children as his own.

Who was the father of James M.? It is a significant question, because James M. was the child who grew up to become the notorious Doc Middleton. Was there a man named Middleton involved back in 1850? It would be said many years later that the father of Doc Middleton was hanged for murder. Or was the "M" in James M. simply associated years later with, say, "Uncle Bill" Middleton, thus invoking respectability and keeping the name in the family? Or did John G. Shepherd continue to father his sister-in-law's children, including James M.? Or was J. B. Riley the real father? That the boy was named James suggests so, since Nancy named her first son John, apparently after John G. Shepherd. The answer? I do not know. Years of exhaustive research have not revealed the secret.

James M. Riley was ten years old when the Civil War came to
Texas. The state legislature convened in special session on January 21, 1861 for the purpose of settling the question: Shall
Texas secede from the Union? Governor Sam Houston opposed
secession and argued that "the destruction of the Union would
be the ruin of all the states," but Texas joined the Confederacy.
James was too young to go to war, but his step-father (or father)
and his half-brother John went.

In March of 1861 J. B. Riley enlisted for service in the Texas
Rangers, being mustered in at Fredericksburg. He was mustered
out at Camp Mason three months later.[3]

John D. Riley's service was more extensive.[4] According to his
statement, he enlisted at the age of fifteen, clad in nothing but a
long-tailed shirt, which attested to the poverty of the family. He
served as a private in Company C, 33rd Regiment Texas Cavalry,
C.S.A. (Dan, son of Rebecca and John G. Shepherd, also enlisted
in the same outfit, but the dates are not known.) John told of a
battle at Fort Gibson, but his more typical war-time action seems
to be reflected in this summary: "We traded bullets with Mexicans
and chased the banditti back into Mexico when they crossed
the Rio Grande." He served under Col. Duff along the Rio Grande,
and recalled getting a good Mexican poncho which later he used
for years on cattle drives. John also mentioned a thirty-day
furlough; returning from his visit home, he met his command near
Shreveport, Louisiana, with 1,300 Federal prisoners. "I went with
my command to the stockade at Tyler, Texas. In the early part
of 1865, I was in camp on the Brazos River, below Waco, Texas.
When news of Lee's surrender reached us, we were camped along
the Brazos River."

The only war's-end bonus the commanding officer could give
his men was to distribute mules among them, and John and Dan
got one big mule between them. They went home to Blanco County,
where John traded his half interest in the mule to Dan for
twenty-five head of range cattle.

While his half-brother was away in the service, young James
Riley had not been idle. He seems to have been getting a very
early start on establishing questionable relationships with horses.

On May 16, 1866, he was indicted in Gillespie County for "taking up and using an estray, a bay mare worth fifty dollars, running on the range without known owner." The horse was alleged to have been taken on or about the 20th of September 1865. James was fourteen years old at the time. Perhaps he simply boyishly cheered his good fortune to find an ownerless horse. In any case, the matter dragged on for two years. Finally, it was called for trial on May 14, 1868, and the district attorney, appearing for the state, told the court that he would not further prosecute, whereupon it was adjudged and ordered by the court "that the said case be dismissed and the defendant go home discharged."[5]

Though this particular incident had a happy ending, happy and prosperous times in general seem to have been eluding the Rileys. This letter, for example, dated Fredericksburg, Texas, September 30, 1867, gives some evidence of their financial situation. It is in the handwriting of a businessman to whom J. B. apparently owed some money.

> Mr. James B. Riley, Blanco Co., Texas.
> Dear Sir: Your favor of the 24th inst has been received and contents noted. I did not expect such an answer from a gentleman in whom I had such confidence but I shall not sue you yet and hope you will come to see me when we can settle the difficulty. If you have two yoke of good work oxen I take them, or a gentle riding horse or I take corn. Hoping that I may soon hear from you here in town, I remain, Yours truly, H. Lochte.[6]

J. B. Riley had served briefly during 1847 in the Mexican War, and when mustered out had been given, in addition to his pay, Bounty Land Warrant 47996. However, this could not be used in Texas, because the U.S. did not own any land in Texas, all vacant land having been retained by the state when it joined the Union in 1845. Therefore, Riley had sold his land rights. Since there is no record of his having acquired other land yet, we can assume that at this time he was squatting on some vacant land or perhaps renting from someone. Indications are that the Riley family lived fairly close to the Joel Cherry family near Twin Sisters. Six-and-a-half years later Riley would, as far as I can determine, acquire the first and only tract of land he ever owned. On March 4, 1874, he took a preemption on 154½ acres about ten miles northwest of Blanco City.[7]

The records of the County Clerk of Hays County at San Marcos, Texas state that on June 23, 1870, the Rev. N. J. Taylor united in marriage one James Riley and a Mrs. Mary E. Edwards. We do know that our James M. Riley was married about this time. We do know that the Riley name otherwise appears rarely in Hays County records. We do know that records in no other county note a James Riley marriage. We do know that James M. called his wife Lizzy. If we assume that Mary E. stood for Mary Elizabeth, a girl's name often used in Texas, we can reasonably assume that the June 1870 ceremony represents the marriage of James M. Riley. The newly-wed couple appear to have lived in the neighborhood of the Rileys and Cherrys, near Twin Sisters, Blanco County.

There are legends of three homicides in Texas committed by James M. Riley. The first has all the earmarks of telling, retelling, and mistelling. I myself have heard the story from widely separated sources, indicating that the story did indeed have considerable circulation in Nebraska, though relatives interviewed in Texas did not know of it. Sometimes in the telling the story of the killing of a soldier (presumably the January 1877 incident) was mixed in. The only possible evidence I have found to support the tale is the testimony of one couple. If this Texas killing did in fact take place, it was probably about a year before James was married. For what it is worth, the story goes basically as follows:

During the school term, the male teacher had an affair with James' sister, but this was not known until after the term had ended and the teacher had departed. He was then working as an intinerant peddler. Young James, about eighteen years old then, set out to track down the seducer. He overtook his quarry near Corpus Christi (Matagorda County, some say). The man had come in from a drive and had just stabled his horse at a livery barn. James called him to the door, shot him, and hurriedly mounted and rode away. Bystanders fired at the fleeing horseman, but only the horse was nicked slightly. The killer was never apprehended.

In later years, three brothers in Nebraska, the Harrisons, told of a young man who gave his name as Albright, who stopped at their home in Texas back about 1869 and inquired after a schoolmaster he was looking for. The Harrisons knew Doc Middleton in Nebraska, and said that a younger Doc Middleton was indeed the fellow who had called at their place in Texas.[8]

The second homicide story was told by Doc Middleton himself to his brother-in-law in Nebraska.[9] Doc said he was working at rounding up cattle in Texas (no date mentioned) and got involved in a fight in the corral with a Negro cowhand, whom he killed. Not only do we have Doc's own telling of this story, but there is a legend among the Rileys in Texas that one of their boys killed a colored man and fled the state. (We will soon learn of other reasons James might have fled the state.) Outside the family, there is no historical evidence known about this matter.

Riley descendants tell the third homicide story: James and his wife were walking over to see his grandparents, Mr. and Mrs. Joel Cherry. The husband was ill and confined to his bed. As they neared the house, they heard screams and shouts for help. James ran on ahead, picking up a broken fence rail as he went. When he arrived at the house, he found one of the Overstreets, his wife's brother (his wife was an Overstreet prior to her first marriage), beating Grandma Cherry, trying to force her to tell where their money was hidden. In the ensuing fight, James hit the Overstreet boy over the head several times with the club and killed him. His relatives all agreed that the only thing he could do was leave the area, as the Overstreets would surely kill him otherwise.[10]

We have no date for this episode, but obviously it occurred while James and his wife were still living in southern Blanco County. We know that as early as October 1871 our couple was living in Coryell County, near Jonesboro, about a hundred miles from Twin Sisters. Therefore, the killing must have taken place sometime between mid-1870 and the fall of 1871.

On August 11, 1871, a multiple killing occurred at Newton, Kansas. A youth named Jim Riley killed several men in revenge for the murder of the town marshal who had befriended him. This youth was tall and slim, as was James M., and about the right age. However, there are indications that James had never been that far from home, as will be seen. He was married, a child was coming in a few months, and he seems to have been a "home boy."

There are in existence six letters written by James to the home folks in 1872 and 1873. The first four were from Coryell County in 1872. The handwriting and spelling are so poor that the letters can be read only with considerable difficulty. The first letter is dated February 1872, and from its contents we can deduce that James and his wife had been in Coryell County since at least October 1871. We also learn that James' and Lizzy's first baby, a boy, was born on November 4, 1871 and died on November 20th.

Otherwise, the letters are not particularly informative. James complained that he was writing frequently but not getting any replies; he inquired after the health of all the family, "father and mother and Sister Margret and the children and grandpop and grandma," and he wanted to contact Brother John. There seemed to be closer affinity between John, Margaret, and James than between these three and the rest of the family.

On October 31, 1872, James M. Riley was indicted in Coryell County for the theft of a mare. Nothing further is known of this matter.

The next we know of James we learn from two letters he wrote home from Grayson County the following year. His handwriting had improved considerably. It was evident that James was now in trouble and that his wife was not with him. Also, perhaps an intermediary was being used in order to avoid his whereabouts being learned.

The first letter was dated June 7, 1873 and was from Denison City, Texas. Again he wanted to hear from John and he wanted the Rileys to contact Lizzy if possible and to write him.

Another letter was written shortly after, also from Denison City. The envelope in which the letter came is still in existence

James M. Riley, c. 1871. This is the earliest known picture of the young man who would soon come to be known as Doc Middleton. The photograph is from a tintype found by Mrs. Geraldine Henson in Nancy Cherry Riley's old trunk (see note #10 for Chapter 2 and note #4 for Chapter 11).

Margaret Riley, second child of Nancy Cherry. This is the sister to whom James M. Riley wrote.

The above is a kind of postscript to a longer letter written by James M. Riley to his father on April 21, 1872 from Jonesboro, Coryell County, Texas. It shows the hand and heart drawings that James sometimes put at the end of his letters.

The following two pages reproduce an April 3, 1872 letter from James to his sister Margaret. It, like the other extant letters, emphasizes his desire to receive letters from his family. James' June 7, 1873 letter from Denison City comprised one page to his sister Margaret and one page to his father and mother; this latter is reproduced as the third page following. James laments "I dont think that I will ever see you all a gain," and he contemplates going to California within two weeks. He did in fact see his family again, though presumably not his wife Lizzy, and he did not go to California.

Coriel county texas 1872
Jones duer po aprile the 3

dear sister I take the oppertunity
of righting you a few lines
to let you now that
we ar all well at this
time and I hope when this
few lines comes to hand
thay may find you
all well an doing
well I havent rollew nuch
to right you only that
I wdnt you to right
to me an tell me how
yean pap an yean mother
is an tell mother to right
to me an tell father to
right to me an I wdnt
you to right to me as
soon as you get this
leter an right soon an
often for I wd not to hee
from you all ~~~~ I havent
hed fom you in a good

While I want you to
right to me uncle father
John is alright to
him to right to me
an I will right to
him I would likes to her
fom him an right to
me when was the last
time you heard from him
Cirley Jds she would
like to see you all
she ses she winds
you all to right
to her tell mother howdy
for me an all
of the children to do
i mest bring this ltte to a
close fay allow you to right to
you for all J Mr Riley to
            Mrs Riley

you drect your letters to Denison city po Johnson
County texas

Dear father an mother I seat self to let
you both now that I am well and I hope
when these few lines comes to hand
thay may find you both well I
think that I will mind you this time
I hant got molee muse to rite you
vell I hant heared fro mee brother john
sentes I see you I would like to hear from
you all I would like to see you
all a gain but I dont think that I will
ever see you all a gaine I am a long ways
a way from thar if you hav heared from
lizy fry I want you to rite to mee
all a bout har I hant hared from har
sentes I left thar Shint befour 100 mules
I will be in Mcforney with brother
if I can find him so I must come
to a close by asken you to Write
to mee you must excuse my bad hand rite
so noth nor I present & remaine sum untell
deth form Riley to J B Riley
you come drect your letter Denison city

Thomas Riley,
son of J. B. and Nancy Riley,
brother or half-brother to
James M. Riley (Doc Middleton).

Andrew Riley,
son of J. B. and Nancy Riley,
brother or half-brother to
James M. Riley (Doc Middleton).

L-R: Dora Riley and Nancy Riley, daughters of J. B. and Nancy Riley, sisters or half-sisters to James M. Riley (Doc Middleton).

L-R: Nancy Riley; Emma Riley; Mannon Kimbrough, brother-in-law to James M. Riley (Doc Middleton); Dora Riley.

Emma Riley,
daughter of J. B. and Nancy Riley,
sister or half-sister to
James M. Riley (Doc Middleton).

L-R: Lewisa Jane Riley
and Mary Jane Shepherd.
Lewisa Jane was a daughter of
J. B. and Nancy Riley and
sister or half-sister to
James M. Riley (Doc Middleton).
Mary Jane was a daughter of
John G. and Rebecca Cherry Shepherd
and cousin to
James M. Riley (Doc Middleton).

David Crockett Riley,
brother of J. B. Riley,
uncle to James M. Riley
if J. B. was actually the father
of James M. (Doc Middleton).

and was addressed to J. B. Riley, Twin Sisters P.O., Blanco County, Texas. The text is given here as written; it will be noted that another child had been born to James and his wife.

Grayson county texas Denison City po June the 25 1873
Dear father I seat myself to ancer your kind leter which come to hand to day I was glad to her from you all an to her that you all was well this leaves me well an I hope that when the few lines comes to hand they may find you all well an doing well I am glad to her that John is in texas I want you to rite to brother John to rite to me I would be glad to see you all I want you to tell brother John to come an see me I was glad to her from lizzy and the baby I would give ever thing to see them but tis so that I cant it does nearly brack my hart to think about them I hant got nary leter from har cents I left thar I want you to rite to har as soon as you get this leter tell har to tak good car of har self the baby and tell har to rite to you an sister an you an sister Margriet rite to me about har I want you to rite to me soon an oftan I am in a heap a truble about you all it is hard to think that I am a way alone so far a way from home tell mother and all of the chrilden houdy for me tell them all to rite to me so nothen mor at present so good by for a while I remaine your sun untell deth margret I hav rote to you sevler leters an I hant got neary one from you yet you musent think so hard of me for this you must excuse my bad hand rite an short leter James Riley to J. B. Riley and M. A. Riley

On March 19, 1874, James M. Riley was indicted in Gillespie County for theft of a gelding, the property of one Mary Jacobs, value $75. It is not known where he was living at the time or whether his wife was with him.

This case was called on July 15, 1874. J. B. Riley, referred to in these proceedings as James Riley, Sr., had given $500 surety for young James' appearance. To quote from the minutes:

James Riley failed to appear. His name was distinctly called three times at the door of the court house but answered not

and wholly made default and James Riley, Senior, the surety
on the bail bond of the said James Riley was distinctly called
three times at the door of the court house and answered not
and wholly failed to bring the body of the said James Riley
into court; it is therefore ordered, adjudged and considered
by the court that the bail bond taken by this court in this
case be forfeited and that the State of Texas do have and
recover of the def't James Riley, principal and James Riley,
Sr., surety, the sum of $500 and that scire facias be issued
for said surety to be and appear before the Ho. Dist. Court
of Gillespie County at its next term and show cause why this
judgment should not be made final.[11]

On July 23, 1875, the Rileys' attorney appeared in their behalf
and excepted to the sufficiency of the bail bond, but this was
overruled. The attorney then asked leave to amend pleadings,
which was granted.

On November 16, 1875, #254 was continued for service.
Seven years later this case was dismissed, since by that time a
key witness was no longer at hand.

On November 18, 1875, in case #355, forfeiture of bail bond,
the Rileys' attorney made application for continuance, but was
overruled. The court ordered that the decision made before be
made final and that the state recover from the defendant and
surety the sum of $500 and all costs.[12]

The name of James Riley appears in the Texas Rangers' list of
fugitives for both the 1872 horse stealing in Coryell County and
this 1874 horse stealing in Gillespie County.

Cooke County, Texas was a resort for fugitives from justice.
It is on the Red River, which forms the boundary between Texas
and Oklahoma (Indian Territory in the 1870s). This is where
James had fled to after his 1874 indictment. However, it did not
prove a haven for him. At the very time his case was being considered in the Gillespie County court, he was having his troubles
in the Cooke County court.

On July 1, 1875, James Riley and Lewis Bell, his cousin, were
indicted on three counts for theft of horses. A week later Riley was

indicted alone on another count. The records are rather sketchy but the following seems to be the substance of these cases:

Riley and Bell were first tried as case #849. They entered a plea of "not guilty," but were found guilty and their punishment assessed at eight years confinement in prison.

They were then tried as case #850; on this they were alleged to have stolen, on May 12, 1875, a gelding worth $100, the property of G. H. Smith. They applied for continuance and were overruled. They entered a plea of "not guilty," but were found guilty and their punishment assessed at fifteen years confinement in prison. Through their attorney they asked that the verdict be set aside, but this was refused. On July 15, they made a motion for a new trial on the grounds that the court erred in not giving a continuance and in compelling the defendants to go on trial when they had already been convicted of a felony. They stated that they could prove that they had traded for the horse they were alleged to have stolen. It is not certain what transpired, but, when they were received at Huntsville penitentiary the following week, this term was not included in their total.

In case #851 it was charged that on May 12, 1875, Riley and Bell stole a gelding, value $75, from one Pleasant Noll. There were eleven witnesses for the state. A guilty plea was entered and a sentence of ten years confinement for each was given.

In the case against James alone, #865, it was charged that he had on March 1, 1875 stolen a gelding from Thomas Tinsley, value $100. James was referred to as "late of the county," which would seem to indicate that the court considered he had been making his home there. There were nine witnesses for the state in this case, yet it was decided not to prosecute further.

The records of the Huntsville penitentiary reveal that James Riley #4643 and Lewis Bell #4644 were received July 22, 1875, from Cooke County, to serve terms of eighteen years each for theft.

When he Riley was interviewed upon entering prison, this inmate stated that he was twenty-four years old, that he was a native of Bastrop County and that he had been living in Cooke County. He stated that he was married, but did not list the name of his wife or any other relatives.

Riley weighed 150 lbs. when he was received. He was six feet tall, had dark hair, brown eyes and a light complexion.[13]

On September 17, 1875, just less than two months after entering the prison, James Riley escaped, but was captured and returned to Huntsville.

Obviously Doc Middleton did not learn horse stealing in Nebraska! Whether James passed on his "talent" to other Riley family members is uncertain. And surely we do not know for sure who influenced whom. We do know that James' younger half-brother, Thomas Riley, was charged with horse theft in November 1876. Joel Cherry, Thomas' grandfather, and John Riley, another half-brother, signed a bond, binding themselves in the amount of $150 for Thomas' appearance in court. Nothing further was found about this case; perhaps it was just more "gathering of stock."[14] We also know that another of James' half-brothers, Joseph, "got in trouble" a year later, after James had left Texas; and that the following year, J. B. Riley himself was charged with theft.

It is easy to imagine that John Riley might have been one of the few stable and solid influences in James' young life. It is clear from James' letters that he felt close to his brother. John was a little more than four years older than his half-brother James and had been a soldier in the Civil War. Indications are that he was a hard-working and law-abiding citizen and was likely the most prosperous of the Rileys. Apparently John was never accused in court of a criminal deed. His name appears once as plaintiff in a suit to recover damages from a hired man for burning down his barn and once as defendant in an action to collect a bill. John's modest prosperity is perhaps evidenced by his real estate dealings. In 1875 he purchased 410 acres of land from one D. E. Moore for $615 and sold this tract several years later at 150% profit; he later bought and sold other land tracts, always at a profit.[15] John may well have gotten into real estate through marriage. About 1874[16] he married Mrs. Sarah Blaylock, nee Sarah Margaret Bell, daughter of Mrs. Elizabeth Bell of Bastrop and sister of George Bell. Sarah was a young widow whose first husband had left her some property. Sarah's and John's first child, a son whom they named Sid, was born at Willow City, Gillespie County in 1875.

It was about the time of John's wedding, maybe even triggered by his announcement of the coming marriage, that John D. Riley was told he was not really a Riley. Riley descendants say that it was Grandma Cherry (Mrs. Joel Cherry), John's grandmother, who told him that he had been fathered by Rebecca Cherry's husband, John Shepherd. Whether he was told out of good will or ill intentions we do not know, but the Riley family members do claim that Grandma Cherry was in general a mean, determined woman and would do anything to get her way or to spite someone if she felt he was trying "to get too big for his britches." At any rate, John changed his name and was known from then on as J. D. Shepherd, even though the Rileys accepted this change grudgingly and were never pleased over it.[17]

During the decade after the Civil War, John had been a trail driver. This may have influenced James' decision years later to flee Texas with a trail drive going north to Nebraska. His memories of John's tales and letters must surely have been vivid. Range cattle originated in Mexico, descendants of animals imported by the Spaniards and developed over three centuries. They spread into Texas when ruled by Spain and Mexico. Before the Civil War, Texas cattle were abundant, fences were few, and thousands roamed at will. To determine ownership, each owner adopted a distinctive mark or brand. During the War, these vast herds grew unattended, neglected by owners who were in the field with the Confederate armies. So it happened that after the War the plains of Texas were covered with hundreds of thousands of cattle, unmarked and unbranded, some wild as the native game, to which no man could establish a title. This situation afforded an opportunity for hard-riding and desperate men who found themselves stranded on this far frontier after the wreck of the Confederacy. As John Riley himself said years later in an interview with J. Frank Dobie:

    The settlers went to branding up their cattle as soon as they got home from the army. Owners paid 50¢ a head for all mavericks branded with their own brand, with parts of ears cut off being presented as proof to the branding. Of course, any range rider who roped and branded a maverick out alone could have put his own brand on it and taken a piece of the ear as proof of his having been in contact with the animal, but this was not done. The ticks were terribly bad and many mavericks were too poor to run. Unbranded stock were thick around waterings, many of them not wild.[18]

Cattle sold in Texas for as little as $2 a head in gold, perhaps $5 in paper money. These same cattle would bring $40 in the eastern markets. It cost about $2 to deliver cattle in Illinois and $17 for shipping by rail to New York. With cattle abundant and local value trifling, the northern and eastern markets had to be sought. Thus the great cattle drives began. Some pre-war cattle drives had gone north from Texas, but the post-war ones eclipsed them in significance. The Texans gathered their cattle into herds of 2,000 to 3,000 each and struck north across the trackless plains. Indeed, this movement reached such proportions that there was scarcely one of the cities and towns between the 98th and 120th meridians which did not have its origin as a supply point for these nomads. It has been estimated that from the time of the first drive after the Civil War until the final herd in 1897, a period of about thirty years, ten million head of cattle were driven north from Texas. Thirty-five thousand cowboys and one million horses participated in these drives.

In the beginning, cattle were driven incredible distances in an effort to reach a market. In 1866 Nelson Story drove a herd to Virginia City, Montana, through Indian country. His original destination had been Illinois but he changed plans while on the trail. A few drives were made to Illinois, Indiana, and Ohio. Since these drives went through settled country there was resistance on the part of the residents. Some drives were made to California, a trip of two years.

A large drive was attempted by Texans in 1866, destination Baxter Springs, Kansas. This failed because of difficulties with settlers, and was a financial disaster. But Baxter Springs, Abilene, and Junction City were to become cow towns. In 1871 Newton was a cow town; in 1874 Wichita had become the leading shipping center. There were 200,000 head of cattle and 2,000 cowboys in the vicinity that fall.

During the seventies, as the rails made headway westward and the settlers solidified their position in eastern Kansas, the drovers were forced to take a route farther west and Dodge City became the cow town.

In March 1866, when John was nineteen years old, he went down to Caldwell County to work for Col. J. J. Myers, who had been to California with Frémont and who was to drive one of the first herds to Abilene. In 1866 there was no established market anywhere for Texas cattle. Myers was gathering a herd of steers to drive to St. Louis. The cow crowd consisted of ten men under a boss named W. C. Burrier. They did not expect to be back until 1867.

They set out with 600 head of steers, from four to fourteen years old. The cook drove a wagon pulled by two yoke of long-horned oxen. The outfit had no horse wrangler; each man had two horses in his mount, no more. John himself had a horse and a mule. He kept the pony for night work. The pony was very gentle and a remarkable camp animal; he would always stay close to his master's pallet at night, whether hobbled, staked, or loose with a drag-rope on. The men all furnished their own mounts and drew $45 a month.

The grub consisted mostly of corn meal, bacon, beans, coffee, and black molasses. Not a beef was killed after the outfit got on its way, but lots of squirrels were eaten. After the herd reached Missouri, it was held while the men gathered blackberries and were furnished sugar, milk, and cream from the spring houses of some of the farms.

There was not a pair of boots in the outfit. Some of the men wore big roweled Mexican spurs, some little spurs. Some of them had Hugh Miller saddles from San Marcos, where Miller had a saddle shop. "The first cow I ever roped on my Hugh Miller saddle," John recalled, "busted it."[19] None of the hands wore leggins (chaps). The men wore common clothes, made by the home women. They had both rawhide riatas and grass ropes. They had very light bedding. John had learned during the Civil War to "rustle grass and weeds for a bed." If it was raining, the trail men did not need a bed much anyhow, as at such times all hands usually had to be on herd to prevent the cattle from drifting or running. Slickers had not come in yet. John alone had a "Spanish blanket," a Mexican poncho with a hole (for the head to go through) slit in the middle of it. A good poncho would turn water.

The route from the Lockhart prairie to St. Louis went by Fort Worth and crossed the Red River at Colbert's ferry, whence an old road led north. At Red River, the Texans, without a great deal of sorrow, saw a Yankee drown. At Boggy Depot in Indian Territory, two of the men got into a shooting scrape. One was left there wounded; the other rode off. The herd trailed on to Fort Gibson and crossed the Arkansas River.

Near Cassville, Missourians began giving the outfit trouble. The trouble makers distrusted the Texans as being Confederates. One day, when the cattle were going along a field fence of shackly stakes, several went through it. A man by the name of Brickens rode out in the high grass and weeds of the field to turn the cattle back. A Missourian raised up, caught him by the beard, and pulled him down. The boss, Burrier, was a 32nd degree Mason; he gave the sign and the sign was all that prevented serious trouble.

Near Rolla, Missouri, the herd stopped for a few days to graze and rest. At the Mississippi River, it was driven on a steamboat, crossed to the east side, and unloaded. (Other accounts of this drive state that the cattle were ferried across the Mississippi River at St. Louis.) The men had to do some tall riding to keep the steers from scattering in timber-lined bottom land, but they held them on the prairie all right that night. At Mattoon, Illinois, Col. Myers met the cattle and put them on corn.

Corn was selling at 8¢ a bushel. The beeves were held out in a pasture or a field. The corn, already shucked, would be hauled out in a wagon and thrown on the ground for the steers to pick up. Some were sold as oxen to settlers to plow up the prairie. After eating corn for a while, the herd was moved to a clover field

John D. Riley (right), first child of Nancy Cherry and half-brother to James M. Riley (Doc Middleton), with friend Sid Crain, late 1860s. John was likely just in from a trail drive when this photo was taken.

John D. Riley,
1870, Stockton, California.

The following two letters are from John D. Riley in Fort Zarah, Kansas to his parents in Texas. The first complains of the bitter cold weather; the second mentions a happier note—a dance.

Fort Zarah

November 27th 1871

Dear Father
and Mother
I take my seat this morining to
write you a few lines on this
beutiful Sun Shiney morining being
it is the first one that we have
had for a bout 10 days the
Snow is laying thick all, the Country
thare was a bout te 12 men Frose to
Deth and 8 with thare Legs Frose off
that we know and I donte no how
meny more that has hapened
with the same misfortion very near all
this month has ben cold and that
biten to to. I was oute in this last
Storme 4 days and I Suferd mire with
Colde and Sever did in my life before
in any Country I think this is the
Colds Plase I ever Saw in life

I think it tis to cold fore
Stock to dowell throw the winter
hear Arkansas River is tros over know
So Stock cun t Drink.
I have nothing mor to write et present
I ame well and I hope that when
those few lins comes to hand thay
will find you all well,
Dan I started hame a few days
a go. give my respects to all
inguaring friends. tell frind
Allick forge to write te
write soon and ofteng I or nothing
mor So good bey fore a while

                                    I, D, Riley,
to Father   and Mother,

        M A Riley

Horf "Zarah"
Febr 15th/(72)

Dear Father

I tuk my seat this Evining
to write you a few lines to let
you how I ame a getiny a long
in this Parte of the World
my heath is good and I
was at a Ball the other night
and how I shuck hevy foot
with the maried Woman it was
al Sin will I have nothing
to write of intruzt I wish you
wold senele me a Austin
Paper so I can see how the
Rale Roads is Progruseing
from Kansas City throue
to Austin I hope these
few lines will find you
all well write soon and often
good by   I. I. Riley.

belonging to a German woman. She made a trade to feed the cowboys, some of whom were now paid off and headed back to Texas. John stayed on.

Fall was well advanced and the steers were fat when they were driven to a railroad station and shipped to Chicago. Col. Myers had gone on ahead. John and another hand named Kelly accompanied the cattle. Myers sold them out without much delay. He and his men took a train to the mouth of the Ohio River. There they embarked on a steamboat for New Orleans, whence they shipped to Galveston, getting back to their ranch homes along in November.

It was not until the next year that the Chisholm Trail became a name and a reality. In 1869 Myers put up three herds of 1,500 head each for delivery in Kansas. When they were sold there, John went on with his herd to the Carson River in Nevada and there wintered. The next summer, Bailey and Wilson of San Francisco bought the steers and drove them to Sacramento. John hung with them until they were sold to butchers at around $90 a head. They were as fat, nearly, as the steers Myers had corn fed.

In 1871, John Riley went on another trail drive, this time to Fort Zarah, Kansas. There are several letters in existence which were written by John to his folks in Texas. The first was dated Fort Zarah, October 1, 1871:

Dear Sister: I tak up my pen this moring to let you no what I ame doing I am still working with the cattle whe are stoped for the winter hear and probley longer that is if he dont sell out there is some talk of it one man was down hear yearsterday on that bisnes So if he sell out I think that I be home a bout the first December. Well I ame note very well to day and cant think of eny thing to write I havent heard from you all sence I left thare. you must excuse this short letter and write soon and give me the news of that country give my respecte to one and all so I will close by saying to you to kiss some of them priety girls for me I don care who it is So it tis the righ one My adress Ft Zarah Kansas yours as ever afectionat Brother untell Deth J. D. Riley.

The next letter from John was also from Fort Zarah, dated

November 19, 1871:

Dear Father: I tak up my pen this morining to ancer your letter that I recd on the 17th I was very glad to hear from you all a gane I hadant heard from you all Sence I left thare and I hade writan Several letter to You I rekan that thare is one on the rode it will give you all the news that I have and whate I expect to dow if nothing hapans out of the way, all thoe I wold like to go in with you in the Cattle Bisnes for I think that it will pay beter thin eny other kind of Bisnes well, you will git my other letter if I thote you note get it wold give you sume idie whate I intended to do, bute I rote all mye intion ans in my other letter. well Folks thare is two Men a going to Ellswarth and that is the ofices wher all the male gose frome, and I ame in a hery and whe have hade a hevey Snow Storme for tow days. I think that Brother James hav forgot he has gote a Brother John. my heathe is good at presant and I hope that when this letter comes to hand thay will find you all well. So I will close by aske to writer soon and oftom and I will do the same. give my respects to all inquaring friends. write to Zarah Kansas this to one and all   Sister, I have writen all I can think of at presant and you mosant think that you are slited a tawl and write evry opoportunity you gite. So good By for a while. J. D. Riley

The final letter from John on this Kansas trail drive was written on April 11, 1872:

Dear Father and Mother: I seat my self to write you a few lines in and ancer to you of the 18th of March I was truly glad to hear from you and to hear the you are all well and to hear from Brother I hade all most givupe ever hearing from him a gan But I am happie to no that he is Still living and too him Selfe. have not much time to write you muste excuse this Short letter I ame a going out on Cow hunt to morro and have to git redey this Evening and hve a beout 18 miles to ride yeat and it is 2 o clock now So give love to all Write Soon and oftan good bey for a while. J. D. Riley.

It was about this time that Joseph Riley, John's and James' younger half-brother, began going on cattle drives. His descendants say that Joe went five times in all, the first when he was fourteen years old: twice for White and Littlefield and three times for Schreiner of Kerrville. On one occasion he went to Cheyenne; on another he saw a stampede go through Dodge City and tear down a lot of adobe houses.[20] Little is known about Joe's trail driving trips, except the 1876 one which we mentioned in the previous chapter.

William, two years older than Joe, may also have been going on cattle drives, but nothing is known of his activities, except that he did go north later, apparently in a hurry. We will encounter him much more later.

Had James been up the trail before his 1876 trip? We do not know for certain, but it seems very unlikely. If he did go on a trail drive it would have to have been prior to his marriage in 1870, because after that we have accounted for enough of his time in Texas each year to suggest that while he may have been moving around he was not on a drive that normally takes two-thirds of a year or more. We even know that at one time he tried to make a go of it at farming. Besides, there is a kind of plaintive tone in some of his letters which indicates that he does not like being away from home and would not choose this alternative. When he was in Denison City, for instance, he spoke of it as a " long ways" from home (and it was, some 300 miles) and he wrote, as he often did, of his desire to be reunited with his wife and child and his brother John.

In the last-quoted letter from John (April 11, 1872) there is a curious statement: "I am happie to no that he [James] is Still living and too him Selfe." What could "to himself" mean? It likely means simply that he was living away from the home folks. One thing we do know: During the fall and winter of 1875-76, James was "to himself" in a way he chafed under, but in the spring of 1876 he made another try at escaping from Huntsville, and on April 1 he was successful. (About a week later Lewis Bell made an unsuccessful attempt, but about a year-and-a-half later succeeded in escaping the penitentiary.)

Joe Riley's son says that after his escape "Jim" came home and he and Joe together went down around Brackettville and helped gather a herd of wild cattle for White and Littlefield, who had also just brought a hundred head of wet horses out of Mexico; they were pretty sorry horses. James and Joe hired on with White and Littlefield to drive the cattle and take the horses north through San Angelo to Dodge City. J. B. Riley gave James a good horse and told him to tell no one where he was from and to make no friends.[21]

It was at this time that James M. Riley changed his name to David C. Middleton. Does the name he chose have any significance or family connections, or was it a name chosen at random? We are not absolutely certain, but the family connections are too clear to be coincidental. Some say David C. was for David Crockett. James had both an uncle and a half-brother named Crockett Riley in Texas. Some say the C. was for Cherry, his mother's maiden name. Bax Taylor, a cousin (at least by marriage) to James, said that Doc Middleton's real name was James Cherry.[22] What about the Middleton name? There is some, but not conclusive, evidence that James' grandmother's maiden name was Middleton.[23] If J. B. Riley were James' real father, then of course the Middleton name would have family significance. When John D. Riley was told that he was a "Shepherd," this surely must have raised the question of parentage of James and Margaret. Possibly James' mother told him then that his real father was named Middleton, as some have suggested. We simply do not know for sure.

In later years, when asked about the significance of his middle initial, Doc Middleton said it stood for "Charley," probably a flip answer to a question he considered too personal.

As to the nickname, Doc, several explanations have been offered: one, that he was just a fairly good, self-educated horse doctor; another, that while on the 1876 drive north, a cowboy broke a leg and Middleton cared for him, thus earning the name of "Doc"; again, that Middleton was an expert at "doctoring" brands on stolen horses and cattle; finally, that when he signed the name, D. C. Middleton, the initials resembled the word DOC.

Whatever the true origin of the moniker, on the Nebraska frontier Doc Middleton was widely believed to have been a doctor during better days because of his cultured appearance and general bearing. These traits, which so distinguished him from the common desperado, were noted by all who knew him and did much to build his legend.

3

Nebraska Panhandle

At the end of chapter 1, we left Doc Middleton in January 1877. He had shot a soldier in Sidney and was running from the law. What happened to him when he got off the stage coach at Fort Robinson? We do not know; he is lost to us for a few months. Some say he spent most of that year in the Iowa State Penitentiary, but the evidence is at best circumstantial, perhaps just conjectural. The *Cheyenne Daily Leader* for August 6, 1879 carried an article on Doc Middleton entitled "Scenes From a Wicked Record." It said: "He cannot clear away the fact that he served eighteen months in the penitentiary at Fort Madison, Iowa, under the assumed name of Wallace, for the crime of horse stealing." This statement has to be at least partially in error, because there was not that much time unaccounted for. But if he was incarcerated at Fort Madison it must have been during 1877.

Two men by the name of Wallace did serve sentences at the Iowa pen during the 1870s. One was received in 1871 and clearly cannot be our man. The other, however, shows more promise. A. Wallace was received March 16, 1877, and went out on August 25, 1877, after expiration of his six-month sentence. He was received from Henry County and his crime was larceny. He was described as "dark"; he stated that he was born in Illinois and that he was married. We remember that Middleton left a wife and child behind when he became a fugitive from justice in Texas.

Another indication that Doc may have served time at Fort Madison is the fact that he and one Lyman P. Hazen became acquainted in some way at about this time. Hazen was a native of New York, married, and thirty-three years of age when received at Fort Madison April 15, 1874. He had been convicted in Polk County, Iowa of an offense involving a girl. His sentence was six years and he was released August 23, 1878, after serving three-fourths of his term. After his release he drifted on west and showed up around Omaha. If he and Doc Middleton met on the outside, it would have to be after August 1878. Some said that the two had met at Dodge City, but it is more likely that they met in prison. We will meet Hazen later.

At any rate, we are not sure where Doc Middleton was during most of 1877. However, he does turn up for certain at the end of the year—stealing horses! According to Wyoming accounts, which were always unfavorable, and perhaps rightly so, Middleton was at the ranch home of William Irvine on Horse Creek in the fall of 1877. He was ill, and Irvine, knowing him to be a fugitive, provided him with shelter and care until his recovery. When he was well enough he left, taking some of Irvine's horses, and is said to have admitted that this was the meanest act of his life.

Earlier that year Middleton had teamed up with John Baldridge, George Smith, and a young Texan named Edgar Scurry. It is a matter of historical fact that the theft of Irvine's horses was part of a larger job pulled off by Doc and his associates. On December 30, 1877 Scurry, Smith, and Middleton stole thirty-four horses and started for Kansas with their booty.[1] A posse pursued the trio and the stolen horses, overtaking them about twelve miles from Julesburg. The three abandoned the stolen stock and scattered to the hills. Scurry and Smith succeeded in making their escape, but Middleton was closely pressed by the posse. After a chase of some twenty miles, with his horse ridden down, Doc dismounted and made a stand among the rocks on a butte. According to one account, after the exchange of a few shots, he surrendered. Another story relates that while Middleton was holding the posse at bay, detective William Lykens charged Doc's position on horseback, oblivious to danger. Middleton leveled his rifle at Lykens and shouted, "Duck, you little Dutch fool! I don't want to kill you!" But Lykens kept coming and Doc tried to fire, but the gun jammed. Lykens rode at full gallop right up to Middleton, threw down on him with a sixshooter, and took him prisoner. It has been said that Lykens did not know what an important prisoner he had caught, but as a matter of fact Middleton was not such an important catch at that time. Aside from the homicide at Sidney, which the posse had no way of connecting with Middleton, the current theft was the only count against Doc, as far as I can determine.

During the two-day trip to Sidney, Middleton made several attempts to escape, but Lykens guarded his prisoner too closely for Doc's success. However, the jailer was less vigilant than Lykens:

> He was lodged in the little log jail at Sidney, but the next morning he was a free man again. He had escaped during the night by tearing up the floor and tunneling his way out by means of an old fire shovel, which, it was claimed by the jailer, had been accidentally left within his reach.[2]

Middleton's brother-in-law claimed that Doc told him he had had an accomplice. A young lad of slight build was also in the jail with Doc, but he was soon freed; he returned with a shovel and helped Doc to escape.[3]

No charges were filed against Middleton, Scurry, and Smith for the time being. However, in May of 1878, Smith apparently made the mistake of showing up in Cheyenne, and the wheels of justice were soon in motion. The thieving trio was indicted jointly on three counts of grand larceny: #433 pertained to the theft of three horses from James M. Carey; #434, theft of eight horses from William Irvine; and #435, theft of twenty-three horses from Charles Coffey. On May 29, 1878, warrants were issued for the arrest of the three, and the following day Sheriff Carr of Laramie County arrested George Smith. On June 3, Smith was arraigned.

He pled "not guilty." Bail was set at $500 and the trial date for June 17. He changed his plea to "guilty" and was sentenced to one year in the Nebraska penitentiary. As to Middleton and Scurry, the case was continued. A later account indicates that Scurry "jumped bond and returned to Texas," yet nothing has been found to show that he was ever in custody.

And Doc Middleton had not heard the last of this matter.

Cattle were introduced into Wyoming Territory and western Nebraska several years earlier than the time of the opening of the Western route through Kansas by way of Dodge City. Texas herds were brought to the Union Pacific Railroad at various places along the Platte River during the late 1860s; some were delivered to Plattsmouth, Nebraska, but Schuyler was a cow town of more importance. Later, Kearney became the cow town, and saw its share of cowboy troubles when the wild Texas drovers reached there after several months on the trail.

Some of these cattle were shipped directly to market, while others were fattened on locally grown corn before being shipped. Some were held in the adjacent country, and the Platte valley began to become populated with cattle. Cattle were driven westward along the Platte to various points in western Nebraska and Wyoming Territory in the late '60s and early '70s; thus began the ranching industry in the Nebraska panhandle. By the time Doc Middleton appeared there in 1876, ranching was well established.

But all the drovers who came north with the herds could not be employed locally. Some, of course, did not wish to remain in the country; they often returned to their homes in Texas, perhaps to come again the next season. Some would take employment with the ranchers or perhaps go on to the gold fields in the Black Hills or some associated work such as freighting to the Hills. Some had been fugitives from justice in Texas and could not return, but were too restless by nature to settle down to the monotony of work at ordinary pay; these were the perpetrators of much of the crime.

The practice of mavericking encouraged stock stealing. An unemployed cowboy could earn $2.50 to $3.00 by placing a rancher's brand on a maverick. Some began mavericking on their own, and some respectable cattle outfits got their start in this way. Other cowboys went on to professional stock stealing.

Many horses had been brought up from Texas, for many were needed in the conduct of the ranching business. Horse stealing was a very lucrative form of crime; stolen horses could be moved great distances rapidly, and often the victim of the theft was left without the means of pursuit. And horses were salable at a good price.

The ranchers were running on public domain and the Indian question had not been entirely settled. There were thefts of stock by whites from Indians, Indians from whites, and whites from whites.[4] On the frontier, the rancher and settler had little regard for the rights of Indians, and would willingly have seen them exterminated. Indians would make a reprisal raid on a ranch and steal a herd of horses in revenge for some wrong done to them by other parties. The general attitude of the white settlers that all Indians were horse thieves anyway made it easier for whites to blame horse thefts on the Indians, regardless of who actually did the stealing. These attitudes helped make a man like Doc Middleton possible. And the instability of the frontier helped too. In the Nebraska panhandle, Lincoln, Keith, and Cheyenne Counties had been organized, and there was a semblance of law and order, but the sheriffs had their hands full. Two typical newspaper stories from 1877 will give a good sense of the problem in western Nebraska and adjacent Wyoming Territory and a flavor of the feeling building up on the part of the citizens.

About the capture of ponies and men on Saturday last, it was reported that some men had been seen about Redington's ranch near Potter and that they had a band of ponies cached in a canyon close by. The men said that they had a herd of animals for Powers' upper ranch. Saturday night, Cowles, who is stock inspector for Cheyenne County, Redington, Jack Mallon and Hamlin went up to Potter and found where the band had been driven across the tracks, not toward Powers' but south in the direction of the South Platte River.

The party returned to Sidney; Hamlin and Cowles procured a buggy, drove to Iliff's Riverside ranch, secured horses and, riding up the river, found where the band had crossed the Platte at the mouth of the Cedar. At Brush's ranch, the pursuers found the men had just left with their animals and four miles farther on in the Sand Hills they were sighted and signaled. After a little preliminary work, both men gave themselves up, were disarmed, and together with the ponies were brought to Sidney. The two men, who are at present in jail, claim that they purchased the animals, twenty-nine in number, but there are those who differ in opinion. Of this, however, the courts or some more competent authority than a newspaper must decide. The animals are at Jenkins' corral.

This action on the part of the stockmen cannot be too highly commended, and should the animals prove to belong to the Indians, when the fact becomes known to them that the stockmen are trying to break up the theft of their animals, it will go far toward ending the predatory raids and stealing done by way of "getting even" on the part of the Indians.[5]

For some months past it has been a very common occurrence with stockmen to have twenty-five or thirty horses cut out of a herd and run off into the everlasting sand hills. The cattle men of Cheyenne, Keith and Lincoln Counties were generally the losers, and not less than 600 head of animals have been stolen within the last three months. With scarce an exception the thieves have eluded capture and the cattlemen are out a large number of horses which it will be impossible to replace this season. For the purpose of either recapturing some of their stock or at least driving the thieves, who are believed to be Indians, farther off, a company of seventy-five experienced and daring men have gone in pursuit of the stock robbers.

The State of Nebraska at present comes very nearly being in the hands of the horse thieves—a regularly organized, desperate and thoroughly trained class of highwaymen and robbers. And there doesn't seem to be any combined efforts to catch these marauders.

There is scarcely a day but what someone loses a horse and it is seldom that they succeed in recovering it. Not only this, but the outlaws kill cattle for meat, taking only what they need for a few meals.

There are a number of large bands of horse thieves and outlaws in that section. The ranchmen lose more by the wanton destruction of their cattle to supply them with meat than the loss of horses. They see no remedy for it. The thieves perhaps outnumber the ranchmen, and if they should shoulder their guns to defend themselves from these raids the chances would be in favor of a victory for the outlaws. Besides risking their lives by attempting to stop the work of the thieves, the ranchmen would be in danger of losing a large amount of stock by indiscriminate slaughter and other property by incendiarism. This is a serious state of affairs, but the people are being aroused to action, and it is hoped and believed that the thieves and murderers will soon be hunted down and dealt with.[6]

It was also in 1877 that the Wyoming Stock Growers Association decided to hire a stock detective. They chose William C. Lykens. This was the man who arrested Doc Middleton in December of 1877 and this was the arrest that would dog Doc for some time to come. Edgar Beecher Bronson described Lykens as follows:

Billy Lykens was one of the most efficient inspectors of the Wyoming Stock Growers Association. A short man with heavy muscular physique, a round, cherubic, pink and white face, in which a pair of steel-blue, glittering eyes showed strangely out of place. A second glance, however, showed beneath the smiling mouth, a set of the jaw which did not belie the fighting eyes. So far as I now recall, Billy never failed to get what he went after while he remained in our employ.[7]

This, then, was the country in which Doc Middleton found himself a fugitive again. Obviously Doc did not invent horse stealing on the Great Plains. However, he did quickly become notoriously associated with horse thefts throughout much of that land. By early 1878 the phrase "Doc Middleton's gang" was in use. Here is a portion from a *Sidney Telegraph* story describing an encounter between two cowboys and some unidentified persons, outlaws or Indians, at Little Springs, seven miles northeast of Sidney. This place had the reputation of being the headquarters of a large part of the deviltry committed in that part of the country. The locality was described as being a "crescent-shaped" valley abounding in caves and rocks where one well-armed man could withstand twenty. There was an abundance of water and browse, the only place where water could be found between Lodgepole Creek and the North Platte River.

1809666

The cowboys rode up to the springs, and noticed some horses grazing; on closer examination the horses were found to be branded. And they gave evidence of having been ridden extremely hard and appeared to be about exhausted. The boys recorded the brands and started off when three shots were fired from the bluffs a few hundred yards away. A little farther on, more shots were fired, the bullets striking the ground nearby. The two cowboys rode for cover, dismounted and exchanged shots with the unknown parties, finally giving up and leaving without seeing anybody. It was their opinion that they had encountered some of Doc Middleton's "gang."

The extent to which Doc Middleton was responsible for Plains horse thefts cannot be known. He was credited with being the chief of a vast operation, but how such organization and discipline could be possible among as large a number of lawless and undisciplined men as were engaged in stock stealing baffles the imagination. Outlawry and thievery were prevalent on the frontier before Middleton's arrival and continued afterward. However much his leadership may have been exaggerated, he became a legend within the brief period of eighteen months, and Nebraska has never quite seen his equal.

Doc was keeping in touch with the home folks back in Texas. His half-brother William had come up to Nebraska, and under the name Charles Fugate had stolen two horses from one Charles Woods of Lincoln County on July 6, 1877. He later joined the "Middleton gang," but he was moving around, as we note in a letter which Doc received from his stepfather as 1877 came to a close and 1878 began:

Dec. the 24th, 1877
Gillespie County, Texas

Mr. D. C. Middleton Dr sir I got your kind letter and was Glad to her from you and her that you was well I just ritten you a letter the other day and you keep movin a round so that I don't now how to wright this leaves us all well at present but we live harder than we ever did in our lives I aint able to worke eney more and all the boys has left me and so I have a hard time as you and Joseph has broken me up and William together and so none of you can help me nor live with me to help along so I will cratch along until I can sell my place. Joseph has got in trouble in our County and hant got out yet but I recon he will come clear next cort we are nearly all naked and I cant make a doller her no way that I fix it only by a little halling once and a while I hant got nows to wright at present but this is the hardest plase live I ever saw in life ther aint no money here cerc a Tall everything is low callico is 20 yds to the dollar and everything in proportion 50 cts will by more now than a dollar would 2 years ago we send our love to you William is at Ogalia Kances [Ogallah, Kansas] last month is the last time I herd from him if you can make eney thing ther you had better stay ther and dont come her for the rangers and polease is a huntin down all theves and convicks and you had better stay away from her until I wright you to come and see us all for William he can come back to see us all but cant stay long yet a while in a few years he can come home and stay at home I aim to move up the country next summer if I can and nothing happins the kindsfolks are all well as far as I know mag bell is married and Ales bell all so is married so I have ritten all I now at present so I remain as ever your friend until deth   J. B. Riley
Direct your letter to Gillespie County martinsburg post office[8]

This letter was later taken from Doc by an officer and reprinted in the *Cheyenne Sun* of August 5, 1879 in derision of "Texas literature, — verbatum et literatum spellatum."

The records of Blanco and Gillespie Counties did not reveal any trouble Joe may have been in. At one time Joe was working for a stockman, rounding up wild horses in company with other cowboys; apparently they rounded up a few which were not quite wild enough. The Rangers swooped down upon them and everybody got away except Joe. He was held for a time at Kerrville and then released, since he was only a hired hand.[9]

J. B. Riley had some theft troubles of his own. On September 5, 1878, on complaint of a William Shelton, he was indicted in Blanco County for stealing a cow. A neighbor, James Tanner, and Nancy's nephew by marriage, John R. Robinson, along with a man named Erlenmeyer, put up bond, which was taken and approved by the sheriff of Blanco County on November 8, 1878. It would appear that Mr. Riley may have been held pending the raising of the money. He deeded his 154 acres of land to Tanner and Robinson, who had put up most of the money; after the affair was over, they deeded it back to him. The case came up the first Monday in March 1879, and was continued. The case was called again in late summer. Some of Riley's German neighbors helped him; his sister, Louisa Jane Ives, came up from San Antonio to give testimony for him. Subpoenas were issued for William Shepherd, who appeared to have been the nephew of Nancy Riley and brother of Mary Jane Robinson, but Shepherd could not be located. Finally, on September 3, 1879, a verdict of "not guilty" was brought in.

At about this time, though the precise date is uncertain, a William Shepherd of Blanco County was murdered, along with his wife and one child. The murderer and the motive are unknown. Several of the Shepherd children were orphaned by the murder, and John R. Robinson made application, unsuccessfully, to adopt one of them, stating that he was an uncle. They appear to have been adopted by a family named Shackelford in Bastrop County. Almost all the documents pertaining to this matter have been lost. Therefore, it is not certain whether or not this murdered Shepherd is the same person for whom subpoenas were issued in the Riley case, but there seems to be more than coincidence at work here. This remains one of the small mysteries of Blanco County.

4

Doc Middleton's Country

We now turn our attention to the upper Elkhorn Valley and the adjacent Niobrara Valley during the middle and late 1870s. Ranching developed here later than in western Nebraska and Wyoming Territory; though excellent ranching country, it was the last area of the state, with the exception of certain parts of the Sand Hills, to come to the attention of the rancher. This region, which became known as "Doc Middleton's country," was near enough to the outskirts of civilization for some conveniences, far enough away to provide a degree of safety from the law, many miles beyond the railhead, and traversed, except for certain variations of route, by a single wagon road, the Black Hills Trail.

The Fremont, Elkhorn & Missouri Valley Railroad reached Wisner, Nebraska in 1871 and paused there several years, not resuming construction until 1879. The setttlement of the Elkhorn Valley preceded the coming of the railroad by several years. Oakdale and Neligh, sixty-five and seventy miles beyond the railroad, were in existence in the early '70s; Antelope County was organized in 1871. In 1874 the O'Neill settlement was founded, about fifty miles farther up the Elkhorn. In the fall of the same year, Troy, later renamed Paddock, was founded on the Niobrara River, north

39

and slightly east of the O'Neill settlement.

By way of General George A. Custer's expedition, the year 1874 brought to the public in a more official and widespread way the cry of "gold!" in the Black Hills of Dakota Territory. By October the first large civilian group was headed for the Hills—against government orders and wary of Army interception. Organized in Sioux City, Iowa, this group was the Gordon party, consisting of twenty-six men, one woman (Mrs. Annie D. Tallent), one boy, twelve yoke of oxen, and six covered wagons. They represented themselves as being emigrants, bound for the O'Neill settlement, at present-day O'Neill, Nebraska. Upon reaching that point, they continued on up the Elkhorn approximately to its headwaters, crossed over toward the Niobrara River, fording at some convenient place; according to their story, they crossed the Niobrara about twelve miles below Long Pine Creek. They reached the Black Hills in early winter and built a stockade where they wintered. The group was later discovered by the Army and removed. Nevertheless, there was a steady stream of goldseekers into the Hills — and by 1876 they were "legal."[1]

Wagon trails developed from the nearest rail and river points. By the spring of 1875, all routes leading to the Hills were beginning to take form. Trails led in from Pierre and Bismarck, Dakota Territory and from Sidney, Nebraska and Cheyenne, Wyoming Territory on the Union Pacific Railroad. Another route proceeded from Wisner, Nebraska westward to the Elkhorn River and up that stream to the Niobrara River — much the same route beyond the O'Neill settlement as the Gordon party had taken. The distance was about 350 miles by wagon beyond the railhead, but this trail accounted for an important amount of emigrant and freight traffic.

Gordon's route became the major one after a time, but not at first. At a point about ten miles downstream from the Gordon fording, an enterprising man, one Captain Giles, established a ferry in the early spring of 1875. This ferry site was very near where the present Holt, Rock, Boyd, and Keya Paha county lines meet. To cross the Niobrara here, the traffic left the Elkhorn Valley at a point some twenty miles above the O'Neill settlement.[2] Giles soon sold his business to Lem Rickord of Neligh. Realizing that this crossing was too far downstream for the best topographic advantage, Rickord moved upstream, after a season, to a point about two miles below the Laughing Water. To approach this ferry, traffic proceeded some forty miles up the Elkhorn beyond O'Neill; then once over the Niobrara, the trail followed the old Gordon route to a great extent. After crossing the Niobrara, the earlier Giles-Rickord route had paralleled the Nebraska-Dakota line for a considerable distance, while the new Rickord route headed the canyons of the Niobrara, though both routes converged before reaching the Minnechaduza.

Rickord appears to have had the field largely to himself for a season or two, but in 1878 John Morris and his son-in-law, Jim Warner, who had settled in the region about 1876, built a toll bridge across the Niobrara immediately below the mouth of the Laughing Water, just about where the Gordon party had crossed. This must have put Rickord out of business, as he disposed of his ferry and left, relinquishing his landholding to James McFarling. In the spring of 1879 the Morris bridge went out with the ice, so for that season Morris operated the old Rickord ferry boat at his own bridge site until he rebuilt the bridge the following year.

Warner lived on the mainland by the Laughing Water, while Morris lived on an island at the south end of his ferry run. A small commercial center developed here at this upper crossing of the Niobrara, and it was the focal point of such social activity as there was. It seemed to be the favorite gathering place for Doc Middleton and his men. By the time they began to frequent the area in the winter of 1877-78, there were a few settlers there. Even as early as April 21, 1875, the *Oakdale Journal* was talking about "the immense travel which is now setting in and which, as the summer advances, will increase to a steady stream." This Elkhorn and Niobrara route to the Black Hills carried a large amount of traffic of all kinds.[3] A century later traces of the old Black Hills Trail still remain in places along the way. Within a few years the Trail became outmoded by the railroad, but it played its part in the colorful history of the region.

In 1876, Holt County was organized, and Paddock, on the

Niobrara at the mouth of the Little Platte, later named Eagle Creek, became the county seat. In 1877, Dr. E. A. Reaves founded a settlement at the confluence of the Niobrara and the Keya Paha Rivers and platted the town of Keya Paha on the table land. Also in 1877, Henry Tienken, an immigrant from Germany, settled in the unorganized territory between the rivers above Dr. Reaves' town. He was joined there by his brother Charles. They were the first settlers and saw some trying times.

A man using the name F. J. Franklin arrived on the Niobrara in late 1877 or early 1878 and located a claim a few miles down the river from the Morris bridge on the north side. This man, whose real name was Barto, had become involved in some difficulties in his home state, left, changed his name, and remarried without getting a divorce from his first wife.

Also in 1877, Henry Richardson and Jake Haptonstall left their homes in Illinois and made a trip to the Black Hills with a load of trade goods. As they passed through the Niobrara River region, they resolved to return and homestead. Haptonstall returned to the country first and filed on a homestead; he built a log house about a mile below Morris' bridge on the north side. He was later joined there by the Richardsons. It was at Jake Haptonstall's log house that Doc Middleton first met Henry Richardson, his future father-in-law.

Outlawry became so bad that some settlers resigned themselves to having nothing but old plug horses and oxen to work, as it was next to impossible to keep a good team except at the whim of the thieves. The country was considered as bad or worse than Missouri in the region of the James gang.

It has been the belief in the Niobrara and Elkhorn Valleys that the Middleton gang did not molest the settlers but stole only from the Indians. I believe that this is true to a great extent. However, Middleton could not enforce such discipline among men of this stamp, and thefts sometimes occurred without his approval. Also, there were more criminals in the region than those known to be associates of Doc Middleton. Finally, Middleton would steal on occasion from a settler who had made the mistake of assisting a sheriff in an attempt at his capture.

The question arises, where and how did these outlaws live? Many communities have their Middleton legends; this or that canyon was a Middleton hideout. As to what sort of domicile they had, no satisfactory answer has been given. Doc and a small band of followers often stayed overnight or for a meal with a settler. They sometimes paid for lodging with gold coin; sometimes they presented their host with a horse, undoubtedly stolen.

It was the custom among the settlers to extend to all comers such meager hospitality as was possible within their means, and to ask no questions. Also, there were some settlers on the frontier who were little better than outlaws themselves, and their places sometimes were places of resort for the thieves. Thus it will be seen that the lawless element was not entirely without a way of making out. It was necessary that the outlaws remain ever ready to move on short notice, thus it was difficult for them to have any permanent abode.

Yet the legend of dugouts along the Niobrara has persisted to the present day and has been magnified beyond any possibility of fact. The pioneer photographer S. D. Butcher supplied a picture of a dugout, out of repair and falling in, purporting to be somewhere along the Niobrara; it was described as a Middleton hideout. Probably it was a settler's dugout and the outlaws occasionally stopped there. It may well have been the dugout of Bill Smith, near Jake Haptonstall's house.

There have been reports of excavations along the creek, colloquially known as the Haptonstall Creek in former times. These were at varying distances along the creek, a mile below Carns on the north side. Some of these have been described as being about the right size to conceal a man in a crouching position; they appeared to have had covers. A larger one was said to be of sufficient size to have been a domicile or to have concealed a few horses and riders. All trace of these has been obliterated by time, and I cannot vouch for the authenticity of the alleged findings. No law officers reported such excavations and no professional individual or group has ever verified them. The accounts are merely mentioned here for the legends they probably are.

Of course, the most persistent and dramatic account of Middleton dugouts and hideouts is the ever-popular story of Doc's huge underground areas large enough to accommodate herds of horses. A stolen band of horses would be secreted underground and land above so well camouflaged that any pursuing posse would ride right over the top without suspecting a thing. So go the tales. And the tales located underground corrals as far away as Boone County. I give as much credence to these stories as I did above to the legends of smaller dugouts. Anyone who has ever cleaned out a stable, as I have, will see how ridiculous the stories are.

An 1879 newspaper story about "the Niobrara bandits" and their "chief," Doc Middleton, referred to still another form of hideout: "It is said that they occupy an impregnable fortress where a few men could defend against many times their number."[4] I have lived in this region the greater part of a lifetime and am two generations descended from an early-day pioneer; I have the advantage of such local legends as exist, and I researched on the subject for over a decade. *Nothing* has been discovered of dugouts where men or horses could hide or of a stronghold where outlaws might make a stand against law officers.[5]

But, insist the believers, how could Middleton and his gang have possibly been so continually successful in their horse thieving without the underground corrals? The answer is undramatically simple. The "secret" was rapid flight for long distances with only a few men—and the hope of leaving the victim without means of pursuit. It was a fairly easy matter to stop and rest in a deep, timbered canyon where water and grazing were available; this was the extent of their concealment. Then after a time the flight would be resumed. In brief, the country itself was Middleton's strength.

Further, Doc himself was very wary, always carrying field glasses, for example, in order to observe people at a safe distance; and the outlaws carried arms and were more or less expert at their use. And let us not forget the settlers, whether their hospitality was genuinely friendly or only self-interested. Especially around Morris' Ferry Middleton was among friends, many of whom would be certain to warn him of the approach of suspicious strangers. Also, there existed on the frontier, even among the better citizens, a kind of disregard for law. While not outlaws, nonetheless when a law worked to their

Early scene on the Niobrara River at the Morris crossing, site of the ferry, the bridge, and Carns Post Office—headquarters for Doc Middleton and his gang. (The makeshift bridge was drawn in with ink by an unknown person; the diagonal line on the left running perpendicular to the bridge is caused by a crack in the original glass plate.) *S. D. Butcher photo. Courtesy Nebraska State Historical Society.*

The Newman Ranch, 1870s, a successful venture along the Niobrara. Drawing by "a young Englishman," from *Nebraska History*, Oct.-Dec., 1927 (p. 336).

disadvantage and breaking it did not put them at odds with their neighbors, settlers were likely to take a broad interpretation of the matter.

For instance, during this period there was an illegal still in operation near Niobrara and whiskey was stocked by the barrel at points along the trail for sale to "Black Hillers." The seller probably never thought of such a thing as a license. Roadside places catering to the travelers would supply a meal — or a drink of firewater.

Another common violation of law was the cutting of timber on government land. Freighters returning empty from a trip to the Hills would stop along the Niobrara and cut a load of cedar posts to sell back at the settlements. The first settlers made part of their living whenever possible by this sale of cedar posts.

During 1878 a number of cattle ranches were established in the "upper Niobrara" region. Notwithstanding its name, this area is actually about midway along the course of the Niobrara River. In August of 1878, A. N. Bassett arrived at the head of the Long Pine Creek with 500-600 head of steers, bought in Iowa. He ranged the adjacent region and the extreme headwaters of the Elkhorn.

Merritt Taylor, who settled in what later became Keya Paha County and who was a qualified observer, stated in 1879 that "during the past year, 55,000 head of cattle have gone up the Niobrara ranches and so far it has been only an experiment."[6]

In present Keya Paha County were the Brockman-Livingston ranch on the Keya Paha River and Theo Barnhart and Capt. Coffman, Texans, on the Niobrara. The Drexels, financiers, also ranged on the Niobrara.

In present Brown County were Cook and Towar, on Bone Creek.

In present Cherry County, the Creightons, financiers from Omaha, had three locations on the Niobrara and tributaries; and Herman Kountze had a location on the Niobrara. Sharp had two locations, on the Niobrara and on the Minnechaduza. Ranging on up the Niobrara were the McCanns, the Poors, and Seth Mabry. The great Newman Ranch was at the mouth of Antelope Creek, and there were others on the watercourses throughout the region to the south of these.

It has been claimed that Poor's ranch was a Middleton hangout.

Probably during the year 1878 an "outlaw ranch" was located on a tributary of the Keya Paha River at a point near the Nebraska-Dakota boundary. This stream, then unnamed but since known as Holt Creek, Keya Paha County, was named for George Holt, alias "Black George," a Texas outlaw. Holt and Little Joe Johnson were positively identified with this enterprise and with Middleton to an undetermined degree. It was apparently the plan to steal Indian horses and trade them for other stock which they would then take over to the ranch. They had some horses and mules at the ranch that they acquired in this way—and other stock which they had stolen. The location was a favorable one, being protected by rather abrupt bluffs toward the northwest.

At the time some of this stock was being accumulated, Middleton entrusted some horses to Franklin to keep for a while, until some disposition could be decided upon. Franklin sold the horses and kept the money, and thereafter did not dare come back up to his claim, but stayed down at Neligh. Some of the time his new wife and her son by a prior marriage stayed at the claim.

In 1878 Atkinson P. O. was established. A little settlement had grown at this point and prominent names there were John Carberry, Frank Bitney, Will Dickerson, John O'D. Nightengale, Pat Hagerty, and others.

Meanwhile, a few more settlers had arrived along the Niobrara. Henry Richardson brought his family—his wife Anne, and children Mary, Tom, and Rene. The Turpins, Belmers, Bateses, and Sam Likens, to mention a few, also settled within a few miles of the "upper crossing."

It was still 150 miles to the railroad. It was thirty-five miles to the nearest post office and trading center, and fifteen or twenty miles further to the next settlement—and to a sheriff, who had no jurisdiction in the unorganized territory.

5

Horse Stealing

In November 1877 Red Cloud's Oglala Sioux band and Spotted Tail's Brule Sioux band moved down to the Missouri. The Brules settled for the winter near the confluence of the Missouri and Niobrara, and in the depredations that followed it was they who suffered.

The first raid by white thieves on this band occurred before winter set in, about the first of December 1877. The Niobrara was partly frozen over; the thieves drove a large band of horses into it and drowned about half of them. Whether or not the remainder were successfully crossed over into Nebraska and sold out of the country is not known. The raids continued throughout the winter of 1877-78. By spring the Indians were becoming furious. The *Pen and Plow* of Oakdale, April 27, 1878, carried an article stating that "the Indians are in a vicious mood. Their ponies have been stolen in large numbers. They think their horses are scattered all along down this valley and have been sold in Columbus." Probably some of them were even then sold along the Elkhorn Valley. Later, a "wholesale" market developed there, at the outpost of the settlements. But another market farther away from the scene of the thefts was on the point of land between the North and South Platte Rivers. The stolen horses would be taken in a southwesterly direction, across Holt County and the unorganized territory adjoining, and then across the branches of the Loup system.

Middleton and a few men, three or four, would accomplish the actual theft and drive the stolen stock to one of these points on the Platte Rivers, on the Elkhorn, in Boone County, or elsewhere, and sell to a man with the means of purchasing the entire herd at a price allowing for ample profit at resale to the settlers, taking their pay in hard coin.[1] In this way the outlaws could afford to pay well for lodging with settlers. They could even be generous and make an occasional gift of a horse to a needy person whom they wished to help or to whom they might feel indebted for some favor. On the other hand, they would steal from those who crossed them.

Other gangs worked at this same nefarious trade, against other Indians and settlers in other localities, but few made the effort to "get along" with the settlers that the Middleton gang made in the Elkhorn and Niobrara region.

The average frontier desperado was far from glamorous. Actually, he was often offensive in person, unclean and unkempt and sometimes seemingly vicious by nature. He stole indiscriminately, particularly from the most helpless; he abused anyone he could; he did few kindnesses. Some of the men associated with Middleton at times were capable of the most depraved of crimes. But generally he was able to hold his men in check along the Elkhorn and Niobrara.

Middleton compared very favorably with the average desperado. He was "dressy" and personable. He ran errands of mercy on occasions and did many kind deeds toward the settlers, in addition to trying to police the valleys. He was welcome in most of the settlers' homes. This rounded out his formula for success: travel light, travel fast, travel friendly. All these qualities, together with his reckless daring when making raids, his escapes from posses, and his rare courage and self-possession in a crisis, account for the Middleton legend.

In mid-May of 1878 seventy-five horses were stolen from the Spotted Tail Indians and ten or fifteen from the settlers around Paddock. Though these thefts appeared later to have been unrelated, that could not at first be known. The Indians decided on a

retaliation raid, but upon learning that the whites had also suffered loss, they were partly pacified, at least as far as concerned
the settlers. A citizens' posse was gathered and a search begun, but
owing to a difference of opinion as to the course they should take,
they returned. They then regrouped and set out again. The trail led
southwest, across the Elkhorn at or near Carberry's (Atkinson), and
at this point the search party encountered four Spotted Tail Indians
under the supervision of Black Crow on the trail of their horses.
Thinking perhaps the two trails merged, they all banded together.
But the Indians were too resolute for the whites. The Sioux had been
riding at the rate of eighty miles a day, subsisting on dry bread and
a small piece of salt pork daily. The citizens group soon discovered
that they could not keep pace with the Indian, and after a few
hours abandoned the pursuit and left the Indians heading westward.

In the meantime, Capt. Wessels, commander of the post at
Spotted Tail, issued orders for a detachment of soldiers to start in
quest of the missing ponies, and took command in person. Arriving
at the Carberry's, he came in contact with the citizens group, and
they set out together, taking the same trail the Indians had taken.
After some days of beating around the country, they discovered
on the horizon a herd of horses and several horsemen. They
grouped, ready for a charge. The order was given; all went
together for the first quarter, when some of the civilians got a
trifle in the advance and discovered in the nick of time that it was
the Indians returning with the property they had recovered from
the thieves. A more scared party was never seen. They said they
imagined that the thieves had congregated and sought their destruction. The Indians reported that they had followed the trail about
four hours after the whites had given up and discovered the object
of their search some distance in advance; they waited until nightfall, crept up on the camp of the thieves, and watched them till
about 2 o'clock at night, at which time the thieves rounded up the
stock and went to sleep. Taking advantage of this, the Indians
drove off all the horses except one, which they generously left for
the four men. The command went twenty-five or thirty miles
farther, taking Black Crow with them to try and capture the men
and bring them in. But tiring of this, the chase was abandoned

and the military returned.

The civilians, then, decided that their horses had been taken in another direction, that their loss was probably a different theft entirely; so they headed off toward the Loup system. They arrived at Fort Hartsuff, had a meal, and beat about the country; finding nothing encouraging, they gave up and returned home one by one, worn out with the chase.[2]

Such is a typical horse-theft story from the Nebraska newspapers of the late 1870s. Whether Middleton was involved we do not know. Butcher tells a similar story, without dating it, but naming Doc as the culprit.

> Milton [Middleton] fell in with a young man about twenty-five years of age, five feet ten inches tall, a fine looking fellow with dark hair and eyes, the last man on earth that one would have taken for an outlaw. . . . For convenience we will call the young man Ed Smith.[3] He and Milton seemed to be natural leaders and planned many daring raids which were carried out by the band.
>
> The Sioux Indians had thousands of ponies in the southwestern part of Dakota and the northwestern part of Nebraska, and this band would go up into that country, four or five strong, find a bunch of ponies ranging in the hills, wait until night and then drive seventy-five or a hundred of them south, traveling night and day until they were beyond danger of pursuit by the Indians. . . . They soon became very well known all over the central portion of the state. Milton and Smith were both men of good address, pleasant sort of fellows, and assumed great credit to themselves because they never stole horses except from the Indians. In the degenerate days of the present, the code of morals by which these men regulated their conduct would appear a trifle lame, but in the wild days of which we are writing the aborigine was considered a common enemy who had no rights which white men were bound to respect or even consider.
>
> It is said that at one time Milton and Smith, with three men, made a dash on a band of horses and succeeded in

getting about 140 of them. The Indians had lost so many ponies that they had become cautious and night-herded them, making it more difficult for the thieves to get the start of them. There was a short time, however, between the watches in the evening when the ponies were not guarded. Taking advantage of this, Milton and his men made a bold dash, knowing that they were taking desperate chances. They crowded the herd at full speed all night, not knowing how soon they would have to turn and fight the pursuing owners of the horses. They headed for the Platte river, as usual, keeping their booty on the move night and day until they crossed the Middle Loup river, keeping a sharp lookout all the time for the savages. Not having seen anything of them, after crossing the Middle Loup they were lulled into security, and as men and beasts were alike worn out by their rapid and ceaseless flight, they concluded to stop in a small valley for a little needed rest and refreshment, and to let the ponies feed. Turning all their saddle horses loose with the herd of ponies, with the exception of one which they put on a lariat, they lay down to take a nap. They little dreamed that savage eyes were watching them from a high bluff a short distance in the rear. When they awoke they found themselves afoot and alone, many miles from any habitation, with very little provision and no horses, except the one that had been picketed near their camp.[4]

During the last week of July 1878, the Brule, or Spotted Tail, Sioux left the Ponca Agency and about September 1 arrived at their newly located home on the western bank of Rosebud Creek some 2½ miles above its confluence with the South Fork of the White River. But when they moved west, the thieves also moved and continued the raids. It is estimated that during 1878 and 1879 Middleton and his gang stole 3,000 head of horses, mostly Indian ponies, and ran them off to various points in Nebraska, Dakota, Iowa, Wyoming, and Colorado. They also dealt somewhat in cattle. They did an immense business and had little trouble in selling their stolen stock.

Butcher relates another incident, but this time Doc came off wtih no horses—and barely with his life.

> Milton and Smith, with two or three others, were reconnoitering a large Sioux camp on the Niobrara river. Just as they had reached a position southwest of the camp a band of Sioux came dashing upon them from the southwest with a war whoop. They were on a ridge. To go west or south meant death at the hands of the savages, who were closing in on them from both of these points. To go east would take them into the Indian camp, which was now all confusion with the savages running to and fro, catching their ponies and securing weapons, having been aroused by the war whoop of their companions. All the show for escape was to the north towards the river, which they proceeded to make for as fast as their horses could carry them, the savages only a little behind them in close pursuit, rending the morning air with their blood-curdling yells. In a few minutes the flying white men were on the bank of the stream, which they found to their dismay to be straight up over ten feet above the water. There was no time to look for a better crossing. The Indians, knowing the situation and feeling certain that they had the enemy at bay, redoubled their yells and rushed forward like a pack of demons. There was but one alternative open to the hapless Milton and his companions, and that was a leap for life into the boiling flood below. The leap was made, horses and riders disappearing under the icy cold waters of the river, but soon emerging and reaching a small island in the middle of the stream, covered with a dense growth of underbrush, into which they pulled themselves and horses and prepared to defend themselves in case they were followed. But the Sioux did not follow, and contented themselves by firing a few shots into the thicket which did no damage.[5]

It is difficult to understand why there would be a large encampment south of the Niobrara and why the outlaws' flight would be northward across the river. This would appear to have taken place when the Indians were on the lower Niobrara near the Missouri. The presence of an island in the river bears this conjecture out; islands are much more numerous where the river is larger and the valley wider. The upper reaches more nearly adjoining the permanent location of the Brule and Oglala Agencies do not have the islands, and it would be more reasonable if the outlaws were fleeing south across the river, the lower course of which at the time we are considering was the boundary between Dakota Territory and Nebraska. In any case, this is the story as Butcher told it.

On occasion, the agent of the Yankton Sioux would issue passes enabling them to leave their reservation and go hunting along the Niobrara and other streams. They sometimes made an appearance in Holt County and came into contact with the settlers there. There was not much friction, but thefts did occur. At one time a party of Yanktons stole some cattle from Orlando Dutcher and offered them for sale to another party. Dutcher recovered his stock by bribing an Indian to tell him where they were.[6]

Sometime during 1878, a party of Yanktons, including Peter Longfoot, the son of Chief War Eagle, were on a hunt far south of the Niobrara, on what has been described as a tributary of the Loup. They were camped for the night. Doc Middleton and two accomplices discovered their presence by accident while on their way back to the Niobrara from the Platte. They charged the camp in the darkness, firing their guns in order to stampede the Indians' horses, and in so doing wounded one of the Indian women. The Indians returned the fire, but the outlaws succeeded in driving off thirteen horses. However, the Indians brought down one of the outlaws, "Tom Brown," probably an alias, possibly supplied for the one occasion.[7]

John W. Douglas, Indian Agent for the Yankton Sioux, writing of this matter, stated:

> The last fellow . . . was shot in his saddle by an Indian rifle. He fell, calling upon his companions for aid, who were off in the darkness with what ponies they had succeeded in stampeding. The dead man was armed with a Henry rifle and

rode a Texas saddle, and his dress and accoutrements, from what I could gather from the Indians, showed him to be either a Mexican or a Texas horse thief, one of those bandits that infest the region of the upper Niobrara.[8]

So now Longfoot and the Yanktons had a score to settle.

One spring, probably in 1878, the Tienkens suffered a theft of most of their horses. The trail led westward up the Niobrara River, so they set out on the trail, walking and leading a pack pony. There was a rumor about that the outlaws were preparing to leave for Montana, that they had a camp on Plum Creek, a tributary of the Niobrara, in present Brown County, Nebraska, and that they were operating from this place until they could move. There is a legend that there was such a place in one of the canyons north of Ainsworth. Some have claimed to have seen the remains of corrals and other evidences of the place, but I have never located it. In any case, the brothers crossed the Niobrara at Morris', inquired but learned nothing of their horses. They were told that one of the Black Hillers had lost a mule the night before. They proceeded to the southwest across Long Pine Creek and lesser tributaries, finally reaching Plum Creek. They encountered other parties searching for stock stolen near Morris' crossing, but found no outlaw camp. They left another search party with what provisions they could spare and went home through a drizzling rain. Their horses were not recovered.[9]

It can well be imagined that the Tienken brothers must have been tempted to leave the country as some of the other settlers were doing. Land could be acquired closer to a market and there would be law and order. Here they were in a no man's land, attached to nowhere, as was all north Nebraska west of Holt County. They were recent immigrants from a well-ordered country and could scarcely believe such lawlessness to be possible. But they refused to give up.

These brothers were the "two German settlers of Holt County" mentioned in Leach's *History of Antelope County,* who did not show "as much friendliness to the gang as was demanded and expected." [10] This "wrong" attitude on the part of the Tienkens toward outlaws explains the stories of depredations against them by the Middleton gang, as opposed to Doc's otherwise legendary friendliness to settlers. As far as is known, the Tienken brothers had not as yet attempted to help bring about Middleton's capture, though at least one of the brothers, Charles, later did. Apparently the Tienkens were at this time only trying to endure until better times.

Charles Tienken went to Niobrara and bought a span of fine young mares which cost $235. The Tienkens knew by this time that thieves would steal them unless they watched them day and night. But they had to go after repairs for some of their haying machinery, so Henry started out for Turpin's place, upriver and on the south side. First he went to Andrew Hupp's place, left the team and wagon there, and then crossed through the river on foot to Turpin's. After getting the repairing done, he went back across to the north side to his team. It being late, he decided to stay for the night. He improvised a sort of corral and tied the horses' halters to his wagon; he slept in the wagon box under a tarpaulin, raising it up to look every few minutes. A thunderstorm came up and Charles' host begged him to come into the house, as no thieves would be out on such a night. But he declined and stayed out in the storm, trying to keep dry under the tarp. In spite of these precautions, thieves who had lain out in the storm crept up, cut the halter ropes, and made off with the team. Upon discovering the theft, Tienken and his host raced about, taking advantage of the flashes of lightning, but could see no sign of the thieves or horses. To quote Tienken:

We decided to get along with some cheap horses and oxen, the way the other settlers were doing. We traded for a fairly good one-eyed horse and an old plug that no one would want to steal. Otherwise horse stealing and holdups went from bad to worse. Meeting anyone on the prairie was done with all kinds of maneuvering. One would generally leave the trail a short distance, dismount and pretend to fix something about the cinch of the saddle until he knew whom he was meeting.

One time my brother and I were riding out of the bottoms onto the tableland when we saw three men riding along the trail. Of course we wanted to know why they were and rode toward them as fast as our plug horses could go; for precaution, one of them rode ahead a hundred yards and one dropped back a short distance, waiting for one of us to come closer so they could see who we were. We knew one of the men and were convinced that they were not crooks.

We had offered a reward for the return of our mares that had been stolen and soon received several unsigned letters, telling us to ride to such and such a place, where we would recover our horses, but we did not walk into any trap like that.

We finally received a communication that looked good to us. It read that the mares were at McCann's ranch on the Niobrara River, fifteen miles west of Snake River. We got in touch with the sheriff of Holt County, who deputized Robert Wilbert of Paddock to recover the horses. Mr. Wilbert and I started, taking William Feuchs along. This was before Fort Niobrara was established.

When we arrived at the ranch, Mr. McCann had not seen anything of our horses, but was very friendly and hospitable to us. One of our horses was sick with the colic and he took great pains in doctoring it.

That evening, one of the cowboys followed me as I stepped out of the bunkhouse; he told me that Doc Middleton had brought the mares to the ranch and that McCann had bought them in order to stay on the good side of Middleton, that he had sold one of them to a surveyor from Columbus, and that the other one had been taken to the Bull Camp on the upper Snake River, but that it would be useless to go there trying to find her because McCann had already sent one of his men to take her away from there. I thanked this man for the information, which made us feel pretty good.

After breakfast the next morning, Wilbert called McCann aside and told him that he was an officer from Holt County, that he knew where the mares were, and that he had better settle with me. Right then McCann saw what he was up against. He told us that all he had in the world was tied up in his horses and cattle, that under the circumstances he had to do things that should be overlooked, etc.

He went to his desk and handed me the check the surveyor had given him for one of the horses, $125, and agreed to let us have a horse to get home with. We left Feuchs there until our horse was O.K., and later McCann sent our own mare down in exchange for the one he had loaned us.[11]

6

Captures

According to the *Oakdale Pen and Plow:*

> During 1878, fifty or seventy-five horses have been stolen
> in Holt County. There is no county attorney, only a district
> judge who lives 150 miles from the scene of the crimes, and
> who has never made one official visit.

At the suggestion of F. J. Franklin, Sheriff Jeptha Hopkins of
Antelope County organized a posse in the fall of 1878 to attempt
the capture of Middleton and his band. Among the fifteen-man
posse were Franklin; Alex Belmer, a resident of Antelope County;
Frank Tappan, foreman for the Boslers, heavy losers of stock;
and Peter Longfoot, the Yankton Indian whose party was assailed
in the night by the Middleton gang. It will be remembered that
"Franklin" was the alias for fugitive Barto, who was not only
fleeing troubles in his home state but was also staying clear of
Middleton because he had cheated Doc on a horse deal.

In some way it was decided that the place built by George Holt
and others on the tributary of the Keya Paha was the location of
the outlaws. Perhaps Peter Longfoot and the Yanktons knew of it;

perhaps Frank Tappan knew something of the place; it is possible that Franklin had had some hint of the location when he was on better terms with the outlaws; or maybe they only guessed. In any case, on October 9, 1978, the posse went to the ranch. They had come prepared to encounter a sizeable party of thieves, but found only Holt, John Morris, and a man named Mason. The only suspicion against Morris was that he was there—that is, he knew the location of the place and therefore must surely be somehow implicated. Actually, the Middleton gang had presumably given him an Indian pony earlier; it had escaped from Morris and gone back over to the ranch, and he had ridden over to Holt Creek from his home on the Niobrara to look for the horse. The posse took the three men into custody and handcuffed them. Also, all the stock found at the ranch was confiscated, including the pony the outlaws had given Morris and the horse he had ridden to Holt's place that day.

Middleton's brother-in-law gives an account of how Doc just missed being caught in the posse's raid and how he reacted when he spotted from afar what was happening:

John Morris was over there to stay all night. They had given him a pony and he pulled the picket pin and—he'd been over there—and some horses he's used to bein' with, and, by god, he took the picket pin and rope and all, and went over there, went home, and the old man went over there; he knew where it was, and he thought he—it was eighteen miles—he thought he would go over and visit with the boys and stay all night, and that's when they handcuffed him and George Holt and took 'em to jail down there.

So, by god, Joe Smith and Jack [at this time Doc Middleton was known as Jack by some in the region] was a ridin', and there was a knoll in about a quarter mile, and when they come they would ride up to that knoll; Middleton had glasses, and he'd get off and go and look and see if everything was clear, you know. They was just gettin' started there, had them mules an' horses; so they was out, an' late, an' hungry, and Joe Smith, he was a stout, young fella, he said, "Aw, everything's all right"—had to ride a mile outa their way to get to the knoll. But Middleton says, "Well, I'm a goin' anyway." So he rides up and gets off and, by god, there was a wagon down there and a team of horses and a team of mules, and a lot of horses in the corral, and they was a carryin' the dishes outa the house. He took his field glasses off and he laid there, and he'd saw Franklin, and, by god, you know, Joe Smith rode up there, and Middleton pulled his Sharps rifle off the saddle and Joe Smith begged him for god's sake. You know he'd have killed Franklin at a quarter mile. He was gonna take a dead rest, and they had George Holt and Old Man Morris handcuffed. Old Man Morris, there after the horse they'd give him, was goin' to stay all night an' visit with 'em. Well, by god, Joe Smith said, "You kill him and if they ever catch us they'll hang us, just as sure as the world," and talked him out of it. They got on their horses and rode off and never went back there again. And they call that creek Holt Creek today. So Old Man Morris he had to stay there in jail till spring, till the term of court, and they didn't have a thing agin him, and he sued Jep Hopkins for false imprisonment, and, by god, I think they bought him off. And he'd write home to his wife, and he had Sam and Dan and Ed, three boys, and they had some cattle, and they had a cow that had twin calves, and he was great for fun, you know. "Oh," he said, "I don't care for anything, only I want to get home so bad to see my twin calves." [1]

Sheriff Hopkins, with his posse and three prisoners, began the trip down the Keya Paha and Niobrara toward civilization, driving the confiscated stock, seventy head of cattle and eleven horses belonging to the Boslers as well as all the other stock, some of which were alleged to have been stolen in Antelope County. After five days on the trail, they reached Niobrara. Here a hearing was granted.

At this point, Joe Johnson came riding into Niobrara, heavily armed and making the threat that he was going to free the prisoners. Sheriff Hopkins heard about this and deputized some cowboys, and as Johnson rode up in front of the Hubbard House, the sheriffs and deputies surrounded him and with cocked revolvers demanded his surrender. He gave up and was taken in with the other prisoners.

A complaint was made and warrant issued before Judge Cooley, dated October 14, 1878, and served by Davis Armstrong of Knox County. The prisoners, George Holt, John A. Morris, Joseph W. Johnson, and A. Mason, were charged with having, on or about the 15th of April 1878, stolen seventy head of cattle, worth $1,000, and eleven horses worth $300. The prisoners were held in the amount of $500 in the default of which they were conveyed to the county jail at St. Helena in Cedar County, the jail at Niobrara being considered an unsafe place in which to keep them. And there they languished in jail, the innocent and the guilty, until the grand jury met in March 1879.

The principal witnesses against them were Charles Lewis and Franklin who stated that they had seen these men and knew them to be instrumental in the stealing of cattle and horses. It was stated that brands had been altered. Franklin, upon inquiry of Judge Cooley as to the truth of the report that there were fifteen more thieves on the Dakota side of the Niobrara who threatened to rob Niobrara and the safes if these men were convicted, replied that he had heard them say it and that they looked perfectly capable of accomplishing the purpose.

By this rigorous prosecution of these four men, the citizens and the court hoped to set a stern example for all the thieves yet unapprehended. Perhaps they would see the handwriting on the wall, leave the Niobrara valley, and do their horse stealing some- where else.[2]

Let us return to Henry Tienken's account, where we witness the lack of friendliness between Middleton and the Tienkens.

One evening as I was going home with a load of cottonwood poles, I met a Negro, and as was the custom in those days, I stopped the oxen to have a chat with the man. He was riding as fine a horse as I had seen in a long time. He told

me that he had been working at the Newman Ranch and that
he had quit because of the cold Nebraska weather. He said
that he was going to ride to Yankton, sell his horse, and take
the train to San Antonio, Texas, where his people and
friends lived. He wanted to know how far it was to Bell's,
and seemed to be in a hurry to get away.

I supposed then that it was the cold that made him uneasy.
I noticed that he had a carbine slung to his saddle. I tried to
persuade him to stay overnight with us; that we would trade
him a pretty fair pony for his horse and pay the difference
in cash.

Now I had seen and talked to plenty of Negroes before
and it seems that I should have noticed that he was a white
man, blackened up, which he was; but the fact was that I
was looking more at the horse than the rider. Furthermore,
he had some Negro features and he knew how to imitate the
Negro dialect.

The next day, when this fellow stopped at a settler's house
near Lavinia, Holt County, the people noticed that he was a
white man, the white showing under his eyes and nose. The
man of the house slipped out and notified a neighbor, who
gave the alarm to another man nearby, and they planned to
capture this suspect right there and then.

The fellow no doubt mistrusted what was going on,
mounted his horse and jogged lazily along, but when the
pursuers got pretty close, and when they were out of the river
bottom and on the prairie, he was out of sight of them in no
time, heading southwest.

This fellow's name was Charles Fugate, better known as
Texas Charley. He knew that Franklin, whom he intended
to kill, was coming back from Niobrara, and but for the
men at Lavinia, he would have met Franklin that very day.

He [Franklin] went to Paddock and tried to get five or six
men to agree to go to his place [upriver, below Morris], hide
in the house, and he would try to decoy the leaders of the
gang there; and he thought it should be an easy matter to
arrest all of those who would walk into his trap. Finally four

or five men from Paddock came to us and insisted that one of us should go with them to Franklin's and help pull off this stunt. My brother finally agreed to go, but I refused to haul them and they had to walk the whole way. They hid in Franklin's house, but no rustlers showed up.[3]

Retaliation was not long in coming.

In late fall or early winter, Doc Middleton, Joe Smith, and Charley Fugate appeared on the south side of the Niobrara River at the lower crossing, intent upon crossing to the north side. Tom Richardson's description of this crossing is so vivid that it has to be used here:

McFarlin lived on the south side down there, and we was down there; we heard they was over there and they was gonna come across. We went down and there was ice on each bank, see, and the current just a runnin' like the devil in the middle, and them boys showed up at McFarlin's over there; so they went a lookin' down there—there was the Means boy and me, and, by god, there was three of us—anyhow, they got off into the river; Middleton plunged off into the river; they had to ride out onto that ice and jump off into the river —they wanted to get on this side. Well, he got over all right. Well, Charley Fugate, he got over; and Joe Smith's horse wouldn't stand the sand, you know; there was current and there was sand. And just as soon as he struck that quicksand, he went under—went down, all but—well, he went down and come up, and that water was ice cold, you know, and Joe Smith was havin' a hell of a time with him out there, you know, and Middleton, I recollect well, he still had his coat on, and he had—well, he had his pants on, and he got out in water up to his coat—and throwed a loop—the horse's head was down an' up, and, by god, he throwed a loop and caught that horse right around the neck, you know, god damn, say, he—and, oh, Joe Smith was damn near froze to death when they got him out. So they hollered, though, from over there, "Build him a fire over there."

Well, there was cottonwood galore, you know; somebody had—we built a big fire over there, and, my god, them boys —why, Joe Smith was wet all over; it was just something awful; by god, we built up a hell of a fire, and they took— Middleton even took off his drawers and wrung 'em out. And they was there about an hour; well, Mrs. Franklin lived in her house on her homestead; old Franklin didn't dare show up there; well, we stayed around there with 'em, and Middleton got to singin' a Southern song, you know, and there they had their six-shooters all wet, and pretty soon they got their clothes back on, cold and wet, you know, and they got on their horses and they started; by god, us kids followed 'em to Franklin's; must have been a mile, and they went in her house without any—never said nothin' to her, just three of 'em went right in her house, and her boy was there and George Callison was there—he helped build that house— they went in there and took their six-shooters out and took 'em all apart, cleaned their six-shooters all up; well, then, Tienken's was the next place—and they went down to Tienken's, and now, that was the worst I ever knew Middleton to do.[4]

For the story of reprisal against the Tienken's, we have the account of the brothers themselves:

While doing the evening chores, we noticed five men coming toward the cabin. Thinking they were from some cow outfit, we hurried along with our chores and feeding the calves, and I went toward the house in order to meet the men and tell them where they could put their horses up for the night. As I was coming around the cattle shed with an armful of hay, one of them stood in front of me, ordering "Hands up;" I threw down the hay and told them they were mistaken. My first thought was that these men were U.S. marshals, especially the one who wore clothing such as I had seen on well-to-do Mexicans [this should be Doc, but strangely Tienken does not identify him], but when they commenced cursing and yelling, "Stick 'em up," I realized that they were staging a regular holdup.

I looked around and saw that they had Charles covered too. A man named Frank Haskell, from Chelsea, Maine, was staying with us and doing the cooking; he was coming out of the cave with potatoes for supper when they cornered him. None of us carried a gun and the bunch had a snap and had things all their way. Two of them kept us covered with guns, another drove in our horses, and the other two ransacked our cabin and trunks.

Texas Charley wanted to know where we had our money hidden, saying that there would come a few Indian tricks on us to make us tell. He gave us quite a lecture, told my brother that he was one of the damned mob that had tried to trap them at Franklin's house and that this was their country and that they needed clothing and blankets and horses to make a final raid on old Spotted Tail's band. They fired off our guns, and took my carbine, our pistols, field glasses, and when my brother asked them not to destroy his heavy Remington rifle, they told him he would find it later. When they left, and got to the top of the hill, they threw the rifle in the grass.

When they were putting hackamores on our horses, we asked them to leave us with one horse. "Well," they said, "the old white horse looks as if he would pitch, and we can't ride him, and that Brownie horse of McCann's, we know all about him." There we were again with an old plug horse. Once more we mailed cards, giving accurate description of the horses stolen.

We received a letter from Con Groner, sheriff of Lincoln County, stating that Fugate was under arrest, that our horses were in that neighborhood, and for us to come and claim them.

The arrest of Fugate had come about in this manner. Late in January 1879, Middleton and a band of outlaws, eight in all, arrived at North Platte and offered eight or nine horses for sale.

They rode in quite nonchalantly, armed with revolvers and needle guns, making little or no effort to conceal their presence there. As they were obviously prepared to fight, and dared arrest, it was decided to use extreme caution. Finally, Sheriff Groner, with several others, some deputies and others who have been described as railroad detectives, decided to attempt the arrest of some of the worst. On January 19 they tackled Charley Fugate in a saloon and succeeded in taking his revolver from him, but in the ensuing struggle he drew a small pocket pistol out of some place of concealment on his person. There was a fight over the gun and Fugate accidentally shot off some of his own fingers, the bullet going through Sheriff Groner's hat.

Fugate was lodged in jail and charged with the theft of horses in Lincoln County on July 6, 1877. The trial did not come up for a couple of months.

As to the railroad detectives, one newspaper said of them that they were

> creating some excitement along the line of the Union Pacific Railroad. They do their work well, and make but little talk about it. They appear to have legal authority for what they are doing and seem determined to have their men. They are breaking up the worst gang of desperadoes that ever infested this region.[5]

To continue Henry Tienken's account:

> My brother and Charles Hoyt went by the way of Fort Hartsuff; from there to a ranch on the Middle Loup, and then to Plum Creek [now Lexington]. Hoyt remained at Plum Creek and Charles took the train for North Platte, made himself at home in the waiting room, and when the agent wanted to lock up, went across the railroad tracks to the round house. There the railroad men let him have some blankets, and he slept on the floor. In the morning he went uptown, had breakfast for twenty-five cents, and looked up the sheriff at his office.

They went to a dance hall where the proprietor turned over to him the field glasses and my Winchester carbine. Sheriff Groner had an order from Fugate to the owner of the dive to give up those things or there would be trouble. He also recovered two of our horses that Fugate had disposed of in North Platte. My brother was now without money and told Mr. Groner that he would like to sell one of the horses to raise sufficient funds to get home; the sheriff replied that there was no need to sacrifice his horse and loaned him the money.

Charles rode from North Platte to Brady Island, where he stayed with a farmer overnight, and the next day rode to Plum Creek to get the horse he had left with Charles Hoyt. From there he rode to Olive's on the South Loup, where he had no trouble in recovering our other two horses. He now had five horses to bring home. This last stop was the place where the two settlers, Mitchell and Ketchum, had been lynched and their bodies burned.⁶

On this same raid which resulted in Fugate's capture, several other lawless characters were rounded up, but no connection appeared to exist between them and the Middleton gang. Charley Reed, a Texan, was jailed; two Smiths were taken in a restaurant while eating with their needle guns across their laps. A murderer from Texas, named Moleskie, was taken; there was a supposed $3,000 reward for his arrest. Middleton and the rest of his group escaped.

So now Holt and Johnson were in jail in St. Helena and Fugate in North Platte. But there would be new recruits and the gang was far from finished. However, the situation of the Tienken brothers appeared to improve.

In late March of 1879, Charles Fugate was brought to trial before Judge William Gaslin in North Platte. He was found guilty on the charge of horse stealing and also on the charge of shooting at the sheriff, Con Groner. Fugate charged that Judge Gaslin had said at Kearney, Buffalo County, in the fall of 1878, that he "would like to get some of the Adams County rogues before him, and that he would sentence them." This was an attempt at proving prejudice. Judge Gaslin swore that he did not make the statement. When found guilty, Fugate is said to have flown into a rage and to have spoken abusively to the judge. Whether for this reason or not, Judge Gaslin sentenced Fugate to ten years in the Nebraska penitentiary for horse stealing and ten years for shooting at the sheriff, a total of twenty years.[7]

So now Middleton's half-brother had been put away for a good long while. Doc himself would continue to elude capture, but the noose to get him was beginning to form with more determined though uncoordinated efforts afoot.

In the spring of 1879, J. L. Smith of the Union Pacific Police Force organized a search party in North Platte to track down train robbers, horse thieves, stage stoppers, and various outlaws. He chose to accompany him "three of the best men in the police service of the Union Pacific." The party went northward until they struck the Niobrara River and then went eastward for several days. They were out ten days in all, on a long, cold chase which netted nothing. They reported that they struck the trails of several parties of rough characters, but were unable to come up with them. In what manner they concluded the character of the persons who made the trails is not clear. They said their discoveries confirmed their beliefs concerning the size and extent of the outlaw organization.[8]

By this time, William C. Lykens had resigned his position as stock detective for the Wyoming Stock Growers Association and had become a railroad detective.

Also by this same time, Middleton and his band were on the Niobrara in the vicinity of the Morris ferry. Doc announced that he and four accomplices were going down around Sidney and run in some wild horses. He left a favorite horse, Red Buck, with Jim Warner, who lived on the mainland, on the south side of the river at the mouth of Laughing Water. Warner had to put Red Buck on the picket rope; no one had a fenced pasture, only a few pole corrals for the close confinement of stock. It would be over a month before Doc would return and not all his followers would be with him.

While Doc and his band were heading for Sidney, a party of

ranchmen from North Platte had set out to attempt his capture. They apparently were unaware that he was heading in their direction. Newspaper articles heralded the ambitious goals of the ranchers. One article stated that the people from around North Platte were determined to bring Middleton to justice; that the party undertaking this was well armed and determined; that there were other desperadoes, notably Jack Nolan and Dennis Gartrell, the latter involved in the Olive affair, for whom there were rewards and who would be taken at the same time; that Creightons had offered $500 reward for the capture of Middleton; and that there were lesser criminals with the gang for whom there were rewards in smaller amount. Finally, it was acknowledged that the desperate character of the gang was well known and they probably could not be taken without bloodshed, but when the gang was broken up, the people would rise up and call the men blessed who accomplished it.[9]

The North Platte group did not get their blessing, but nonetheless the Middleton gang would not go untouched.

Doc and his four men went first into Custer County, where they remained for some time, staying at Olive's ranch. When they moved on, they took with them some horses in reprisal for their owner's serving on some of the sheriff's posses. From Olive's they proceeded to the Cottonwood Ranch and stole Phil Dufrand's prize horses, Frank and Fox. Jim Gray, a cowboy who was sleeping in the barn, put up a stiff fight, but the outlaws returned his fire with interest whenever the flash of his revolver gave them a target. After leaving the Cottonwood Ranch, they moved on to the Brighton Ranch; then to Frank Cozad's spread. The outlaws next showed up north of Sidney at the Water Hole Ranch, a road ranch on the Sidney-Black Hills route.

Sheriff Hughes, of Keith County, and a posse of three men, had been following Middleton and outfit from near Ogallala, up the south side of the North Platte River, for several days, always camping a day behind the gang. They followed them right into Sidney, arriving there on Sunday, April 27. The local officers were immediately apprised of the presence of the outlaws and on Monday located them precisely. The party had gone through town and put up about a mile and half west of Sidney.

Accounts vary as to the following events. A Texan named Charley Reed,[10] something of a gambler and desperado, was induced to go out to the place where Middleton and his men were staying and attempt to lure them into town, where a trap would be waiting. Middleton was too wary to go in, but Smith fell for it. According to some accounts, Smith was riding Phil Dufrand's horse, Fox; Tom Richardson said that Smith left his horse and got on behind Reed and rode "double" into town. This account may well be correct, since at the first sign of resistance on the part of Smith, the gambler jerked Smith's gun away from him, which he could not have done so easily had they been riding separate horses.

I asked Middleton's brother-in-law whether it was indeed Charley Reed who came out and enticed Smith into town. Here is his reply:

> Well, it could have been; he was from Texas and knew Joe down there, and I don't know what his name was. Well, he came up to the Grout House, a mile, and I don't know how he knew they were up there. But they was runnin' in them—they failed on them wild horses—and they come in and slept and was goin' to leave that night, make a night ride, and this feller showed up on a big bay horse, that Joe Smith used to know in Texas, and, by god, this feller says, "Don't leave to-night," says, "I've come up to take you boys down and show you around town." I don't know how he knew they was there, I don't know how he found it out. The Fitch boys, they knew a lot—they owned the Grout House, you know, up there a mile.
>
> So, by god, Middleton, he gets Joe to one side and he says, "Say, I'm not a goin'," he says. "You don't know what that man wants with us." And Joe, he got about half mad, and he says, "Why, I used to go to school with him in Texas." "Well," Middleton says, "you can go with him, and I'll stay her and get another night's sleep." And they had their horses saddled up, and hitched there, and was goin' to leave, and go right up over the country, and, by god, this feller showed up.
>
> So, Joe Smith had a Winchester on his saddle, you know,

and a six-shooter on, so he went to get his horse, and this feller says, "Oh, leave your horse, and get on behind me." So, he got on behind this feller. So they got down there, it was only a mile, and this feller says, "We'll ride around this alley and tie my horse." Well, by god, they rode right in there, and they just showed up on both sides.[11]

Joe ought to surrendered there; 'stead of that he slid off and started to run and they shot him, you know. And they pulled him into a building, and—shot, you know. Oh, I don't know how many times, but he called for him [Reed]; they says, "He's out here." He says, "Bring him in here." They brought him in—and the Fitch boys said Smith was on his elbow—Fitch boys found out some way—and so he says, "You're the son-of-a-bitch who gave me away," and slumped right down and died.

Well, then twenty of 'em on government horses, here they come on a dead run; if they'd give Middleton until eleven or twelve at night they'd had him; they'd a surrounded the Grout House, but he heard 'em, them big horses with them shoes on, on the hard road—he heard 'em, and, by god, he goes out there, he takes Joe's gun off the saddle and broke it over the gate post, and skinned his slicker and everything he had on the back of his saddle, and got on and took right up over the hills, and, by god, they run him—the best he could get at it, they run him for twenty miles, but they couldn't catch him. And he saw 'em—the moon come up and he saw 'em comin' over ridges behind him, and, by god, they gave up and went back.

And now he knew a man on the Running Water, a horse man, and Middleton knew him. He headed for that ranch, he rode that horse all that night until two o'clock the next day, about wore out, and he hadn't had nothin' to eat, and so he headed for that ranch—he knew that feller—to get a fresh horse. Well, the feller was gone and a boy was out there herding seventy-five head of geldin's, unbroke, so, of course he was hungry, so they went down and got dinner, and he told him what he wanted. "Well," this boys says, "we're short on saddle horses, but you can have your pick outa the bunch out there."

So he goes out, and he looked them over and he picked on a gray horse, and with the help of the boy, he roped that gray horse and throwed him and saddled him down and rode him up, and took his hat and herded him, by god, clear back to Morris's Ferry. And sir, I don't know how he done nights, but when he got down there, the horse was so damn poor you could see his ribs a hundred yards, and he gave that horse to old George Holt. George was down there workin' for Tarbell, and he give him to George. And say, that man was a judge of a horse; nobody paid much attention to him, but he began to pick up pretty soon, and when he picked up and got some meat on him, he was—oh, he was a fine horse.

So, he had Red Buck picketed at Warner's—he was gone forty days on that trip—Red Buck was fat, so he got on Red Buck and just rode around, day and night, visiting, and, by god, McFarlin was down there at the lower crossing, you know, and he rode into McFarlin's at twelve o'clock at night, he hadn't took the saddle off for two days and nights, and, by god, he turned his horse loose in the stay pen, and Red Buck and just rode around, day and night, visiting, and, by lin had a young wife, and she got up and—she knew that he liked—they had a milk house—that he liked cream and cake, and she baked a cake for him that night, twelve o'clock at night, and he stayed there and visited there till morning. Now, you can tell how he stood around that country. The Robisons, the Warners, the Morrises, everywhere but Likens, the only place but what really wanted to see him.[12]

Accounts vary not only about Joe Smith's death but also about Doc Middleton's escape. Some stories have him crossing the bridge at the town of North Platte, others at the bridge across the North Platte River north of Sidney, on the Sidney-Black Hills road. Some tales include a picture of Doc with the reins in his teeth firing a six-shooter in each hand as he roared across, believing the bridge to be guarded.[13]

The most appealing story comes from the *Sidney Telegraph,* which outdid itself with delightful irony:

> Our friend, Doc Middleton, who is a sort of cousin germaine of Claude Duval, hasn't been heard from since his visit to Sidney last week. The doctor, it will be remembered, had an engagement that suddenly called him out of town, and with the professional good sense of an M.D., did not state the nature of his business or the direction in which it lay. We are informed that the gallant boy crossed the North Platte bridge on the 3rd of May, riding a fine gray animal. As he neared the bridge, with the detestation all thoroughbreds have for matters of small detail, the doctor gently sunk the spurs a half inch into the equine's flanks, and gallantly doffing his hat to the gate-keeper, with the remark that he "would pay when he came back," dashed onto and across the bridge.
>
> He next appears at a ranch some ten miles above the bridge, and it being supper time, what more natural than to indulge his appetite, always good, but in this case keenly whetted by a brisk morning ride. He satisfies himself on that head, and bidding his newly made acquaintance a regretful bye-bye, he takes his departure unattended, not wishing probably to encroach on the sleeping rights of the occupants. And out on the cold, bleak, uninviting prairie, the chivalrous doctor makes his bed.
>
> The next morning dawns, bringing with it a renewed appetite, which is allayed at the same ranch, after which the gentleman takes his final and somewhat accelerated departure in a northwesterly direction. Prior to this, to wit, on the 1st of May, two other gentlemen crossed the North Platte early in the morning, their clothes being somewhat saturated with the water flowing in that turbulent stream. They crossed the Platte west of Chimney Rock, and were solicitous as to the whereabouts of a man who was supposed to be riding a fine gray horse. The man not having yet put in an appearance, the two men cantered up the Platte to Mitchell's Bottom, remained all night, and in the morning went on in a north-

westerly direction, after a man who was supposed to be riding a fine gray horse and wearing a sombrero.

We hope in all goodness they will find him, for it must be terribly lonesome sleeping alone on the broad, bleak prairies with coyotes and an occasional wood wolf prowling and howling around.

Still farther up the river, the doctor passed a pleasant evening playing high, low, jack and the game of cards, and being fearful that some thieving cuss might nip his Winchester, took the precaution to fondle it in his lap. So watchful was he that the gun should not part company with him, that when his temporary partner in the game had occasion to go outside the door, the doctor left the table, and backing up against the wall, nursed his gun until his partner returned. And that's all we know about it.[14]

Likely there are grains of error in each account. Whether Doc raced immediately for Morris' ferry on the Niobrara or made his way leisurely along the North Platte River for a time, we do know that there was a chase and that he arrived back at Morris' alone.

Joe Smith was dead, and the other three men were scattered, though they did return in due time.

Shortly after Doc had left the Niobrara for his trek to Sidney, George Holt and Joe Johnson appeared at the "upper ferry." They had escaped from the St. Helena jail. This explains why Holt was around for Doc to give the skin-and-bones gray horse to when he returned to Morris'.

Also on the scene when Doc returned was a mysterious outlaw known variously as Curly Grimes, Lee Grimes, Lew Curly, and Lew Wilson. He was another Texan, very reticent about his past. Jack Nolan also threw in his lot with the Middleton gang. Nolan, it will be recalled, had been targeted for capture by the North Platte vigilante group. He had earlier escaped from jail at Plum Creek where he was being held for the murder at Sidney of one José Valdez, a Mexican cowhand.[15] Nolan appeared on the Niobrara riding White Flanks, a prize horse belonging to Print Olive. Butcher says that Middleton traded Nolan out of the horse and sent it back to Olive;[16] since the Olives were Doc's friends, it would be like him to do that. Also at about this time the names of Dick Bryant and Bill Shebley (variations: Scheeble, Sheeby, Sheblits) began to be associated with the Middleton gang. Shebley, as we will call him, was from Iowa, as was Black Bill; perhaps they were the same person.

By the time Doc had arrived back at his haunts on the Niobrara, Charley Reed, the desperado who had tried to lead him into a trap, had come to an untimely end. Reed shot a local citizen of Sidney, named Loomis, in the thigh, breaking the bone. The leg was amputated and within a day or two, Loomis died. Loomis was said to have declined an invitation from a "bad woman," and she considered it an insult and called upon Reed to avenge the insult. After the death of Loomis, a mob took Reed, escorted him to a telegraph pole, rigged the rope, and leaned a ladder against the pole. "The miserable wretch, seeing that there was no escape for him, climbed the ladder, adjusted the rope about his neck, said 'good day, gentlemen,' and jumped off into eternity." [17]

7

Dances, Candy, Thread, and Things

The Niobrara-Elkhorn valley area has been particularly rich in Doc Middleton lore. Some of the tales are rather vague as to time and place; some are clearer but not completely authenticated. Some are probably very nearly the exact truth; some are wholly true. Others may be considerably in error but contain elements of truth. Many items from the narration of Tom Richardson are folksy stories of Middleton's kindnesses toward the settlers or other matter exhibiting the conditions and the social climate in which he moved in this region during his heyday. All in all, these anecdotes make their contribution to history. From Tom Richardson:

You see, they'd steal these Indian ponies and take 'em off down there and trade 'em off; and they give some ponies away; they give my dad a pony, and them Irish down on the Elkhorn River, they was all just stuck on Middleton. He was always giving them something.

Well, up on the river, when he would leave, the women around there, they'd say, "Now, when you come back, will you bring me some thread, will you bring me—," by god, them women on the river in our neighborhood would all say,

"Will you bring me—," oh, little damn things; well, sir, he wouldn't write nothin' down, and he'd get every little darn ol' thing any of 'em told him to get; he'd come around by Atkinson or O'Neill, and, by god, he'd come up there and visit, be for dinner, stay all night, and he never wrote nothin' down, and he never forgot nothin'. I never seen such a man.[1]

We remember that Middleton had a score to settle with F. J. Franklin. Here is how he got even in a round about way. Richardson continues:

And, by gosh, everybody—Middleton had everybody solid friends, except there was Franklin over there, and Sam Likens. Sam Likens claimed he was a cousin to that Bill Lykens, the detective from Cheyenne, but he lied. Franklin was afraid to come up there. His wife, or she thought she was his wife, she come up, and Monte Barto, pretty soon he come from Iowa with this gray horse, Chief.

Well, by god, it took a little while, and Black Jack Nolan was there, and Middleton seemed to find out and know that Monte Barto was Franklin's son; you see, his name was really Barto.

Well, he found out that that horse really belonged to Franklin, so Matt Timms, who drove a yoke of cattle back and forth, and Jim Prosser up there, by god, they was all friends of Middleton; so he found out the horse was down there. Well anyhow, he goes to Matt Timms; he come along with a yoke of cattle—you know, the road went around this way, and a road went up this way by Franklin's house, so he had Timms drive by—McFarlin kept the mail, and Matt Timms took some mail, and drove by and went in, and gave them their mail, and set and visited with 'em, while Middleton went around this way and stole the horse outa there. By god, next morning Chief was gone, and Monte got into an awful lawsuit; he replevied Chief, or he thought it was Chief, you know. Man told him, "No, that's *my* horse," told him how long he'd had the horse. Monte thought it was Chief; I guess

it did look like him—Chief went over to the South Loup—
feller said, "No, that's *my* horse." Monte replevied him, and
this feller, he replevied him back, and they had a lawsuit, and
this man proved this horse clear back to where he was suckin'
his mother, and Monte lost the case.

And, looka here what they done; he was there at Likens
for dinner, him and Joe Smith [It is questionable whether
Joe Smith was in the region at the time, though he could
have been], and a coupla fellers came across the river up
above this country with some Indian horses they'd stole—oh,
I don't know how many; you see, Sam Likens would plow
prairie in the forenoon and turn his horses out—he just settled there, you know, but he had a cabin built and a stable,
and a milk cow and a team, and he was puttin' in a crop,
and he worked the team a half a day, and then he'd plant
corn with a spade; by god, he opened the sod with a spade.

So these fellers came along with these stolen horses—they
crossed way up there, and they left them out there and
picketed their horses out near by the house—and they got
done, 'bout done eatin', and they heard a shot fired, and
Likens' team had grazed, and had got out there, and they
didn't look after them, and was in with these horses, where
they left 'em out there—and here come the Indians across on
the trail and got around the whole business, and when they
got a goin' good, they fired a shot, and they went outa there,
and Sam Likens' horses was gone in that bunch. And there
he was, puttin' in a crop, and, by god, he like to died off; he
had a family—now there he was, don't you see? He just had
a milk cow. Now, looka there what they done; Middleton
asked him if he could get along a couple of days, and him
and Joe Smith went over on the head of the Calamus River—
'twas settlin' up—now, there was nothing' said—there was
never nothin' owned up 'bout that—so Sam went out one
mornin' to milk, and there stood a work team in his stable
out there, and, by god, he just harnessed 'em up and went
to plowin'.

Now, Middleton done that, but there wasn't nothin' said

about it; wasn't anybody would guess who done it, but we all thought—he went out to milk that cow and there was a work team in there and by god, their collars fit 'em pretty good, and he went right on farmin'. Now, they done that for him, still he claimed he never had no use for him, and, by god, I told Middleton about it, and then when he come back up here, I figure five years later, Likens wanted to shake hands with him and Middleton says, "I don't know you at all." Now that's the truth. Robisons, Sheldons, McFarlins and clear down eight miles down to Means, well, I tell you, they was all for him.[2]

Bill Huntington in *Good Men and Salty Cusses* tells of Doc Middleton and another cowboy rescuing his mother and himself, he a babe in arms at the time, from drowning in the North Platte River.[3]

From several sources comes a story of Middleton's finding an immigrant family stranded along the trail, one of their horses having died. In one version the people were near O'Neill and heading for the Black Hills; in another it was in western Nebraska; from Tom Richardson the story is that they were heading for the Long Pine Creek country.[4]

In the one case Middleton dismounted, unsaddled his horse, and hitched it with the immigrant's horse, leaving himself afoot with the saddle; in another he went some place and returned with a horse, which is more likely. Perhaps this even happened more than once. Here is Richardson's account:

A man and his wife and two kids had a covered wagon and a goin', pullin' for Long Pine to get a job, and they watered at a spring and one of the horses drank too much and took the spasmodic colic and died, and there they was, three miles from this spring and a dead horse there; and Middleton and Joe Smith came ridin' along, and the woman, she was cryin' —they was awful friendly, and got 'em dinner, and so Middleton and Joe talked this over, was there for dinner and they was awful good to 'em, so they made up their minds.

Then they talked to 'em and says, "Can you make it, are you fixed to stand it here for two or three days?"

Well, they could go back three miles and get water, water this horse see, and they said, "Yes." And now they says, "Don't you worry," and they went over there somewhere and came back with a black horse, and, by god, hitched it up, and went on to the Long Pine. Now that's helpin' people; that's all true. Middleton and Smith was awful good to everybody.

The *Norfolk Journal* published about him havin' a gang of ten or twelve and there never was but three that I knew of. You see, this stuff gets out big, but when it comes to the truth of it, it's different. They said he had a gold tooth which shone like a yellow kernal of corn.[5]

Talking about some of the social activity in the community in the vicinity of the "upper ferry," Richardson recalled a dance in Jake Haptonstall's house:

We were living in Ol' Jake's house; he stopped there, and he came with some boys and they had a dance in Ol' Jake's house, and Middleton could play the fiddle, you know—god but he could play, oh, good old tunes that would make you lonesome—so he set up there and played a couple of tunes, and that didn't suit him—he wasn't gettin' to dance any—and Jim Prosser, he lived up there in a dugout, and he played the fiddle, so there was several boys there, come to the dance, you know, and some women from the other side of the river, there was two Robison—Lizzy Robison, Turpin girls, and I believe a Wyman girl—so, by god, he just slid off a bench and got on his horse and went on a run up to Prosser's, and here he come with Prosser on behind, with his fiddle, so they just danced, by god, till morning.[6]

There were many country dances and the Middleton gang attended them and were well-liked by the settlers. Nolan was with the group by now and was a polished sort, with apparently a better education than average. He had a good voice and would sing at these country get-togethers.

Doc was a good fiddler and took turns at playing; he was also a good dancer and popular with the ladies. When not otherwise occupied he would care for children so their mothers could dance. He brought candy to children and had a way with them.

On one of the occasions the dance was at Jim Davis'. Davis was a good fiddler, and someone had a bass viol and another a cello. Middleton was at this dance, danced once or twice, and complained of being tired and wanted to lie down. So Mrs. Davis told him to go into an adjoining room and rest, which he did. He was there only a short time, however, when he got up; he said that he had a dream that the detectives were closing in, so he went out, saddled up, and rode off. He had these premonitions and apparently believed in them.[7]

Another curious incident is related: Middleton was going out to Jim Davis' to see a horse. He encountered some horsemen, one of them Davis, whom he thought he recognized, but did not take the precaution of scanning them with his field glass. Suddenly, Davis, who was carrying a plow lay, raised it and pointed it at Doc, as a joke. Quick as a flash, Doc was off his horse and had drawn his rifle from the scabbard. The approaching horsemen hastened to make their identity known, and when they had come up, Doc was nearly in tears. He said, "Don't *ever* do that sort of thing again!"

There was always a certain amount of trouble with Jack Nolan. There was a story of a freighter having his horses stolen while he was encamped at night. A small group of horsemen rode up next day, observed the freighter in his plight, and pronounced it the work of the Black Jack gang; the leader, of striking appearance and with the familiar piercing eyes, said he would see what could be done. They later returned with the freighter's horses.

Nolan stopped by Slaymaker's homestead on one occasion; the Slaymakers had just come to the country and were breaking sod and laying up a sod house. Nolan rode up at dinner time and expected to be asked to dinner. When, however, they did not ask him, he took offense; he left, swearing to himself that he would get even. Upon his return to Atkinson, he broached the subject of stealing Slaymaker's cattle. Doc refused to countenance this, saying that they did not want these people down on them.

On another occasion, Nolan planned to rob Will Dickerson on one of his freighting trips to and from the town of Niobrara. He was going to do this on his own. Fortunately, Dickerson did not go the day planned because of a visitor who wished to have a ride back to Niobrara; Dickerson delayed a day, so Nolan lay in wait for nothing.

On still another occasion, Nolan suggested robbing Pat Hagerty's store and post office at O'Neill. Middleton was unable to dissuade him, so after they had gone to bed in Atkinson, Doc got up and made the ride to O'Neill and back, totaling forty miles, and warned Pat Hagerty. He was back at Atkinson before daybreak. When Nolan and accomplices entered Hagerty's store, several armed men rose up from behind the counter. Nolan and his boys heard Hagerty's voice, "Throw up your hands, ye bloody devils, yez!" They beat a hasty retreat and were allowed to depart.

Pat Hagerty is credited with saying, "Why, Doc was as straight a man as the best of us."[8] When I told this to Tom Richardson, this was his reply: "Well, Pat Hagerty told me that, and he says, 'Doc can come in here any time and get anything he wants, whether he has the money or not, and he don't owe me a dime.' "

Some diary entries by a former county clerk in Nebraska furnish us with additional personal recollections about Middleton:

> Doc Middleton was of the Robin Hood type, robbing the rich to help the poor. He had many, many friends and was generally well liked because of his good deeds, especially among the ladies. He attended many of their social events, and was an especially good dancer. Always well dressed, according to those times, with his high Montana boots well shined, corduroy trousers and fancy shirts. He was of medium height, dark haired, and of a rather striking appearance.
>
> James Ewing settled in a log house across the river from the present town of Ewing. He had a caller one night, who asked to spend the night. Like all Westerners he did not ask any questions of the stranger. During their conversation, the

visitor mentioned that he did not see any stock about the place and the old man remarked that Doc Middleton had stolen them. Just how he knew or what he suspected was not mentioned. However, the guest was given the back part of the room and the old man lay down across the door with his gun handy. Some time in the night, the guest left, and a couple of nights later, the old man's horses were back in the corral.

An old Irishman by the name of Con Keyes, who lived two miles west of O'Neill, missed an old cow and horse and swore they were taken by Doc. He walked all the distance of 75 miles to Doc's hideout and demanded their return. Doc took him to the corral, had him pick them out and told him they would not be bothered again. Some of his boys had done the job without his knowing about it.[9]

In A. J. Leach's *History of Antelope County* a story is told of a horseman arriving just at evening at the house of a Mr. Caldwell, about three miles from the southwest corner of Antelope County, and asking to stay all night.

This request was readily granted for in those days a traveler was always welcome at the home of any of the settlers. . . . The stranger was a good looking young man, of slender build, somewhat above medium height, and had a gold tooth that plainly showed when he smiled or when engaged in conversation. His horse, a good one, appeared tired and jaded, as though he had been ridden a long way. The horse cared for, and supper served, the young man, complaining of being weary, was shown to his bed. The next morning Mr. Caldwell's son, on going to the stable to look after the horses, found the stranger's horse in the stall all right, but their own riding horse was missing. On going to the house to report the fact, the stranger's bed was found empty. He had gone in the night without disturbing any one, leaving his own tired horse and taking Mr. Caldwell's fresh one instead. Mr. Caldwell, thinking he had no great cause to be dissatisfied, the horse that was left behind being a better one than the one taken, let the matter go and made no effort to recover his own horse.

That same morning, just after the family of D. E. Beckwith had finished breakfast, a stranger rode up to the door and asked for something to eat. He stated that he had lost his way, and had slept in the straw stack the latter part of the night. Mr. Backwith, at that time, lived on his claim just six miles south of Neligh. The horse was taken to the stable and fed, and Mrs. Beckwith at once prepared breakfast for the stranger. She noticed that when her guest removed his coat to wash and comb, which he did with great care, that he carried a belt filled with cartridges and a revolver attached. These he did not remove. She also noticed that in talking he exposed a gold tooth. Her guest was the same one that had stopped the night before at Mr. Caldwell's, on Beaver Creek. After breakfast he offered to pay his fare, and, asking the distance to Neligh, mounted his horse and rode away. Mr. Beckwith's boys observed, however, that he followed the Neligh road only about half a mile, and then, turning to the west, struck off over the prairie at a gallop. This was the notorious "Doc" Middleton, or "Gold Tooth Jack," or just "Jack," as he was known to his confederates.[10]

Middleton had ridden about twenty miles that night, and the change of direction was, of course, for the purpose of confusing any possible pursuers.

Ben Arnold told this story:

On one occasion, when I was running a road ranch, a man came to stay over night with us. According to custom, strangers were taken in and no questions asked. The weather was cold and of evenings the guests sat around the large stove in the sitting room. Later the same evening, another man came for lodging, who proved to be a peace officer, on the lookout for some of the bandits who had been making travel unsafe for several months.

After supper, we all sat around the stove, the peace officer made known the fact that he was out looking for some of these robbers, and especially for Doc Middleton, known to be the most dreadful of these lawbreakers. He didn't mince matters in the least and told us emphatically what he would do to Middleton if he ever run across him. When he had about talked himself out, my other guest, who had sat silent and unperturbed throughout the peace officer's monologue, spoke up and asked:

"You say you have a warrant for Doc Middleton?"

"You bet I have," was the prompt reply.

"Well, I'm Doc Middleton," said the stranger, composedly.

The peace officer gasped, and it became immediately evident that he had decided that he was not looking for Doc Middleton after all.

"Well, why don't you serve your warrant?" asked Middleton. "I'm here."

With trembling fingers, the deputy sheriff pulled out the warrant and began to unfold it in the uncertain light of the kerosene lamp, whereupon Middleton reached over, and in an unconcerned sort of way took the paper and threw it into the stove. The deputy had taken off his revolvers before eating supper, but Middleton still carried his buckled around him. The deputy hadn't a chance and he knew it. Middleton was not only a desperate character but fearless and unbeatable in gunplay.

I have never seen anyone whose face revealed less of what was going on in his mind; he permitted the deputy to go on his way without his guns and never joked or said anything about the affair. As soon as it was over, it was as if it had never happened.[11]

The following is taken from *Adventures of a Tramp Printer* by John Edward Hicks. As an itinerant printer, Hicks was making his way westward and journeyed to Norfolk, Nebraska but found no work there.

One of the printers gave me a tip that there might be a job

at "O'Nale's" if I were willing to "kiss the Blarney Stone." . . .
The wag added further that doubtless the judge [Judge G. M.
Cleveland, editor of the *Holt County Banner*] would arrange
accommodations for his printer at the Grand Central Hotel
in O'Neill.

What more urging would one need? There were visions of
setting type on the *Banner* for the kindly judge and of spend-
ing my evenings in a comfortable wicker chair on the broad
veranda of the Grand Central Hotel. The culinary advantages,
too, would be equally great—no doubt.

But disappointment awaited Hicks. There was no work at the
Banner, and "the hostelry with the highsounding name was only
a sod house." Further, the area seemed plagued with "devilment"
and "merry hell."

O'Neill was in that part of Nebraska often referred to as
"Doc Middleton's country," because up to that time there
had been a minimum of organization in behalf of law and
order, and the doctor, though lawless, was a sort of law in
the land. His cattle rustling activities [Middleton has often
been erroneously identified with large-scale cattle stealing]
were extensive and he had a large retinue of followers among
the "pony boys" of the area. This ilk went heavily armed and
usually could be counted on for any sort of devilment, but
all in all, their major crimes were cattle stealing. . . .

Opposed to the pony boys were the cowboys, who, while
counted on the side of law and order, could raise seven kinds
of merry hell and still stay within the rather elastic code of
behavior known as "the law." Invariably they rode into town
on Saturday nights and spent their wages and just as invariably
the good citizens went home and locked their doors—"hunted
their holes" as the cowboys expressed it. . . .

[Doc Middelton] was a tall, dark man with a natural gift
of leadership and a glint in his eye that boded ill for those
who dared oppose him. He was a sort of Rob Roy of the
sand hills and many tales were told of his helping the wretched

settlers. It is no reflection upon the law-abiding proclivities of early-day Nebraskans that they would endeavor to shield Middleton when he was hiding out from the law. It simply is a psychological manifestation that has appeared among the common people in many places and at many times.[12]

Many more stories could be told of the doings of the Middleton gang. Every unexplained theft of stock was blamed on them; crimes of such a nature as to seem out of character for Middleton, hundreds of miles from his haunts on the Niobrara and Elkhorn, were credited to him. In the brief period of eighteen months, it seems impossible that he could have been implicated in half of what has been credited to him, but these tales demonstrate how he had captured the public's fancy.

8

Sioux

By spring of 1879, the forces of law and order were beginning to coalesce. True, the sheriffs had made some attempt at holding lawlessness in check, but without conspicuous success. The unorganized territory of Nebraska was a vast emptiness, with no law enforcement of its own; the comparatively few cattle ranches scattered far and wide were unable to defend themselves from either Indian or outlaw. The sheriffs of the adjacent counties sometimes penetrated the region but usually without much success. They had their hands full in their own respective counties without attempting to police such a vast area so far from home. There were the occasional attempts at recovering some stolen stock and, of course, the forays of the reward hunters.

Holt County was eventually to attach a strip of country about sixty miles in breadth and 170 in length, for taxation and judicial purposes, but this had not as yet been done, and when accomplished it did little toward bringing law and order to the country.

As early as the spring of 1878, the *Oakdale Pen and Plow* had recognized the existence of a den of outlaws on the Niobrara and suggested that there was a job for U.S. marshals.

In late December 1878, it was reported that the Indians were burning off the ranges of the "upper Niobrara" ranches in an attempt at driving the ranchers out. Troops were sent from Fort Hartsuff to investigate, and while they found that there had been extensive fires, there was no proof of Indian hostility. However, it was becoming recognized that the activities of white desperadoes were jeopardizing the peace between the Indians and the ranchers and settlers. By the early spring of 1879, there were more fires. The *Cheyenne Sun* of March 20, 1879, published the following item:

A letter just received from Mr. James Creighton and published in the Omaha papers Tuesday gives some interesting news from the cattle ranges northeast of Cheyenne. The writer says: "One of Poor's men came from Spotted Tail Agency and stayed at your ranch on the night of the 5th. He says that the Red Cloud and Spotted Tail Indians are killing cattle as they come to them, skinning and selling them to the buyers at the agencies, and are also burning the prairies. The stockmen will lose a great many of their cattle if they don't put a stop to this immediately. We need protection right away and if we don't get it soon, further trouble is looked for. We can see the Indian fires every night in every direction. A good many cattle are dying but not as many as I expected. I got here yesterday morning the 10th, and will remain here for a few days. The news reached here from Atkinson that there were 100 Sioux there yesterday, hunting their ponies, and they met Wallace and several others fifteen miles this side of Kountze's ranch."

It was soon after this that Creighton's ranch offered $500 reward for the capture of Middleton.

Mr. Sharp and some of the other ranchers of the "upper Niobrara" had made a strong appeal in late 1878 to Senator Algernon S. Paddock for the assistance of the military in securing the arrest of both Indians and desperadoes, who were allegedly riding into the ranches and stealing stock. Paddock had sent the appeal on to General Sherman and received the following letter in reply:

My Dear Sir: I beg to acknowledge receipt from you of what

amounts to a petition to Congress to repeal the 15th section of
the Act of Congress approved June 18, 1878—the posse
comitatus clause of the Army bill. I recognize the great importance of protecting and encouraging the growing and most
valuable cattle interests of Nebraska, but with most profound
respect for yourself and for Congress, I don't see how soldiers
can do impossibilities with both hands and feet tied. Should
Indians or white desperadoes come into Nebraska from the
Indian country, you make it a fine of $10,000 and imprison-
ment for two years if soldiers help your sheriff. Now, our
officers don't usually have $10,000 handy about them, nor do
I feel disposed to advise them to spend a couple of years in
the penitentiary by trying to help your sheriffs arrest and punish cattle and horse thieves. On the other hand, in the Indian
country, soldiers can only act upon application of Indian
agents, and these same Indian agents think that your constitu-
ents steal the ponies and cattle of their Indians.

So we soldiers occupy a most unpleasant position, and I
prefer to sign my name to the petition itself, for I sympathize
sincerely and deeply with Messrs. Sharp and others in their,
desire to add to the wealth and prosperity of our nation. But
I must frankly say that the law takes away from the Army the
only legitimate way of helping them by supplying the sheriffs
of border counties with the necessary "posse comitatus" to
make arrests. It would be a waste of money to establish any
new posts because the Indians and cattle thieves know the law
as well as we do and laugh at the soldiers who are forbidden
to help the peace officers of your State. With great respect,
W. T. Sherman, General.[1]

In December 1878 Senator Paddock secured quick passage of
a bill providing that the posse comitatus section of the army bill
not be applicable in "the States of Nebraska, Kansas, Colorado,
Oregon, Nevada, and Minnesota and Territories subject to Indian
incursions." It was sent to the House but died in committee when
the 45th Congress adjourned in March 1879.[2]

Around April 20, 1879, Kid Wade, Sneaky Johnson, Bud Wilson,

Charles Lightner (alias Lightning), and Sam Morris ran off a large number of ponies from the Rosebud Agency. Here is at least one horse theft from the Sioux which Middleton did not participate in; he and his four companions were at that time leaving Custer County for Sidney, where Joe Smith would be tricked and killed and Doc would have to make a hard run for it to escape capture. Except for Smith, and maybe Black Bill, we are not sure who Middleton's group were on that April 1879 foray down into Custer County and over to Sidney, but at least we know five men who were *not* with him.

On April 30 or May 1, 1879, the "Black Jack Gang" stole eighty-three ponies from the Spotted Tail Indians.[3] It will be remembered that at this time Joe Smith had been dead less than three days and Middleton was making his ride back to Morris' ferry after eluding his pursuers. Therefore, Doc could not have been involved in this horse theft. Nevertheless, many folk thought of the Black Jack gang as Middleton cohorts—and with just cause, since they were closely associated. Though Jack Nolan and Middleton were often at odds, Nolan did run with the Middleton outlaws. However, Nolan was beginning to make a name for himself. Little Joe Johnson teamed up with him and sometimes Curly Grimes would throw in his lot with them. But it is difficult to imagine Grimes accepting authority from anyone; he was said to be the "fastest gun" west of the Missouri. He had perfected a system of snap shooting without seeming to aim; and as for cool accuracy, when taking careful aim, was said to be able to put every bullet in an oyster can at a hundred yards.

On one occasion, this trio dispossessed Deputy Sheriff Valentine of Dawson County of his horse, guns, and money near Atkinson, leaving him to carry the saddle. This occurred in broad daylight and was observed by settlers who were at the moment laying up sods for a house. They kept their heads down and made no sign that they saw it. The deputy had come up from Plum Creek to return Nolan to jail to await trial for the murder of the Mexican cowhand at Sidney.[4]

The remarkable thing about all these thefts from Indians and pursuits by them is that there was so little loss of life, but at last, on

May 6, 1879, an innocent party, a cowboy, was killed on one of the "upper Niobrara" ranches. James Williamson and Felix James were out driving a few horses belonging to Paxton to the ranch on Snake River when fired upon by a party of Indians. Felix James gave the spurs to his horse and escaped by leaping into the river, while Williamson returned the fire but was shot down, three bullets piercing his body. His body was brought to McCann's ranch a few days afterward and buried. His grave was for many years marked by a board marker, which has since been replaced by a granite marker and the wooden headboard placed in a museum at Fort Robinson. The Indians no doubt mistook the herders for horse thieves as they had lately lost many ponies.

Six Indians, Two Calf, Gray Dog, Bull Thunder, Horned Horse, Bear Man, and Turning Bear, were surrendered to white authorities and held in custody at various forts. They were finally brought to West Point and placed in jail, the idea being to try them in district court there. When the case came up, in 1881, they were freed on the ground of lack of jurisdiction and were escorted back to the Spotted Tail agency.[5]

There are records and oral tradition in Cherry County about the killing of two other cowboys by Indians under circumstances similar to the death of James Williamson, but the identities of these men have been lost. As indicated, considering the provocation the Indians had, the death toll for whites was *very* low.

In May 1879 a character known as "Black Hank" (Frank Slaven[6]) stole twenty-nine Indian horses from the Pine Ridge Agency. Black Hank was said to be a member of the Middleton gang, but then the same was said of almost all desperadoes in the area. This theft prompted the Indian agent, Dr. V. T. McGillycuddy, to empower one William Kellum to reclaim stray or stolen Indian ponies wherever he found them. Kellum proceeded, with his instructions, to Fort Hartsuff. He stated that hundreds of horses had been stolen from the Indians, and if no effort were made to recover them, the Indians were liable to make a raid and recover them by force. He reported that a large number of horses were held by farmers in the Loup Valley and that he had seen a number of them. There was an indifference to this wholesale horse stealing among the settlers;

they seemed, in fact, to connive in the practice and partake of the benefits by buying horses at cheap rates from the thieves.

After resting overnight at the fort, Kellum went to the county seat, accompanied by two soldiers from the fort, Pvts. Eppelt and Jacobs, who volunteered their services. Securing the help of the sheriff at Ord, they proceeded up the valley again, and about midnight they arrested the suspected horse thief, Black Hank, at a settler's house. All of the stolen ponies had been disposed of when he was captured; some had been sold and others traded for cattle, a wagon, and various articles. The outlaw seemed to feel no apprehension, as he was making his way out of the country in leisurely fashion in a wagon drawn by a yoke of oxen. Illustrative of the cooperation between the settlers and the thieves was the fact that the occupants of the house in which Black Hank was arrested endeavored to mislead Kellum and the sheriff.[7]

This is the opinion of the *Black Hills Journal,* which reprinted news reports of this affair:

> The interests of this entire region demand that the agents succeed in restoring ponies to their original owners. The Spotted Tail Indians have been uniformly friendly to the whites during the late war, and the Red Cloud band nominally so, at least, and this nefarious practice of carrying off their ponies causes a just indignation among these bands, which may at any time lead to an outbreak, when troops would have to be sent to punish the savages for seeking to recover their own property wrongfully taken from them. The courier, Kellum, is entitled to great credit for the zeal and energy he has displayed, and especially his courage in alone defying the gang that has so long defied law on the border.
>
> We are not of that class, and thank God, they are not numerous anywhere in the West, who think the Indians should be despoiled of their property at every opportunity—that it is not a moral offense to steal from them. Our view is that a white thief who steals from an Indian is tenfold more criminal than the Indian who steals from a white man, because one pretends to be civilized and the other is a barbarian. Is it to

be wondered that we are "in the midst of alarms" from Indian raids where the infernal outrages are tolerated?

On May 19, 1879, Governor Albinus Nance received a telegram from Thomas Henry Tibbles of the *Omaha Herald,* requesting the governor to come to Omaha and meet with a large group of cattlemen who had "desperate trouble with Doc Middleton and Indians."[8] Governor Nance next received a letter, dated May 29, 1879, from V. T. McGillycuddy, Indian agent at the Pine Ridge (Red Cloud) Agency, reporting that ninety-seven head of horses had just been stolen from the Indians and requesting that action be taken.[9] This letter does not mention Middleton, and for good reason; it is known that Doc did not participate in this raid, for he was otherwise occupied at the time, as will presently be shown.

Of course, Doc Middleton had participated in plenty of other raids on Indian ponies. The following incident was related by Middleton himself to Captain J. H. Cook of Agate, Nebraska, who later told the story. Doc claimed that it was his last attempt to raid the Indian agencies.

> He and three others, all of whom I knew, conceived the idea that they could go up into the country near the Red Cloud Indian Agency, . . . where they thought the Indians would not feel that they had to guard their horse herds very carefully; and run off a big band of ponies, which they could turn over to some confederates, in the country lying just north of North Platte city. They all had good horses and took no pack horse with them, but each man had an extra blanket, and a little food, which he carried on his saddle horse. All of them were well armed. Three of them carried Winchester rifles. The other man carried a government "Long Tom needle gun" across his saddle. When they arrived within a few miles of the Agency buildings, they discovered a large encampment of Indians on a creek named Little White Clay, near the Red Cloud Agency. . . . These Indians had a big band of ponies, but they kept a guard consisting of several men with it, both night and day. Doc, and his associates, were concealed in the rocks and timber

on an elevation where they could overlook the Indian camp and horse herd. They waited for a favorable moment to arrive, when the herd was left unguarded. Food ran low, and the horse thieves were none too comfortable, or safe, from discovery by the Indians. One evening, Doc, who was watching the herd of ponies from his perch among the rocks, saw a fresh lot of Indians ride out of camp to night-herd the ponies. Acting on the impulse of the moment, Doc pumped a lot of lead out of his Winchester into the midst of the Indians' camp. Naturally the camp swarmed out after them. The only thing left for those enterprising horse thieves to do then was to make a very hasty departure for Ogalalla [sic], Sidney or North Platte city.

They certainly did so, with all the might and main they and their horses possessed. In speeding over some open ground the horse ridden by the man who carried the long needle gun across his saddle, stepped into a gopher hole and turned a somersault. His rider was not injured much, so the moment he and the horse could get on their feet, and the gun had been secured from where it had been thrown as the horse turned over, all were off again for the land of safety. Not until they had ridden an hour or so from the place where the horse fell, did they discover that the barrel of the long gun was bent into the form of an arc of a circle, and was a worthless impediment to their flight, when, in their imagination, the whole Sioux nation was pursuing them. They arrived safely in the white man's country, but that was the last venture in stealing a big band of Sioux ponies.[10]

There is no date affixed to this abortive raid, but I have no doubt that it happened. It is plain that this sort of activity could not go on indefinitely; the forces were gathering to put an end to it. But whereas previously the direct approach was taken (according to the western mind, there was no other way), a devious method would soon be used. However, now another chapter in Middleton's life was unfolding.

9

Marriage and Pardon

Doc Middleton, the notorious Great Plains outlaw, turned up in a new role. The story, as reported in the *Omaha Herald* of June 28, 1879, was as follows:

> Sometime since, Middleton became enamoured of the daughter of a ranchman in the region through which the outlaw raided, and the girl would have been less than woman if she had not returned his affection. He revealed his passion, proposed marriage, and was accepted.
>
> Then came the question of where the marriage should take place and by whom the ceremony performed. There were no county officials in the neighborhood to grant the license, and no clergyman to perform the ceremony. With about twenty detectives on the lookout at the several points where these incidents of civilization could be found, this seemed by no means an easy task. He hurried off to Holt County and without trouble procured a license. Returning with two ponies and this formidable document to the abode of his charmer, the loving couple started together for the Niobrara where a clergyman was found to perform the necessary offices.

Mary Richardson, second wife of Doc Middleton. In her letter to Doc's mother (infra, p. 136), Mary mentions a picture taken "when I was fifteen years old"; this is in all likelihood that photo.

MARRIAGE RECORD, *Holt* COUNTY, NEBRASKA.

Mr. *J. M. Sheppard*
Mrs. *Mary Richardson*

No. *12*

Before the County Judge of _____ County, Nebraska

18____

MARRIAGE LICENSE.

The State of Nebraska,
Holt _____ County. } ss.

OFFICE OF THE COUNTY JUDGE.

License is hereby granted to any person authorized to solemnize marriages according to the laws of said State, to join in marriage Mr. *J. M. Shepford* and Miss *Mary Richardson* of the County aforesaid, whose ages, residence, etc., are as follows:

NAMES OF PARTIES	AGE	COLOR	PLACE OF BIRTH	RESIDENCE	FATHER'S NAME	MOTHER'S MAIDEN NAME
J. M. Richardson Shepford Groom	25	white	Illinois	*Long Pine Nb Co.*	*D. Shepford*	*Boone*
Mary Richardson Bride	18	"	"	*Keny. Neb.*	*Henry Richardson*	*Ann Richardson*

And the person joining them in marriage is required to make due return of the annexed Certificate to the County Judge of said County within ninety days, of the names of the parties, time and place of marriage, and by whom solemnized.

In Testimony Whereof, I have hereunto set my hand and affixed the seal of said Court, at my office in _____ *Paddock Neb.* in said County, this *24th* _____ day of *May* A.D. 187*9* *Wm Mullen County* Judge.

CERTIFICATE OF MARRIAGE.

To the County Judge of *Holt* County, Nebraska:

This Certifies, That on the *28th* day of *May* A.D. 187*9*, at *8 A.M.* at *Bridgeline* in said County, according to law and by authority, I duly joined in marriage Mr. *James M. Shepford* and Miss *Mary Richardson* and there were present as witnesses *Warren & M. Morrow*

Given under my hand the *28th* day of *May* A.D. 187*9*

Rev Pming H. Skinner

Marriage record of J. M. Sheppard (Doc Middleton) and Mary Richardson, May 1879.

The reporter who wrote this article was not entirely familiar with the surroundings. The license was indeed procured in Holt County, but no trip to the Niobrara from the "abode of his charmer" was necessary, since she lived on the Niobrara, as did also the clergyman. The girl was Mary Richardson, daughter of Henry Richardson, who lived on the north side of the river, at Jake Haptonstall's house, a mile below the Morris ferry. The clergyman was Rev. Irving H. Skinner, who had lately come into the country and lived in a tent on the south side of the river, not far from the ferry.

Holt County Marriage License No. 12 was issued to Mr. James M. Sheppard and Miss Mary Richardson on the 24th of May, 1879, at Paddock, Nebraska, by Judge William Malloy.[1] "Sheppard" gave his age as twenty-five, his birthplace as Illinois, his residence as Long Pine, Nebraska, his father's name as D. Sheppard, and his mother's maiden name as Boone. Mary Richardson's age was listed as eighteen; birthplace, Illinois; residence, "Ferry," Nebraska; father's name, Henry Richardson; mother's maiden name, Anne Richardson. (Anne Richardson was Mary's stepmother.) Four days later, on the night of May 28, 1879, at eight o'clock, James M. Sheppard and Mary Richardson were united in marriage by the Rev. I. H. Skinner.

Not long after this, Rev. Skinner's wife, in an interview, told their story of the affair:

My husband had been in very poor health for some time and in the spring of 1879, with the hope that he would regain not only his health, but much he had spent doctoring, we sought a home on the Niobrara. Ignorant of the existence of the "pony boy" clan, we pitched our tent on the south side of the river about a mile from where Morris' Bridge was since built. We had been there only a few days when a couple of young men came, one by the name of Morris and the other Doc Middleton, the noted leader of the gang of horse thieves that surrounded us, but who was introduced as James Shepherd. After asking Mr. Skinner if he was a minister, he requested him to come to the little house across the river and perform a marriage ceremony. On the appointed evening Mr. Skinner

forded the river and united him in marriage with a Miss Richardson. The room was crowded with armed men, ready for a
surprise from the Indians, they said, while the groom laid his
arms off while the ceremony was being performed. Mr. Skinner, judging the real character of the men, left as soon as his
duty was performed.[2]

The bride's younger brother, Tom Richardson, told the story of
the courtship and of his father's opposition to Middleton's marrying Mary.

We was livin' at Ol' Jake's house, and he got to stoppin' there.
Oh, Mary, she just got plumb nuts about him, you know. My
dad didn't pay no 'tention much. Bob Ferris was—god, he was
a fine feller. Ferris and Barnhart had in a bunch of southern
cattle up there; of course, they come out broke in the spring,
but Bob Ferris was a fine man, and, my god, Mary could have
got him, and my dad was for him. Bob Ferris was a fine man;
but, hell, he wasn't swift enough, you know. Ohhh Christ, and
so when my dad seen how things was goin', he was pretty rough
about it.
     And you see, my sisters and my stepmother didn't get along
very well, and that caused both to marry men they hadn't ought
to. And anyway, I heard—I went right by—Middleton come
right up and asked my dad for her like a man, and my dad was
—we was a comin' from the upper place, my dad's homestead,
had been workin' up there, and Middleton had been to the
house, and then they met right down in here. Of course, I
didn't dare stop, but I listened as I went by; I slowed up. And
my dad went to work and talked to him, and told him, he says
—and told him what was goin' to become of him—says, "You
boys is either goin' to be hung or go to the pen." He says, "You
boys can't keep this up." And he says, "If you was a clean,
clear man, I wouldn't say a word." But he told him right there
he couldn't have her.
     Well, then, don't you see, he began to scheme. So they got
around to Morris' over there; he forded the river. Well, he

comes along down here, and Smith lived in the dugout down there, and Mary used to go down. You see, Smith moved his family in that dugout, down at Ol' Jake's till he could build a house up above Tarbell's. Mary was lonesome; she was eighteen years old, and she'd go down, oh, two or three times a day, down to the dugout to visit with Mrs. Smith; she didn't care to visit with her stepmother, you know. Anyway, they met down there. . . .

And she set right on behind him sideways, on that big bay horse; girls didn't ride astraddle them days. The boys, two of 'em anyway, was on the other side of the river up there with throw ropes, you know; well, by god, he went off the bank into the river, and that horse swum, and fought quicksand with both of them on there, and got out and didn't need no help.

Richardson said that after the marriage the couple went to Morris' place, where a team and wagon were waiting, and then went to Atkinson. I asked where the couple lived, and this was his answer:

Well, my dad let 'em come back home; they was down at Atkinson, and around—so it run along. And my poor dad, when he was on the way with a load of posts, and camped right down there by Atkinson, and Middleton had the guts to ride out there and see him; he was camped out, him and Ol' Jake, with posts, takin' posts to Neligh to trade for straight grade flour. And he rode out there to see my dad—had guts, you know; my dad had told him he couldn't have her, and it run along, oh, I don't know, about a month, I believe. And he rode out there and talked to him and—"Now," he says, "Mary wants to come home." So, by god, they had a visit, and 'twas no time till he had Mary up there, before we had our house built and was at Ol' Jake's house.

You see, my father, after he asked for her, he give Mary— my father give Mary an awful goin' over and a talkin' to, see, and that put a scare in her, but she was stuck on him, and of course she got with him and told him, and he promised her— and old George Holt was at Tarbell's then, and he's the one that built up the outlaw ranch over there on Holt Creek—and they was a goin' to go to Canada,[3] and he told Jack [a nickname for Doc around the region], and he says, "I haven't got a chick nor a child." And he says, "I'll just go with you." And Middleton had give him that gray horse, you know, and he got up in good shape, and they traded for a wagon from Beeman's up there, to leave the country in, a light wagon, and Middleton had them two good saddle horses, you know, and he had this other bay horse he rode across the river, and they says, "We'll be on our way inside of two weeks." So, the two weeks went by, and then, when she—he got so when she would say, "When are we going to go?"—you know, she was anxious, she'd go anywhere; she had a stepmother to live with to home, and he got so he'd say, "Well, now, I'll go when I get ready; I ain't gonna be run out."

Well, then, he met up with these detectives, don't you see, and he grabbed that. And old George Holt tried to talk him out of it. He says, "They're gonna kill ya." And, by god, he wouldn't believe it; he thought they wanted him to go on that police force, because he could ride and shoot and had guts and all that.[4]

But we are getting ahead of our story. At about this time, there began circulating in the Niobrara-Elkhorn valley region rumors to the effect that a pardon for Middleton was in the offing. This is from the *Niobrara Pioneer,* July 11, 1879:

For the last 18 months, the upper Niobrara and Elkhorn regions have been infested with a set of bandit horse thieves, keeping in danger the stock of the settlers and causing trouble with the Indians. They have been daring outlaws, and have had free access to the whole country. Various expeditions have started out to catch this notorious gang, led by Doc Middleton, but in vain.

A new wrinkle has just come to light. Doc has just got married and is anxious to reform, and it is stated that Fred J. Fox, an attorney at Niobrara, gave the governor an interview not long since, relative to Doc's pardon, but the governor, having nothing to pardon, would not lend himself to any such low proceeding as interfering with the law for the arrest of criminals at large. At any rate, it is a well-known and disgraceful fact that Fox is interceding for Middleton, and Bruce, while in charge of the Knox County News, took occasion to speak a "good word" for this man, who, for the last 18 months, the whole upper country has been in fear.

Petitions are being circulated in Holt County and the unorganized territory West, for the freedom of this man, and we learn, with successful results. It is acknowledged by most of these people that it is not out of respect but fear that they sign such papers. Why should they fear? Are there not a sufficient number of settlers in the upper Niobrara country to clean out this notorious band, who by their simple desire to free this man, show that their power is weakening by the increase in population?

We do not know much of Doc Middleton's past history except what he bears in a criminal point. It is quite reasonable to suppose, however, that if he is an innocent man, he would not flee from justice and become an outlaw in the wilds of the Niobrara. If he were an innocent man, why has he allowed himself to become so prominent as the leader of this gang of banditti? It appears to us rather late in the day to bring him up as a "much abused man," and those settlers in Holt County and citizens in this, are taking a very wrong course to rid this country of men who have no way of making a living but to steal stock.

If it is done to protect the heavy stockman alone and intimidate the farmers, further this way, it is indeed a very wrong and selfish interest in the good will of the country and its people. This gang has turned the immigration from this country a great deal, and while it may be policy to keep in with these men and allow them all the rope they ask, it is surely not very gratifying to the law-abiding people of this section.

For a word on the other side, the August 5, 1879 *Sioux City*

Journal had this to say:

> Although Middleton has such a gentlemanly and even romantic bearing as we have described, he has in his band a lot of the worst scoundrels yet unhung. One of the chief of these is Jack Nolan, who escaped from jail, where he was awaiting trial for a fiendish murder. Other cut-throats and desperadoes from Kansas, Colorado, Nebraska and Texas, having been compelled to fly because of other crimes committed by them, very naturally sought refuge in the ranks of Middleton's followers. Sheriff Gillen, and Armstrong, two of the worst men concerned in the lynching of Ketchum and Mitchell[5] in Custer County, and who broke jail at Plum Creek, are said to have cast their fortunes with this robber band. Of this, nothing definite is positively known.
>
> There is no doubt that many of the crimes charged to Middleton and his men were committed by other parties entirely.
>
> We know of no case of deliberate murder, in which these men have engaged, but they are robbers and the hand of the law is against them. It is only safe to say, therefore, that they are ready to defend themselves, and to take life in making such defense.
>
> And yet, with all the general charges made against Middleton, there are very few well-defined crimes laid positively at his doors.

The *Daily Press and Dakotian,* Yankton, August 1, 1879:

> Middleton has lived in the Niobrara valley since last fall and during his residence there, no crime has been charged against him. He is a fine looking man, six feet in height, well proportioned, and with a frank and manly countenance.
>
> A gang of desperate thieves and outlaws infest the upper Niobrara region, but it is claimed that Middleton has no connection with them.

By the spring of 1879 there had been sufficient clamor for justice toward the Indians that the Department of Justice decided to act. It was decided to hire a man as special agent of the department, whose duty would be to obtain evidence against persons guilty of violations against the Indians as wards of the government, sufficient to secure convictions in federal court; and when a satisfactory case had been developed, to lay the matter before the U. S. District Attorney for that particular state or territory, and to be able to act as a witness himself. There were certain other violations which came within the jurisdiction of the federal government, such as illegal traffic in whiskey, cutting of timber on government land, etc., but the principal offense was theft of Indian stock.

Letters of recommendation were received by the Department of Justice favoring one William H. H. Llewellyn of Omaha. Llewellyn was born in Monroe, Wisconsin, in the early 1850s; the date has been given variously from 1851 to 1854. Nothing is known of his earlier years; it was said that he worked with a surveying party on the plains for a time—and he did claim to have considerable knowledge of the western country. During the years 1877-79 he was listed in the Omaha directories as a city tax collector and a deputy city jailor. And it was said that he had become a "rookie" patrolman by the time he made contact with the Department of Justice.

L. P. Hazen, we remember, served four-and-a-half years of his six-year term in the Iowa State Penitentiary at Fort Madison and apparently drifted out to the vicinity of Omaha. In 1879, he was living in Papillion in Sarpy County, south of Omaha. It is uncertain as to how he and Middleton became acquainted, but, as noted, it was perhaps possible that it was at Fort Madison. Otherwise, they might have met on the outside; Middleton was reported seen as far east as Blair, Nebraska, and it has been said that he had connections in Iowa. Nothing is known beyond this.

At any rate, Llewellyn and Hazen became acquainted in some way, and here was born the plan for the capture of the notorious Doc Middleton. There were, of course, the rewards; and, certainly, the man who could accomplish what others had failed to do would achieve fame. Hazen was enlisted in the plan because he knew Middleton and could make the introduction and perhaps gain his confidence.

The Department of Justice sent this letter to Llewellyn, dated May 27, 1879:

W. H. H. Llewellyn Esq.
Omaha
Nebraska
Sir:
I am reliably informed that a large number of persons have located themselves in northern and northwestern Nebraska in the vicinity of Niobrara, and subsist in unlawful traffic in whiskey, and by stealing horses and other stock from the Indians and honest white men, and are engaged in other occupations in violation especially of the Intercourse Acts of Congress. It is said that offenses of this character in that particular neighborhood are extended and that in addition to their being in contempt of law, they have the effect of endangering the peace, and are against the treaty obligations of the United States with friendly and peaceably disposed Indians.

Upon his subject, I have received several communications in which wrongful acts of this character are alleged and I am desirous, as far as I have means appropriable, to punish those who are guilty, and in this way, at least, so discourage and put an end to the illegal practice. The proper method for this department to use to this end, are by prosecutions, institutable upon evidence first obtained, and I accordingly wish to make employment of suitable person to collect the evidence and see that the same is duly reported for prosecution.

Such a person should be perfectly familiar with the country, and must have courage, vigilance and promptness to be successful. I have had you recommended to me as in all respects fitted for this duty, and I address you to acquaint you with what I desire, and so make the employment, which I understand, you will accept. The principal duty as I have said, is to obtain testimony against offenders, which can be used to obtain indictments under the Intercourse Acts of Congress. You should conduct the work, if possible, so as to be a direct witness yourself, and also furnish the prosecuting officers with other and material witnesses.

If the offenses you discover are committed against the U.S. laws in the Indian country itself, they should be reported to H. J. Campbell, Esq., U.S. Attorney, Yankton, Dakota; on the other hand, if they are offenses against United States laws, committed in Nebraska, they should be laid before the U.S. Attorney for that state.

I hope by this employment to reach results, and its intention is not to be merely supervisory for the purpose of inspection. I will for the present allow you a per diem of $5.00 while engaged, and actual and necessary expenses when stated in items of account and verified by affidavit.

You will inform the respective District Attorneys of this letter in order that they may aid you in carrying out your duties. I fix no time when this employment will terminate, as that will be determined, to a great extent by the results reached, and the condition of the appropriations. You should make written reports from time to time to this department through the District Attorneys.

Very respectfully,
Chas. Devens, Atty General[6]

Llewellyn, upon receipt of the above communication, replied May 31st, accepting the employment. He made contact with G. M. Lambertson, U.S. District Attorney for Nebraska, and promised to communicate with H. J. Campbell, U.S. Attorney for Dakota at Yankton. He then made ready to proceed to the "upper Niobrara."

Llewellyn appears to have been out several weeks on his first trip, during which time the thieves were not idle. For example, the *Sidney Telegraph* for June 14, 1879 carried this item:

By telegram wired from Fort Robinson, it would appear that the ubiquitous Middleton was paying attention to our friends, the Sioux Nation at Pine Ridge Agency. The telegram states that on the night of June 4, Middleton's gang ran off, under cover of night, 45 head of ponies belonging to the Sioux, and accomplished the feat without alarming a single red although there were 7,000 of them at hand. The Indians went wild over their loss and started on the trail, threatening to tear the outlaws to pieces in case they overhauled them.

Since the first of June, Little Wound, chief of the Kiyaksa band, has lost over 50 head of horses and ponies.

At this moment, Middleton had been married barely a week and was presumably honeymooning at Atkinson.

The *Cheyenne Daily Sun*, June 18, 1879, carried an entirely different sort of story:

The Sidney *Plaindealer* says that it is reported there that Doc Middleton, the notorious outlaw, was recently killed about twenty miles northwest of Fort Laramie. The story goes that a detective put up a job on Doc by representing himself as a horse thief; that he knew where a convenient bunch of mules were being kept and desired the assistance of the experienced fakir in stealing them. Middleton fell into the trap, and while attempting to escape, was riddled with bullets. The *Sun* gives this story for what it is worth.

When Llewellyn made the initial trip to the Niobrara, leaving Omaha the end of May or first of June, he went by way of North Platte, a distance of 251 miles on the Union Pacific Railroad, and from there proceeded overland on horseback 190 miles, striking the Niobrara at a point some thirty miles below its confluence with the Snake. Why such a circuitous route was taken is not clear; the same point could have been reached with nearly 200 miles less travel by going directly to the Niobrara. Possibly he wished to confer with the railroad detectives who worked out of North Platte.

After Llewellyn's return to Omaha, he wrote to the department on June 24, 1879:

I have known this section of country for a number of years from having personally traversed it on various occasions. It is broken by many deep gullies and canyons, which furnish good hiding places for outlaws and horse thieves.

There are of this class of men engaged in stealing Indian and government stock about 150, who are occupied directly or indirectly. They extend from Niobrara City on the Missouri River, west to Snake Creek, over on the headwaters far down the Elkhorn, and have numerous agents at different points on the line of the Union Pacific road and as far south as Solomon River in Kansas. These agents are not infrequently men of financial standing and of fair repute. It is their business to receive and dispose of the stock.

Of the class actually engaged in stealing stock, the number will not exceed thirty-five; this latter class are generally Texas outlaws who from time to time drift north to Nebraska with the great cattle drives from Texas to Nebraska. Doc Middleton, alias Texas Jack, alias Jack Lyons, a murderer from Texas[7] who, since his arrival in Nebraska, has committed murder, is the chief of the active operations. His operations would fill volumes. From personal and reliable information, in the last three years Doc and his gang have successfully stolen and have disposed of not less than 2,000 head of Indian and government stock.

I am personally acquainted with this outlaw, and to effect his capture will be my first and most arduous task toward breaking up this unlawful business which is so openly carried on in contempt of United States laws. I have evidence sufficient from what I have seen personally, and other and material witnesses, to bring a dozen indictments against him. I think I can turn him into the hands of a U.S. marshall within the next four weeks. I also have evidence accessible to subpoenas by the proper United States officials to indict and convict other principal members of this gang. It is more a question of getting them into the hands of U.S. marshals, than of convicting them after they are in custody.

In regard to receiving and disposing of this stock, I shall await the instructions of the District Attorneys before furnishing them with the names of persons engaged in this branch of the trade, and the names of witnesses necessary to make a case.

I start again today for the Niobrara River; this time, via the

Elkhorn Valley route, to be gone two weeks and on my return
if District Attorney Lambertson is back from the east and the
U.S. marshal is ready, I will submit the testimony on the cutting of timber on the Niobrara River by sawmills, and will make
a specific report on other unlawful acts committed in this
district.

Yours respectfully,
Your ob't servant,
W. H. H. Llewellyn, Omaha

Though he does not say so explicitly in the report, we learn from
his next report that Llewellyn presumably made some contact with
Middleton while on this first trip, enough of a contact to arrange a
future meeting. He does say that he was "personally acquainted with
this outlaw," but whether this represents an actual meeting during
the trip is moot. If he did visit with Middleton, perhaps Hazen
accompanied him and made the introduction.

In writing about his second trip, and its preparations, Llewellyn
develops more of a day-by-day account. On June 23, 1879 he was
in Lincoln, for the purpose, as he said, of making an arrangement
whereby he could get the assistance of state officers if he so desired,
and to induce the governor to instruct the sheriffs of the various
counties to assist him in arresting horse thieves and holding them
until a U.S. marshall could be summoned. From this time onward,
there is less and less mention of the U.S. marshals in connection with
the Middleton affair. Obviously Llewellyn had something else in
mind.

On June 24, Llewellyn returned to Omaha, and on the 25th, he
went out to Kearney on the Union Pacific Railroad to interview
Black Hank, who was being held in jail there for the theft of Indian
ponies from the Pine Ridge Indian Reservation.

On the 26th of June, Llewellyn returned to Columbus. Coming
back from his first trip, he had left his saddle horse there, presumably having come on down through the Niobrara-Elkhorn valley
country and thence to the U.P. at Columbus. Now, his second time
out, Llewellyn was going back into the valley, and not by such a
circuitous route. Also, on this trip he was definitely accompanied by

William Henry Harrison Llewellyn. *Courtesy Museum of New Mexico Collections.*

The State of Nebraska, } ss.
Antelope County.

               Of the June term of the District
Court of the Sixth Judicial District of the State
of Nebraska, within and for Antelope County in
said State, in the year of our Lord one thousand
eight hundred and Eighty. The Grand Jurors
chosen, selected, and sworn, in and for the County of
Antelope of the State of Nebraska, upon their
oaths present that Doctor Middleton alias Gold
tooth Charley late of the County aforesaid, on the
13th day of April in the year of our Lord one
thousand eight hundred and Seventy Eight—
in the County of Antelope and State of Nebraska
aforesaid,

               Feloniously did steal, take
and lead away, one Gelding of the value of One
Hundred and Fifty (150) Dollars, the goods,
Chattels and property of A.A. Sloan.

          Contrary to the form of the statute in such
case made and provided, and against the
peace and dignity of the State of Nebraska.

                     C. C. McNish
                        District Attorney.

               Indictment.
        Antelope Co. District Court.
       The State of Nebraska
            vs
Doctor Middleton alias Gold Tooth Charley }
              Indictment for Horse Stealing.
           A. True Bill.
             W. C. Gallaway
                 Foreman of the Grand Jury.

Filed June 18th 1880
                   R. Wilson, Clerk.

            Witnesses
A. A. Sloan, Zebulon Beroy, Lemuel Pickard,
F. W. Tarbell.
              C. C. McNish
                District Attorney.

Indictment in June 1880 against "Doctor Middleton alias Gold Tooth Charley" for the theft of a horse from A. A. Sloan in Antelope County on April 13, 1878.

Hazen. From Columbus they went horseback to the Niobrara River. This is Llewellyn's account:

> On the 29th, I met by former appointment, the celebrated Dr. Middleton, alias Texas Jack, who is, as I informed your department by former report, the chief of all the Niobrara outlaws. Middleton is a man of keen instinct in his line of business, and his record is well-known to all Indian Agents and Army officers on the frontier. *I will not trouble your department with the details of the plan I am pursuing* to effect the arrest and land him in jail as a U.S. prisoner. But as I intimated in a former report, I hope to be successful within the present month. Middleton is regarded as the great obstacle to be removed. His capture will be hailed with joy by the Indians who both know and fear him, and will go far to stop the unlawful raids on the Indian Agencies. I have conferred with the Hon. G. M. Lambertson on the subject, and he fully agrees on the importance of Middleton's arrest. [italics added]

It has to be a matter of curiosity as to what could be the subject of a conference between Middleton and the man plotting his downfall, and, to such a purpose, how it was possible for Llewellyn to contact the man who had eluded numerous posses and faced down sheriffs. The exact circumstances of the first meeting cannot be known. Llewellyn later stated, from a safe distance, that the approach was made by simply riding into Middleton's camp, the implication being that he had ridden in "cold turkey," accepting his chances on what might happen; but it will soon be seen that these latest aspirants for the reward had no such courage. They had to have something to offer and it had to sound good.

Hazen came along to make the introduction and Llewellyn represented himself as being an emissary of the governor, with the authority to negotiate the terms for granting a pardon to Middleton. Doc had long wished for some assurance of immunity for the killing of the soldier at Sidney, since this was the only charge against him in the State of Nebraska at this time. Later, there would be a charge of stealing one horse in Antelope County, probably a reprisal. In

return for the pardon, Middleton was to give up the old life and lend
his assistance to eradicating outlawry in the Niobrara-Elkhorn valley country. Hazen's presence seemed to attest to the authenticity
of the offer. Llewellyn's trips to see the governor were explained as
being incidental to the securing of the pardon.

Llewellyn and Hazen spent a few days investigating other violations of U.S. laws around the headwaters of the Elkhorn and Niobrara. They headquartered at O'Connell's near Atkinson. Llewellyn
did not watch his horse closely enough and it was stolen from
O'Connell's barn by Jack Nolan; no report of this was made for
some time. However, it was reported that John Carberry had sold
liquor at his place at Atkinson, without a license; this was one of
the places along the Black Hills Trail that supplied the demand of
the freighters and Black Hillers without thinking of a license so far
beyond any well-established society. Llewellyn also stated:

> I might add that the said John Carberry has kept a den and
> place of resort for lawless men, horse thieves and villains,
> knowing them to be such. He has bought and sold stolen Indian
> and Government stock and is dangerous to the peace and good
> order of the frontier.

Again, it should be pointed out that when one ran a roadside place
catering to the trade, one accepted all customers without asking
questions. John Carberry ran such a place at Atkinson, and also at
Stuart, ten miles upriver.

Llewellyn also reported whiskey being sold nineteen miles west
of Atkinson (which he always referred to as "Atchison P. O.") and
a sawmill being operated on Long Pine Creek in government timber,
by one D. J. Sparks.

He arrived back in Omaha on the 8th of July, in order, he said, to
carry out the plan for the capture of Middleton.

As the days passed, Doc began to grow impatient for word about
his pardon; he consulted H. M. Uttley, an attorney at O'Neill City,
asking him to look into the matter. Middleton had accepted the terms
offered him, but for some reason, he became suspicious.

Meanwhile, Jack Nolan and Little Joe Johnson, together with

Curly Grimes, robbed the Bone Creek post office near the present site of Ainsworth, Nebraska; the post office was located at the Cook and Towar ranch, and Ed Cook was postmaster. Grimes had worked for Cook and Towar, but had been discharged by them. He resented it, returned with the other two outlaws in broad daylight, and stole everything of value, holding Cook at bay. When they left, they threatened him with death if he reported the matter. It became known, however, and months later, Nolan and Johnson were brought to trial and convicted; the following winter, Grimes was shot-gunned near the Black Hills while attempting to escape while under arrest for this crime.[8]

On July 19, as the trap was being prepared for the elusive Middleton, this article appeared in the *Sidney Telegraph*, as a reprint from the *Cheyenne Sun*:

The Man With the Golden Tooth

There is much about the career of this remarkable man which reads like the old-time stories of Ned Scarlett, Sixteen String Jack or Dick Turpin. Middleton was born to command and is now the acknowledged chieftain of at least one hundred men.

These desperadoes are scattered over Kansas, Nebraska and Dakota; some of them have dared venture into Wyoming. About two weeks ago, one of the gang, known as Texas Long, even penetrated Cheyenne and remained two days.

The Sun sometime since gave an account of how Doc fell in love with a buxom lass named Richards [sic], a resident of Holt County, Nebraska, who eloped with and married him. A gentleman with whom we recently conversed says Middleton protected the people of Holt County and refused to allow the members of his band to steal from them. In this way, he had access to that section without fear of arrest.

Miss Richards fell in love with him "on sight." He could have ruined her but said that was a crime he would not add to his other short comings.

Middleton's real name is Rily [sic]. His father was hanged in Texas three years ago for murdering a man named Lyons. Middleton is about thirty-three [actually twenty-eight] years old, tall but of slight build, has light brown hair, light complexion, dark hazel eyes, black beard and moustache. He has no education but is a smooth talker, and was born to command. He is loved by his men, and yet they fear him. With them his word is law.

He carries two trusty revolvers and is regarded a dead shot. During the past two years, the gang of which he is the chief, has stolen over 2,000 horses, including those taken from the Sioux. Middleton gets the name of "the man with the golden tooth" from the fact that one of his front teeth has been broken off and is built out again with gold. He is one of the most remarkable and successful desperadoes in the West.

10

Treachery

About two weeks had elapsed since Llewellyn's and Hazen's departure from the Niobrara. Mary was ready to leave the country, but Doc, though suspicious, half believed that he was to have a pardon and a place on the detective force. Llewellyn appears to have made some sort of commitment as to when he would return for the final transaction. After his June 29th meeting with Middleton, he spent about a week investigating illegal whiskey traffic and illegal cutting of government timber along the Niobrara, before returning to Omaha on July 8th. Then he turned his attention again to the main matter at hand—Middleton. Here is his report of events for the next ten days:

On the 10th of July, I went into Sarpy County, south of Omaha some 20 miles, to see a person who knew considerable concerning Middleton, that I thought to be of service to me. [L. P. Hazen lived in Sarpy County.]

On the 11th, I went by rail to Lincoln, the capital of Nebraska, to again confer with the governor on matters pertaining to Middleton. [Later, when asked about this precise matter, Llewellyn told an *Omaha Herald* reporter that he had wanted something under the seal of the state as to rewards.]

On the 13th, Sunday, having completed my arrangements to carry out my plans, I took the 6:00 P.M. train, going west, on the U.P.R.R., reaching Columbus, 92 miles from Omaha, at 2:00 A.M., taking with me a Mr. Hazen, who formerly had been with me in the Niobrara country.

On the 14th, I had to remain at Columbus till 1:00 P.M., awaiting a Mr. Lykens[1] from Cheyenne, who was to accompany me to the Niobrara region as an assistant in the capture of Middleton. At 1:00 P.M., Hazen, Lykens and myself started on horseback, passing through Nance County, and arriving at Albion, county seat of Boone County, at 12:20, midnight, a distance of 51 miles from Columbus.

On the 15th, traveled some 25 miles up Beaver Creek, striking across the hills to Frenchtown on the Elkhorn, total distance from Albion 55 miles.

On the 16th, Hazen and myself went openly up the Elkhorn, passing through O'Neill City in Holt County, to O'Connell's [near Atkinson]. Lykens passed off into the hills to the north, and thence west, keeping off the public road in order to avoid observation, reaching O'Connell's at daylight on the morning of the 17th.

On the 17th, I expected Middleton at Atchison P. O., as per agreement. However, he did not come on account of new suspicions, and I had to employ a man to travel over to his camping place, 45 miles, to see him and carry a note to him for me. I spent the day in gaining additional information concerning Indian stock and found such at nearly every house.

The settlements up here are quite numerous; it is on the headwaters of the Elkhorn River and the land is good for farming. I also found 6 U.S. horses which I will return to the U.S. marshal at Omaha.

On the 18th, it rained hard in the morning, and at 10:00 A.M., Mr. Hazen and myself saddled our horses and rode up to the extreme head of the Elkhorn, a distance of 12 miles. Here we met the man I had sent, returning from Middleton's camp. Retracing our steps we arrived at O'Connell's again the same day, at 6:30 P.M., and at 9:30 P.M., taking Lykens with us [he had remained in concealment at O'Connell's], we crossed the Elkhorn to the south side and rode off onto the plains and camped for the night.

The man whom I had sent to Middleton's camp brought word that the chief Middleton would condescend to again meet me and had fixed the place of meeting at Peacock's, a place some 6 miles from the Niobrara River, and distance some 40 miles from our present camping place.

On the 19th, at 3:00 A.M., our sleep was disturbed by a hard shower and sharp lightning. Got soaked through. Day broke about this time, and giving Lykens minute instructions as to road and place I wished him to go and conceal himself, he started, but never having visited this section of country before was something of a disadvantage to us.

Our party consisted of Hazen, Lykens and myself, no others operating with us. There were two other detectives in the vicinity but Middleton knew of their presence and who they were. This had caused his suspicion, alluded to previously, and was the reason he failed to meet me at Atchison as per former agreement.

I had intended to have Lykens go to the head of the Elkhorn, thence on main road toward Peacock's and the Niobrara to head of Ash Creek, a distance of 22 miles from our camp.

Hazen and myself crossed north again to the main road. On going a distance of three miles we met Lykens, who had turned around and was on the road going down the river. All depended on his concealment at the place intended and as it was now nearly daylight, hastily giving him new directions, he galloped off.

It continued to rain hard. Hazen and myself met a bull train, camped, and took shelter from the rain for an hour. At 11:00 A.M., we came to a sod house, where we procured coffee and breakfast.

On coming to the head of the Elkhorn, the place Lykens was to turn off to go to Ash Creek, to our surprise we found him seated in the willows, his horse tied up some half a mile from him. All would be lost if any of the Indian and government stock thieves were to see the third man with us.

No one was now beyond the settlements on the Elkhorn. Between us and the Niobrara River, a distance of 38 miles, there is only one house, Peacock's, which I have alluded to before.

Again instructing Lykens to proceed cautiously, he rode off into the hills toward Ash Creek. Hazen and myself rode rapidly on in the main road. At 2:00 P.M., we discovered the tracks of two horses, freshly made in the road, going toward the Niobrara. We then knew that we had been closely watched.

At 3:00 P.M., we arrived at Peacock's and were greeted by Middleton. He had with him George Holt, alias Black George, Count Shevaloff [Bill Shebley], and Richard Bryant, alias Limber Dick, all well-known Indian and government horse thieves.

I had a long and close conversation with Middleton.

At 5:00 P.M., we all took supper.

A newspaper account, from the *Omaha Daily Bee,* July 26, 1879, gives a few details of the meeting:

On Saturday last Llewellyn and Hazen met Middleton five miles this side of his retreat, at Peacock's. Middleton had agreed to meet them there alone, but when they came there Middleton had three of his men with him, Holt, a jailbird from Niobrara [meaning St. Helena], Sheeby [Bill Shebley], a new recruit but a desperate man, and Limber Dick. It seems that the meeting was arranged for a consultation about a pardon, or "conditional papers of help or immunity," which were bona fide, but about which it is not necessary to say much at this time. [Why it was "not necessary to say much at this time" about this important item is a mystery.]

While Llewellyn and Middleton were talking, one of the party said to Hazen, "You think you are going to take Doc away from us but I'll let you know that we handle Doc as much as he handles us. You have got a string of detectives around us all the time and we are going to give you a hot reception anyway."

The man wanted to find out if Doc would be allowed to work "half and half"; that is to say, break up horse stealing except to work with the rustlers in running off Indian ponies.

Hazen warned him that would never do, that being one of the things they wanted to have stopped and that they need not make any calculations on anything of the kind. The man then turned and left them.

The men had been visiting for an hour and a half when Mrs. Peacock called them in to supper. All went in except Middleton and Hazen; Middleton then said to Hazen, "Is this thing all on the square?" "Yes, sir, it means business on the part of the government," said Hazen.

To continue Llewellyn's report:

At 5:00 P.M., we all took supper, and proceeded on over to the Niobrara River, some six miles. We rode all together. Arriving at Skinner's place on the Niobrara, Middleton and his comrades rode off to the ferry and crossed to the north side of the river.

As soon as it was fairly dark I dispatched Hazen to bring up Lykens. I had made an agreement with Middleton to meet him at the place of a man named Larkins [Sam Likens], about a mile and a half up the Niobrara from Skinner's and I wished to have Lykens concealed in the brush so we could capture him as he passed through.

On Sunday, the 20th, about daybreak, Hazen came up with Lykens. I had remained up all night watching our horses in order that we might not awake to find them gone and ourselves afoot. We concealed Lykens in a dense growth of brush on the Niobrara River near where I knew Middleton would pass with Hazen and myself on our way back from Larkin's house.

Lyken's horse was concealed in a deep ravine.

At 9:00 A.M., Hazen and myself went to Larkin's house, waited until 10:00 A.M., when Middleton and a fellow called the Kid [Kid Wade] came up on horseback. Just at this time, Bryant, Holt and Count Shevaloff crossed from the north side of the river, coming near Larkins's house and stopped. Also noticed two men on down on the bench of land toward Skinner's place.

I talked with Middleton until 10:30 A.M., when we started to go down the road back to Skinner's. Middleton accompanied us, riding by my side. When we came up to the three men before mentioned, Holt rode up by Hazen's side, riding just behind me. By this time we went some three-quarters of a mile, passing down on to the first river bottom among the brush.

When within a short distance of Lyken's place of concealment, he was discovered by Middleton who at once pulled out his revolver and shot at Lykens. A general fight therein ensued, spoiling my plan of capture.

Note that Llewellyn is still talking of *capture*. While attempts were made by the detectives at making this matter appear honorable, it was actually as cowardly an *assassination* plot as ever was laid. By a one-in-a-million chance it did not succeed. Middleton was wounded, Hazen was much more seriously wounded, and Llewellyn received slight bullet creases.

Various accounts of this scene differ so that it is difficult to conclude exactly what happened in the melee of discovery and shooting. Were there any other of Middleton's men near at hand except the Kid? What was the order in which the men rode? Did Middleton's spotting of Lykens provoke Doc's shooting? Did Middleton see Lykens only after he had tried to fire at Doc? Did Middleton ever see Lykens at all? Who wounded Middleton? And so forth.

It would be comforting if the word of a law officer were always good and that of an outlaw always false. But when each of the three detectives in this case tells conflicting stories, when one of the lawmen even contradicts himself, and when Middleton, Tom Richardson, Mrs. Skinner, S. D. Butcher, and local oral history even down to the present day are in substantial agreement, whom are we to believe?

We do know for certain that the last of these "conferences" about

Thomas Peacock's home where Doc Middleton met with W. H. H. Llewellyn and L. P. Hazen for discussion about Doc's "pardon." Mr. Peacock is standing in foreground, in front of team and buggy. This photo was taken in the mid-1880s, when Peacock's place was the Mariaville Post Office; in 1879, when Middleton conferred there, the house was under construction. From *Western Nebraska: A Compendium* (p. 234).

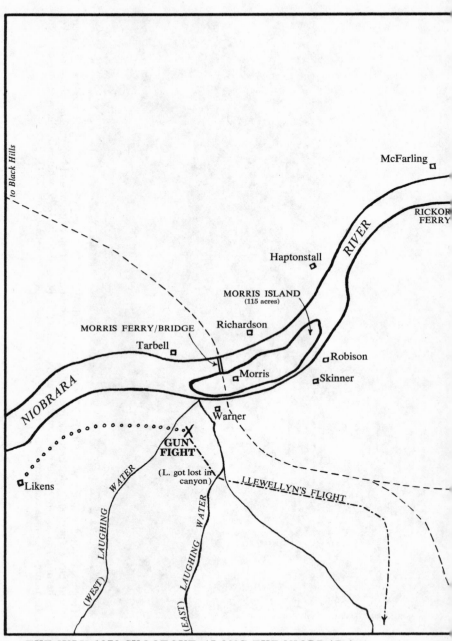

THE JULY 1879 SHOOTOUT ALONG THE NIOBRARA

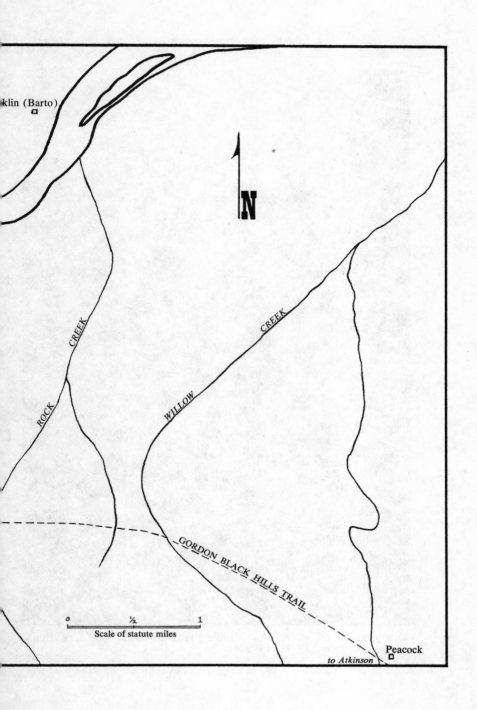

klin (Barto)

N

ROCK CREEK

WILLOW CREEK

GORDON BLACK HILLS TRAIL

0   ½   1
Scale of statute miles

Peacock

to Atkinson

Laughing Water, where Doc Middleton's showdown with Llewellyn's party took place, July 20, 1879.

the fake pardon was held at Sam Likens' place, which was about two miles upriver from Morris' crossing and out on the flat. Also, it seems almost certain that a spurious document, purporting to be an official grant of amnesty from Governor Nance, was forged and handed to Middleton, either at Likens' home or on the way back down the river. That Bryant, Holt, and Shebley crossed the river from the north side and lingered about in the vicinity of Likens' house while the "conference" was being held is very probable; it is equally logical that they trailed along with the detectives and Middleton and the Kid on the way back down the river. But nobody, except Llewellyn, ever said that they were at the scene of the gun fight or took any part in it, even at a distance. In Lykens' account, they were a couple hundred yards behind, and at the first indication of trouble Doc shouted to them to "go back," which they did. Tom Richardson mentioned no one at the scene except Llewellyn, Hazen, Lykens, and Middleton. Middleton placed the Kid with him, no one else.

Regardless of the number of men in the group and the distance between the men, Middleton and Llewellyn and party began riding downriver from Likens'. About one-and-a-half miles away Lykens was concealed in the brush on the river bottom between West Laughing Water (now known as Coon Creek) and East Laughing Water. Llewellyn had to get Middleton to ride past Lykens. But how? Doc had his pardon in his pocket and all was well with the world. And it appeared now as if Middleton was going to leave the trail and head back toward the Niobrara River; this way he would not pass Lykens' hiding place. At this moment, according to Mrs. Skinner, the detectives brought up the matter of another paper to sign, necessitating Doc's accompanying them further.[2] Later Llewellyn would explain that they had been going to the Skinner place to get dinner. Dinner, indeed! It was no part of Llewellyn's intention that Doc would ever see another dinner. He would ride past the thicket, there would be a blast of rifle fire, he would topple from the saddle, and the detectives would then repossess the "pardon" and tell the world that Middleton had fired first. Hazen dismounted in anticipation.

The moment the shooting began, sixteen-year-old Kid Wade drew a revolver and fired on Llewellyn from the rear, and a chase ensued, with Llewellyn in full flight, firing an occasional shot back, and the Kid emptying his gun at Llewellyn. When his gun was empty, the Kid rode off into the timber. Llewellyn kept going, leaving the river bottom and riding up on the bench between the creeks, then through the canyon of the East Laughing Water. He was soon seen racing across the prairie toward Rock Creek. Llewellyn had suffered slight wounds under an arm and on one hand, possibly both from the same bullet.

Each of the detectives afterward tried to place himself in the best possible light. Both Hazen and Lykens claimed to have wounded Middleton. Hazen claimed that Middleton discovered Lykens in the brush, and at the onset, before anyone else had fired, Doc fired at Lykens and then fired upon him, Hazen.

Eventually, all agreed that a man was hidden in the brush, although at first there was an attempt at concealing this fact. And, finally, no one claimed authenticity for the so-called pardon.

Here is the story as Tom Richardson told it:

> You see, when he fell on the side of Red Buck—he was ridin' him and he had been on the picket rope forty days and was fat and felt good, and when that gun snapped—you see, if Lykens had commenced sooner down there, and the gun snapped, he'd a had time to put in another catridge [Tom's pronunciation of cartridge], but he waited till he got so damn close and he had his six-shooter and he—bang he went with that—but when the gun snapped, Middleton fell down on the side of his horse and was pullin' his six-shooter when Lykens shot with the pistol; and Middleton, when he got out of the pen, told me he didn't know where that bullet went, and Llewellyn rode up a hillside steep as a haystack, and Hazen stood back there off his horse—Middleton knew he stopped back there but thought he stopped to fix his saddle blanket. [Hazen had dismounted and got his rifle out.]
>
> Well, just as soon as he heard the gun snap he knew everything was off, see? Well, just as soon as Lykens shot with the pistol, and Middleton—the horse jumped and he fell in

that mud hole—Lykens must of thought he killed him, and, by god, he heard Lykens runnin' through the brush, so Llewellyn went up the hillside through them jack oaks, by god, and Red Buck whirled, you know; that shot scared him, and he went right back past Hazen and went up to Warner's where he'd been on the picket rope, don't you see? Well, Middleton got up, you know, he had his .45 six-shooter—you see, Red Buck run with his rifle, and he says [afterwards], "I didn't know but the brush was full of men." So, by god, he started back, you know, and he told Hazen to drop that gun, and when he dropped it he pulled it off—hit him right there [indicating the side]. So he shot Hazen in here, he shot him twice, and course he fell, and when he got up there—Hazen flat on his back with his hands up beggin' for mercy—he went up there and pulled the gun off—went clear through his lung and into that hard road a coupla inches, and Middleton went right on carryin' the gun, after his horse—went on after his horse—and Jake and I had went down the Elkhorn with two loads of posts and we was just a gettin' back and seen Llewellyn comin'—we didn't know who it was, you know, on a big horse, and he was goin' to meet us, he saw, and then he turned off, and he hit Rock Creek way up above the crossing there. And then all he had to do was go to the fort over there [Fort Hartsuff]."

Middleton's own story was that he had met Llewellyn and Hazen a month or six weeks previously on the Niobrara, and when they had returned to Omaha, he had accompanied them as far as Atkinson on their way. He never suspected treachery on their part until he was fired upon by the man in the brush. He was to have his pardon and in return was to assist the detectives when called upon to put down crime along the Niobrara. Llewellyn and Hazen, in fact, had brought him his "pardon" and given it to him; he was riding along a few yards ahead of Hazen, Doc said, with Llewellyn about two hundred yards behind.[3]

I thought I heard the click of a gun in the brush by the

roadside; imagining I had been mistaken, and that it was a wild turkey that had made the noise I had heard, I passed along, but had not gone more than a few feet when it clicked again. This time I was certain it was a gun, so I slipped down on the opposite side of my saddle, not intending to dismount altogether, when a shot from the brush caused my horse to jump away from me. I then turned around to Hazen and said, "There's some dirt here. You don't want to kill me, do you?" "No, I don't," he said; and he tried to say something about explaining it all, but he was so scared he couldn't say anything. At that moment, a man raised up in the brush, and Hazen said, "There's a man down there, see him?" I turned to look, and as my head was averted, he blazed away at me with his Winchester rifle, the ball hitting me about two inches below the navel. I then fired two shots at him, which were all the shots I fired. I then looked to see how I should escape Llewellyn and I saw him going for dear life over a hill away from us.[4]

Upon being asked by a reporter if he was sure it was Hazen who had fired the shot that wounded him, Middleton answered: "Sure! Well, I guess I am. I don't see how I could be mistaken when I was almost close enough to him to catch the muzzle of his gun." Doc wondered why Llewellyn troubled with such an elaborate ambush. He said that if they had simply told him to put up his hands, he could have done nothing, and they would have taken him without firing a shot.

This was the story as given to the *Niobrara Pioneer* by Chipman Robison, a resident of the upper Niobrara country:

Llewellyn and Hazen had been working up a case by which they promised to make Doc Middleton a detective, to ferret out the dens of robbers, going on the principle that it takes a thief to catch a thief, and Doc had the promise of his freedom. Last Sunday he was enroute in company with Hazen where it was said he would receive his papers of pardon from the governor. On their road some person in ambush shot at Doc and missed him, and Hazen then shot Middleton in the abdomen and in return Hazen was then shot three times by Doc, receiving one dangerous wound in the lung and he was not expected to live. It was thought by Mr. Robinson that the party in ambush was one of the detective party.[5]

An O'Neill City correspondent wrote to the *Pioneer* that Doc Middleton was shot in the abdomen on the 20th by Mr. Hazen, a detective; Hazen and Llewellyn had been prowling around the country for several weeks, he said, but never accomplished anything until a rival set of detectives was sent up by the governor.

These might well have been the "two other detectives in the vicinity" mentioned by Llewellyn in his report about July 19th. In any case, nothing further is known of them.

Lykens' story of the affair is reported in the third person by the *Cheyenne Daily Leader* for July 27, 1879:

> Lykins [sic] allowed him [Middleton] to approach within about twenty paces from him when he drew a bead on him with his carbine. Something being the matter with his gun it would not go off, although he tried it ten or a dozen times. Middleton heard the snapping and turned his horse in the direction from which it came, saying, "By G— there's something wrong here."
>
> Lykins was lying on the ground, and fearing discovery, jumped up and blazed away with his revolver. Middleton returned the fire, and turned to run, crying out to his men to "go back." While on the retreat Middleton met Hazen, one of Lykins' men coming towards him, and as soon as he got close to him he (Middleton) jumped from his horse [a very unlikely thing to do] and shot at Hazen three times, each shot taking effect. . . . At this time Middleton's horse had escaped, so he run for some brush which was close at hand. Lykins again took up his gun, and this time it went off, just as Middleton was entering the brush. He believed he hit him, but could not then be certain.

According to the first statements made by Hazen, Doc discovered the man in concealment, ordered him to come out, and fired a shot into the thicket. Hazen then spoke to Middleton saying, "It is no use for us to exchange shots for I know nothing of this proceeding."

Middleton: "I think this is all your treachery, god damn you. I'll give it to you in the guts!"

Hazen: "No, you won't."

Then the shot from Middleton's gun.

This would imply that Doc was still on his horse, since nothing was said about the horse getting out from under him, and therefore seems false; nor did Hazen say anything about a shot from the thicket or shots by Llewellyn.[6]

The story that differs (in spellings as well as content) the most from the others was related some years later by Edgar Bronson, who had Llewellyn and Middleton meeting for the first time only a few minutes before the shooting:

> One morning Llewellyn and Hassard started up the creek, mounted, on a scout, leaving Lykins and his horse hidden in the brush near the trail. At a sharp bend of the path the two ran plunk into Doc and five of his men. Both being unknown to Doc's gang, and the position and odds forbidding hostilities, they represented themselves as campers hunting lost stock, and turned and rode back down the trail with the outlaws, alert for any play their leader might make.
>
> Recognizing his man, Billy lay with his "45" and "70" Sharps comfortably resting across a log; and when the band were within twenty yards of him, he drew a careful bead on Doc's head and pulled the trigger. By strange coincidence his Sharps missed fire, precisely as had Doc's Springfield a few weeks before [actually a year-and-a-half earlier].
>
> Hearing the snap of the rifle hammer, with a curse Doc jerked his gun and whirled his horse toward the brush just as Billy sprang into the open and threw a pistol shot into Doc that broke his thigh. Swaying in the saddle, Doc cursed Hassard for leading him into a trap, and shot him twice before himself pitching to the ground. Hassard stood idly, stunned apparently

by a sort of white-hot work he was not used to, and received his death wound without any effort even to draw. Meantime, the firm of Lykins and Llewellyn accounted for two more before Doc's mates got out of range.[7]

These are the various accounts of the unsuccessful assassination. As to most of the details, the truth asserts itself; some matters are cloudy and will necessarily remain so.

The shooting was over. Llewellyn had his slight scratches on the hand and under the arm; Hazen had been wounded three times and was in critical condition; and Middleton had been wounded once, superficially by a miracle.

No one knows how he will perform in a crisis until he has met the test. Outlaw or not, Doc Middleton had given a better account of himself than his enemy. If he had any companions, he had shouted to them to go back, and had taken on the field without knowing what the odds were. The advantage of surprise had been in favor of the detectives; they had the drop on him and had gotten off the first shots; he was on the ground, wounded and alone. And yet, when it was over, all had fled, and Middleton was on his feet, shooting. In the words of Hazen, afterward, "I could see Doc standing over me, blazing away."

As to Hazen's wounds, one shot was through the side of the neck, the ball passing out the back of the neck; another through the shoulder, passing down and out through the arm; and the last, between the third and fourth ribs, puncturing a lung and passing out near the backbone.

Middleton apparently was wounded by a bullet from Hazen's .44 Winchester rifle; the bullet entered the abdomen below the navel, never penetrating very deeply, and passing out through the corner of the hip bone, traveling around the inside of his belt and lodging in the clothing near his spine.

Lykens fled the country, heading back toward Columbus. His presence in the region had been so well concealed that it was some time before the truth was known about the mysterious man in the thicket; of all the old-time residents of the Niobrara country with whom I have talked, no one, except Tom Richardson, had ever heard of Billy Lykens.

Llewellyn was on his way to Fort Hartsuff, a distance of eighty or ninety miles by the most direct route across country. The outlaws said he was leading a horse, but that was probably their explanation for the disappearance of Hazen's horse which they themselves had appropriated. Upon his arrival at Fort Hartsuff, Llewellyn sent a report to U.S. District Attorney G. M. Lambertson at Omaha, which said in part:

> I encountered Doc Middleton and several of his gang of Indian horse thieves. They at once opened fire upon us and killed a Mr. Hazen, who was in company with me, and I think a Mr. Lykens, who was also in company with me, as I did not see him after the fight commenced. We killed Black George and an unknown outlaw.

It would be helpful to lay to rest once and for all here the mistaken notion that any outlaws were killed in the Laughing Water shootout. Llewellyn presumably originated this misinformation, Edgar Bronson continued it in 1910, and a few writers have recently revived it. However, all other evidence points clearly to the conclusion that no fatalities among either the outlaws or the lawmen resulted from that July 1879 encounter.

After the shooting, Middleton went to Jim Warner's place. Hazen was lying out on the field of battle. Mrs. Skinner said that her husband, hearing the shots, was soon on the scene (it was just over a mile away) and helped convey Hazen to their tent. Lykens said that he helped Hazen to Skinner's. Hazen, mentioning nothing of any help, said that he walked to Skinner's tent. Mr. Skinner then went to look for Llewellyn, whom they thought had been shot. Eventually going to Warner's, the Reverend found Middleton there, lying on a cot, wounded. Middleton said he guessed Hazen had given it to him this time and wished he could go down and finish him.

A messenger was sent at once to O'Neill City, fifty miles away, for Dr. Daggett to come to attend Middleton. It has been claimed that this ride was made in four hours, but this seems unlikely. It is not known when Dr. Daggett arrived back at the Niobrara, but it may have been a day-and-a-half; during the first night Warner and the Morrises moved Middleton across the river to Richardson's. First reports said that he was guarded there by forty of his men.

Mrs. Skinner told the story in this way:

There the two men lay, not a mile apart, the one surrounded by a host of followers and friends whose lives were already dark with crime and wickedness and swearing vengeance on the betrayer of their leader, and also on anyone who would help him; the other with only us two to stand in defiance of all their threats, and to render him what aid we, in our weakness, could, and believing we defended a worthy man. Mr. Skinner declared he would protect him with his life, and would shoot anyone who would attempt to force an entrance into our tent.

Fearing someone would persist in coming, and knowing it, I went to the brow of the hill and entreated those who came to turn back.

Our oldest son, Adelbert, then thirteen years old, was started to Keya Paha for a physician [Keya Paha was Dr. Reaves' town at the confluence of the Niobrara and Keya Paha Rivers and was thirty to thirty-five miles distant; Dr. Reaves came to attend Hazen], and at night our three other little boys, the youngest but two, were tucked away in the wagon, a little way from the tent and left in the care of the Lord, while Mr. Skinner and I watched the long dark night through, with guns and revolvers ready for instant action. Twice only, when we thought the man was dying, did we use a light for fear it would make a mark at long range.

We had brought a good supply of medicine with us, and knowing well its use, we administered to the man, and morning came and found him still living.

Once only, did I creep out through the darkness to assure myself that our children were safe.

Monday, I went to see Middleton, and carried him some medicine which he very badly needed.

After nightfall, Adelbert and the doctor came and with

them two men, friends of Hazen, whom they met and who inquired of the doctor of Hazen's whereabouts. The doctor, after assuring himself that they were his friends, told them his mission and brought them along, and with their help, Hazen was taken away that night in a wagon, they acting as guards, the doctor as nurse, and Mr. Skinner as driver.[8]

Tom Richardson said it was thought that the detectives had earlier used Skinner's place as a headquarters for their plot and that Mr. Skinner himself was more than a mere bystander in the matter. And Doc always thought that Sam Likens also knew a trap had been laid for him.

Ironically, on the day after the gun fight, while Doc lay wounded on the north side of the river, H. M. Uttley, the attorney at O'Neill City, not having heard of the recent events, wrote a letter to Governor Nance in Middleton's behalf, asking for an answer to the "proposition," speaking with contempt of the "ten or twelve who have been skulking around, seeking blood money," and stating that it would be "an act of humanity and justice to help this man all that it is in our power to, to become a citizen and reform from his old ways."[9]

Within a day or two, Doc Middleton was taken to a spot about seven miles from the Morris ferry: a deep canyon near the head of the east branch of the Wyman Creek. This was done by his friends, Jim Warner and the Morrises, and possibly others. A tent was pitched; there was water from the spring, and supplies were furnished by his wife's people and friends. Dr. Daggett, when he arrived at long last, treated Middleton at this hideout. Just possibly the doctor arrived at Jake Haptonstall's house before Middleton was taken to the hideout.

11

Doc Middleton's Capture

An unnamed informant "from the northern part of the state" arrived at Grand Island on Wednesday, July 23rd. He reported the essential details of the Middleton fight on the Niobrara River. This was published in the *Omaha Daily Bee* and reprinted on Saturday, July 26, 1879, in Yankton's *Daily Press and Dakotian*. The story stated that Middleton was in a helpless condition, but guarded by sixty of his men; it was estimated that he could muster 200 men on short notice, to defend against any party sent to attack him. The traveler from the northern part of the state said that the rewards for Middleton totaled $2,000.

Yankton lost no time in trying to turn the world to its advantage. Two days later the newspaper reported that the man "wounded on the Long Pine Creek [sic]" was actually *not* Middleton, as Middleton had been seen *in Yankton* on Saturday night. The next day, July 29th, the *Daily Press and Dakotian* reported:

> It is quite certain that the noted Niobrara desperado was in Yankton Saturday night. It was reported in Yankton yesterday that the noted outlaw of the Niobrara, Doc Middleton, was in town. As the rumor gained currency, considerable ex-

citement was manifested and a determination developed to capture the celebrated ranger and the reward. The city and county officers, while properly on the alert, did not place implicit confidence in the rumor, but one W. Reinhardt was so confident that the man was in town that he swore out a warrant before Justice Roberts, which was placed in the hands of city marshal Gemmill for service.

From parties who claimed to know Middleton, and to have seen him in town, he received a minute description of the man, and last night between 9 and 10 o'clock, succeeded in arresting the man whom the complainant and others were confident was the Niobrara outlaw and lodged him in the calaboose.

This morning the marshal was beset by a large number of steamboatmen who claimed that they were well-acquainted with the arrested man and that he had been engaged during a portion of the summer on the steamer Dakota and that he had arrived from Bismarck on that boat a few days ago.

Rumors, however, continued rife that Middleton had been in town and that he had been seen by persons who were well-acquainted with him. To ascertain, if possible, the facts in this case, a reporter from the Press and Dakotian made diligent inquiry this morning and was informed by persons who claimed to know Middleton that he was in town Saturday night, but beyond this no information could be obtained.

It is asserted, and apparently with truth, that Middleton enjoys the friendship of every settler in the Niobrara Valley. This is accounted for on the ground that notwithstanding the fact that he is reputed to be a murderer, an outlaw and a horse thief, he respects the property of the settlers, and will not himself, nor allow any of his men, to molest the property of the permanent settlers and stockmen of the valley. He acts as a sort of police for the valley and scrupulously protects the property of the settlers while he levies a heavy tribute from the Indians and outsiders generally. For this reason the people of the valley and those who have interests there are unwilling to give him away, claiming that if they did, their property and probably their lives, would pay the forfeit.

Consequently it is very difficult to obtain information in regard to the whereabouts or movements of Middleton. The conclusion we have arrived at, from the information we could obtain, is that Middleton was not in the fight with the detectives on the Long Pine, that he was in Yankton Saturday night and Sunday morning, and that he is not here now.

What happened to the false Middleton, "the man whom the complainant and others were confident was the Niobrara outlaw"? He was soon one afternoon brought before Justice Roberts for examination. Upon being arraigned, he stated that his name was James McMullen and that he had lived in Nebraska three years and that during the summer he worked at steamboating. William Reinhardt, the complaining witness, stated that the prisoner had been pointed out to him as Doc Middleton by a man who represented himself as being from the Niobrara Valley and well-acquainted with Middleton. Upon this information, a warrant was sworn out for the man who gave Reinhardt the information. The man was already present in court, and upon being called as a witness, gave his name as A. W. Johnson. Upon being sworn, he claimed that he knew Doc Middleton and that the prisoner was not the man.

Question by the Court: "What kind of a looking man is Doc Middleton?"

Witness: "That's none of your business."

The Court thereupon emphatically informed Mr. Johnson that he was in contempt of court and that his case would be properly attended to.

Witness: "Are you the Court? I didn't know."

The Court then repeated the question as to what kind of looking man Middleton was.

"He's a better looking man than you are."

The witness then went on to describe the appearance of Doc Middleton, and wound up with the remark, "He's a damned sight better looking man than this fellow," pointing to the prisoner. Another admonition from the Court and Mr. Johnson's testimony was concluded. He was placed in charge of an officer with the instruction not to allow him to leave the room.

This concluded the testimony, and its effect was to reduce the prisoner from the terrible Doc Middleton to a harmless steamboat rooster. He was discharged.

Then Johnson was brought to the front again and was informed that for his language in contempt of court he would be required to pay a fine of three dollars or go to jail. Johnson paid his fine and then he too went his way.[1]

The *Press and Dakotian* voiced the opinion that A. W. Johnson was not usually in a condition to remember his utterances from one moment to the next.

And thus ended the Yankton arrest and trial of "Doc Middleton."

There was a Doc Middleton excitement also at Deadwood. A local officer arrested a man who he claimed was one of the Middleton gang, but the examination proved this find to be more insignificant than the Yankton affair; the Deadwood desperado turned out to be a drunken saloonkeeper.

Back on the Niobrara, Doc Middleton was convalescing in his camp on Wyman Creek.

On the 23rd of July, Rev. Skinner and party had arrived at Neligh with the wounded man, Hazen, and here Hazen first told his story of the happenings on Laughing Water. Lykens had come to Omaha. Llewellyn had started out from Fort Hartsuff with sixteen infantry soldiers under Capt. Munson.[2]

On the 24th, Llewellyn and the troops were at the mouth of Bloody Creek, a tributary of the Calamus, in the Loup system. At the instigation of Billy Lykens, Sheriff Kilian of Hall County, Sheriff Krew of Howard County, Detective Leach of the U.P. force, a man named Eisley, from Indiana, and J. L. Smith, a deputy sheriff from Cheyenne strongly identified with the railroad detectives, had set out for Fort Hartsuff, not knowing of Llewellyn's arriving there. They expected to combine with the troopers at the fort and proceed on to the Niobrara with them.

On the 25th, Rev. Skinner and party arrived at Columbus with Hazen, who was taken by train to Omaha to a hospital. Llewellyn was at the head of the Bloody.

On the 26th, Llewellyn and the troopers arrived at the Bassett

Craggy bluff
overlooking Wyman Creek canyon
where Doc Middleton was captured
by a posse of sheriffs,
detectives, and U.S. Army troops.

A view southward
toward the Niobrara River
from hills
overlooking Wyman Creek,
a tributary of the Niobrara.

Kid Wade.

Black Bill.
Courtesy National Archives.

Ranch on the head of Long Pine Creek.

On the 27th, Llewellyn and the troops were back at Skinner's place on the Niobrara. The civilian party from Grand Island had reached Fort Hartsuff with the order for the troops, and upon finding that Llewellyn was alive and that the troops had left with him, hastened and overtook them as they arrived on the Niobrara. Happy Jack, a trapper and guide from near the fort, had come along.

First, John Morris of the ferry was interrogated as to Middleton's whereabouts. He refused to tell the detectives anything, and no amount of threats could induce him to change his mind.

Next, the party crossed the river and proceeded to Richardson's, where they took Henry Richardson into custody, and by threatening his life persuaded him to escort the party to Middleton's hideout on Wyman Creek. As mentioned, this was about seven miles from the ferry. The canyon walls were very steep at this point and covered with a dense growth of pine timber. The soldiers and detectives arrayed themselves about the tops of the bluffs, and someone fired a shot into the tent. Richardson pleaded with the men to hold their fire, as his daughter Mary was in the tent. What these armed men were thinking of in firing into the tent is not known. This could not have appeared to be anything resembling an outlaw stronghold; there were no fortifications of any kind. All sources say it was Llewellyn who started the firing.

At the first shot, Kid Wade and Black Bill, aged sixteen and eighteen, ran from the tent. One made good his escape, the other was captured; it was not recorded which one was taken. Mary ran from the tent, screaming, and Doc crawled under the back of the tent and was making his way down the ravine, taking advantage of all the cover available. This is Tom Richardson's story of the capture:

> —twenty soldiers, armed, and four detectives and Leach was one of them; so, by god, they found him up there, you know—he surrendered to Leach—and that Llewellyn was with these soldiers, and it was steep up there, and, by god, he shot through that tent, and Jack told me, when they had him up there on a bed, I got out there, and I went up and

just sat down and cried like a baby—and they had his bed
and him so's they could get to him with a wagon, and Jack
told, he says, "Tom, he shot a hole through the tent, and hit
that big tree, and," he says, "that bullet didn't miss Mary's
head two foot"—and he went this way under the tent, down
there where there was a spring runnin', and the ditch was
covered over with rose bushes and grass, you know, and he,
wounded like he was, he got down on his knees there and he
crawled way down there, and, by god, Llewellyn up there,
and the soldiers, shootin' at all the logs down there, and Leach
had a double barreled shotgun, and, by god, he quit 'em, and
he knew Middleton—they knew one another personally, they
had visited together somewhere—he just come right down
there like that, and he—they didn't think he was in the creek,
they didn't know where he was, they thought he crawled out
under that grass, you know—and Leach was around with his
shotgun, lookin' around, and when Middleton saw him, why
he hollered to him; he knew him, you know; and Leach didn't
come over with his gun ready or nothin'; hell, he carried his
gun in one hand and came over and shook hands with the
other and he [Doc] just unbuckled his six-shooter and handed
it to him, and that was that. Then, by god, that cowardly
Llewellyn, he went with him to Neligh—they took Jack down
there in a wagon, you know. They got into Atkinson, "Hurrah for Doc Middleton." They got into O'Neill, "Hurrah for
Doc Middleton." He wanted all the credit for capturin' him,
the damn coward; he had credit for runnin' like a son-of-a-
gun, but with them soldiers up there, why, when he shot, he
ran back and laid down, and Leach was the most honorable
man of all of 'em. And so they took him—I don't know why
—I never knew why they took him out of Nebraska to Cheyenne; I don't know; he was captured in Nebraska, and, by
god, they took him to Cheyenne.

In Llewellyn's report of this matter to the Department of Justice, he mentioned sharp firing by Middleton's men which was returned by the detectives and soldiers, with what result he was

unable to ascertain. The fact was that there were only two of "Middleton's men" present, and no firing was done by Middleton or either of the two youths. This is the only reference made to any exchange of fire. When the group arrived back at the river, whichever of the two young kids had been captured, Wade or Black Bill, was released.

After the capture, the tent and supplies were piled up and burned. The "contraband" consisted of food and books, reading matter to help pass the hours away. But down in Omaha, far from the scene, this act would be praised. There were headlines: "Huge Quantities of Provisions and Ammunition Captured." "The Camp Gutted and the Tents Piled Up and Burned." Other newspapers, however, severely criticized this destruction. This is the opinion of the *Sidney Telegraph:*

> In the camp was found a large quantity of fresh fruit, green corn, canned fruits and many luxuries, and a fine class of papers and literature. This, we understand, was utterly destroyed and tent burned, a piece of vandalism ill comporting with the general reputation of U.S. officers. We say editorially that Doc Middleton may be a way off, bad man, but he has his excellent qualities and they are as redeeming as any man's can be and it is a shameful, disgraceful, imfamous deed to burn his private property, much of which belonged to his devoted wife.

The detectives and Llewellyn proceeded down the Elkhorn with the prisoner, and Leach was in charge. Lykens had gone back to Cheyenne, where he talked freely of having tried ten or twelve times to shoot Middleton without warning and the Sharps rifle failing to fire. When the cartridges were returned to the store from whence they had come, they were found to be for a slightly different model of a gun, and when tried in the correct gun, worked perfectly; this little oversight had saved Middleton from being murdered in cold blood.[3]

The rather pathetic letter following was written to Nancy Riley by Middleton's wife, Mary, the day her husband of a few weeks was taken down the Elkhorn by the detectives:[4]

> *Atkinson Holt County Nebr*
> *July 29 79*

Mrs Riley
   Dear friend   I will answer your letter that you all wrote to Jack he is well at present and I am well I hope this will find you all well and doing well
   I want you to write and tell me for sure if Jack's Brother [William Riley/Charley Fugate] *is up in this country yet ore not I hav tried to find him but cant I want you to write and tell me if Jack has got anything against him in Texas now ore not you can tell me and it will all be the same no one else will never know it he has got himself in a pretty bad shape here but I guess he will get out all write in time*
   He has got a wife that will stick to him as long as he livs no matter what his fate is I knew him well before we was married and I will stay close to him in all truble never one has his truble sooner ore latter Jack sends his love all best respects to you all and to the girls he says if he lives and lucks well he will come and see you all
   I will now send my picture that was taking when I was fifteen years old I have none that has been taking since then I want you all to have your pictures and send them to me if I could any way I would come to Texas and stay a while but I guess I cant now
   Joseph Smith if you know him got killed he came from Texas he was a good boy I always thought
   Well you must do the best you can and I will do the same I am staying at home now we have not went to house keep yet I want you to be sure and tell me where Jack's brother is if he is up here any place I wish you would write and tell him I want to in a pretty bad shape here but I guess he will get out all write in time see him he can find me on the Niobrara River
   Well I want you to write to me I am a doing well but I am mighty troubled but I will half to get use to it I guess
   That little sister of Jack's wrote and wanted to know what he was doing he said to tell her he was doing all write and wants her to write and nother long letter to him as she did before Well crops

all good here and times are getting better here
Well I have wrote all I know to write now all write soon and
often to Jack and I and be good to yourselves good by yours truly
Mrs. Mary Middleton
When you write you can sign my name that

Doc Middleton's capture raised hopes along the Niobrara that perhaps now horse thieving could be brought under control. It also raised fears of reprisal against those who had aided in the capture. This mix of emotions is reflected in a remarkable letter by Mr. Skinner that asks the State of Nebraska to legitimatize vigilantes who plan to rid the Niobrara of outlaws:[5]

August 8th, 1879
Ranch near the Running Water
Nebr.
Mr. Nance
Governor of the State of Neb.

Dear Sir: After due consideration & in view of our situation as settlers upon the frontier, who have come here seeking a quiett home and a peaceful life we do find it necessary to appeal to your honor as our legal protector, asking your assistance & advice. The situation is one that is no way novel, but imbraces the destruction of property & the threatning of human life. We have about us here a class of men who are called rustlers or in a plainer term, horse thieves who do nothing for a living but to steal & rob, & the majority of the settlers seam to be in sympathy with them, or act thus for self protection. We a few names of us are not of that class, but are strictly legal, & outspoken. We have lent our assistance already toward the capturing of one of thear leaders, Doc Midleton & have thear anathamy & threats resting upon us. They have said they would leave us not a hoof, and that they would shoot us so full of bullet holes that our shirts would not hold straw. We have been looking & expecting attacts boath by day & by night. We don't like the idea of acting alone on the defensive, but wish to hunt them out of thear hiding places & shooting them down & so spread consternation & fear among them. We may lose life in our endeavers but we carey our risks if the governer will stand between us and all legal harm. We don't wish to kill outlaws & desperadoes, & then be punished by the penalty of the law. We are seeking our own safety and that of the legal settlers & the good of the Comonwelth. Since Doc Midleton was taken thear has been 5 head of horses stolen, or four horses and one mule, & these sufferers have no helper near. If we could we would like to have military assistance, but if not, will you pleas send to my order to Oneal in the care of P. Haggardy ten guns with one hundred rounds of ammonition each & I will see that the guns go into the hands of such men as will assist if called upon to take the outlaws. Jack Knowland, Doc Palmer or limber Dic, Cap Kid or Albert Wade, George Holt, Bill Shebley are among the leading outlaws in these parts. Thear are others but we do not know thear names. Mr. Nance if you wish any knowledge of myself, I would refer you to Messrs Hazen and Lewellen, Omaha Neb. I should like very much to hear from you, & as soon as possible in refference to this matter & whether you will send the guns &c. Messrs Wm Wood J. Wood & G Wood and myself have joined in Ranch for mutual protection. These men you will remember. You furnished guns to them last Spring also Mr. Likens. For refference as regards the Woods boys W. P. Philips Lincoln, Neb.

You will pleas address me to Atkinson

Holt Co.

Neb.

I subscribe myself yours in confidence

Revd I. H. Skinner

Pleas reggister letter

12

Prison

Doc Middleton languished in jail in Cheyenne for over a month. No Federal case was made and it appears that it had been decided to try him on the charges there. We remember that in May 1878 he had been indicted along with George Smith and Edgar Scurry on charges of stealing varying amounts of horses from three ranchers.[1]

In early September it was discovered that Middleton was communicating with friends on the outside. The *Cheyenne Daily Sun* reported:

> Through the vigilance of Sheriff Draper and Deputy Sheriff Martin, the details of a deep laid plan for the rescue of Middleton have just been brought to light. It seems that he has friends in Cheyenne who are willing to aid him in his scheme to kill Martin, break jail and escape, but he and his friends have been foiled in their attempt. Women, too, who belong elsewhere, were taking a hand in this scheme and to them was committed the task of conveying to the wife and pals of the desperado the intelligence of what was wanted of them and what he expected them to do in order to effect his escape.

Some days ago, Sheriff Draper and Deputy Martin became suspicious that a correspondence was being carried on between Middleton and parties on the outside. They set themselves to work to ascertain what was on the tapis. A certain party on the outside (whose name we will not mention) was suspected of having received communications from Middleton, though by whom these missives were conveyed to him was not known, although now well understood.

Draper and Martin proceeded to put up a little job on the party who was suspected of receiving the communications. The party was arrested and the following letters which explain the plot that was set on foot to release Middleton were found on his person before he had time to forward them to pals and friends of the desperado. The introductory part of Middleton's letter, as will be seen by our readers, is written somewhat after the style of "cypher dispatches" and cannot, of course, be understood except by the parties for whom the letter was intended.

Cheyenne Wyo.
Sept 9 1879

My friend:

Go and Bi and Di and J.C. and Jo and the other Bi I have an opportunity of writing you all about times to let you know how this place is situated in here. I understand that you are in the country and if so I wish that you boys would come and git me. It is easily done. Two men or three can take this jalor without any truble whatever. I will tell you as well as I can about this jalor. He carries the keys in the jail with him when he feeds ov mornings between 8 and 9 o clock, evenings between 4 and 5 o clock. Either of these times will do to make the break. There is no danger of doing this at all. Bi and Di can come in their own teams and not be bothered by anyone. Come in a wagon and tell folks they come from the Hills. It is all that I depend on in gitting out of here. If you boys dont come and git me out I will never git out. That will settle it with me for some time. For God's sake do something for me for this is the damdest place I ever got into my life.

I can kill the jalor but I dont want to do that if I can help it, but before I will stay here another month longer I will have to do it. I would suicide but I am afraid I would go to hell. Cant you come and see what can be done, I must git out of here. Will you git me out? You can if you want to. I would go to hell for you.

Following this is a few lines to his wife and an envelope in which the following letter was found:

Mrs. Middleton
Dear Madam
Enclosed find a letter from your husband. He requests me to impress it on your memory to attend in person to what he requested in case that his friends fail to assist him. He desires you and your father to be up here to his trial in November. Court commences on the 4th. Be careful of some papers. You understand and have the lawyer to bring them when he comes up, also to save all the money you get until you hear from him—send by the boys or bring with you his gun and revolver providing you can do so without attracting too much attention and be sure and get the watch and chain from Dickerson [Will Dickerson of Atkinson, Nebraska]. Mr. Middleton desires me to tell you that his health is improving rapidly and he is all right. Lots more he told me to tell you but as you have already heard from him doubtless you will do as instructed. Don't forget to burn all Texas letters. Do not write anything to the jail to denote that you hear from him privately —do as he requests and you will be happy yet.

Respectfully, A Well Wisher
P.S. I will write again. Somehow, I do not feel just right although I shall mail this letter on the train. It would be fearful if the mails were watched. I would go up sure but I guess it is all right.

Thus it will be seen just what their plan was. The Well Wisher will also be seen as well aware of the fact that he is engaged in a nefarious business and now that he has been discovered at his work and the whole plot revealed he would probably be doing a good thing for himself to take a skin at once.[2]

Now wtih hope of escape gone, Middleton decided to plead guilty to one of the charges and not await the fall term of Court. Through his attorney, he offered to plead guilty to case #433, the theft of three horses from James M. Carey; this was the least of the three thefts contained in the 1878 indictment. The offer was accepted. He was arraigned on the 18th of September 1879, and pleaded guilty the same day. The prosecuting attorney moved for sentence, and Middleton was sentenced to five years in the penitentiary. Indictments #434 and #435 were dismissed. Doc was sentenced to the Nebraska State Penitentiary for the reason that there had been a fire at the Wyoming Territorial prison, rendering it useless.

The *Cheyenne Daily Sun* carried this item on September 30, 1879:

Doc Middleton, the golden-toothed lover of other folks' cattle and horseflesh, who has been a guest at the Hotel de Draper for several weeks, was taken from our midst Sunday afternoon. By this time he is undoubtedly safely lodged in the Nebraska State Penitentiary at Lincoln, where, unless he effects his escape, he will remain in durance vile for five long and lonesome years.

He left us in charge of Deputy Warden Nobes, whose principal mission to our territory was for the purpose of taking him under his protecting wing. His departure was managed almost as quietly as his arrival, owing to the fact that Deputy Nobes wanted to skip him along the railroad incog as it were, to prevent either his rescue by his friends or a lynching on the part of his Sidney enemies. It was known to the Sun on Saturday night that Middleton would be taken hence the following day, but by special request of Mr. Nobes, nothing was said in our Sunday morning issue about the matter. Consequently there were few at the depot to see the bandit start on his journey. His going, however, became known to several during the afternoon, passed from mouth to mouth, and by the time the train pulled out with the prisoner, about thirty spectators were present to see him off.

He was taken to the train in a bus. His wrists and ankles were ornamented with that peculiar kind of jewelry occasionally worn by men of his ilk. The escort to the train consisted of Deputy Warden Nobes, Sheriff Draper, Deputy Martin, Officer Smith and a Sun reporter.

The prisoner is a tall, lank, cadaverous looking individual, has black hair, worn somewhat long, has black, determined though not desperate looking eyes, carries a stiff upper lip, around which plays a suppressed and somewhat ironic smile. He sat in the bus a half hour perhaps before taking a seat in the car, and while thus occupied the Sun reporter held a brief conversation with him.

"How do you feel over this matter?" asked the Sun man.

"Well," responded Doc, "It's pretty hard but I've made up my mind to take it philosophically. I expect five years down there will seem as long as ten out here on the free prairie."

Deputy Nobes here remarked that most of the prisoners down at Lincoln seemed to think the time flew rapidly.

Middleton said, "I'm glad to hear it. I'm not used to being caged up that way. I don't think my punishment is just. I've been misrepresented by the Omaha papers. To read their accounts you would think I'm the worst man in the world."

The Sun reporter asked, "Why didn't your wife come to Cheyenne to see you as was reported?"

Middleton: "Because she didn't intend to come. I did not expect her. There was no truth to the report that she was on her way to Cheyenne. That was another lie."

While alluding to his wife, the prisoner sighed, his voice trembled and the tears rushed uncontrollably to his eyes. Though an outlaw among men, his better nature was deeply touched when his mind reverted to the woman of his choice.

After some conversation of a general nature, Middleton

said to the reporter, "I'm well-acquainted in this section. I used to work for Judge Tracy. Do you know him?"

The Sun reporter responded in the affirmitive and in a few minutes the judge, who happened to be at the depot, came up to the bus and the following colloquy took place between the prisoner and his former employer.

Middleton: "Well, Judge, I'm going to leave you for a while. I suppose you haven't forgotten how I used to break bronchos for you?"

Tracy: "No, I remember you very well, but I never expected to see you in this fix."

Middleton: "I didn't think of anything of this kind then either. I ain't so bad as they make me out. Just you wait till about the year 1884 and I'll come back and ride your bronchos; see if I don't."

After some more chin music, the judge bade Doc goodbye and walked away. The prisoner, walking slightly lame on account of his wound, was conveyed from the bus to the car and was soon on his way to Lincoln. Unless he manages to escape, Doc Middleton will, during the next five years, be almost forgotten in a land where his name was at one time on almost everyone's tongue.

The following article comes from the *Omaha Daily Bee,* October 1, 1879, as a reprint from the *Lincoln Journal* of September 29:

Doc Middleton, the noted outlaw and desperado who has been the terror of the stockmen of the northwestern part of the State for the past several years, arrived on yesterday's train from the West in charge of Deputy Warden Nobes and taken to the pen to undergo a sentence of five years. Middleton in appearance is not what we expected to see. He is neither a large nor a small man, and his physique does not indicate great strength. Taken all together, he is rather a good-looking man. He has very high cheek bones, a piercing black eye, and a mouth indicative of great firmness.

He was seated in the waiting room of the depot for fifteen

minutes after the arrival of the train, conversing with a stranger, and to look at him, not knowing who he was, he would be the last person in the room taken for an outlaw or desperado. When the carriage which was to take him to the penitentiary was ready, he arose from his seat and walked to it quickly as though anxious to get to his new home. The carriage passed up "O" Street to 11th, where it turned and went south. Middleton was seated in the back seat and his restless eyes seemed to take in everything as he moved along.

From a reliable gentleman who came down on the same train with the prisoner, we learn that an unsuccessful attempt was made at Sidney to capture and lynch him. At this point four men, with their hats drawn down closely over their faces, entered the car, and seeing Mr. Nobes, remarked, "Hello, you here? I thought Doc was coming down with the sheriff of Cheyenne." [The men were disappointed in encountering Mr. Nobes instead of the sheriff?]

Mr. Nobes remarked, "Yes, I am here, and I want you to leave this car immediately."

The leader of the party, who, by the way, our informant says is one of the heaviest stockmen in that country, replied: "We have come after Middleton and we are going to have him. We have a party outside fully able to take care of him and it will not cost the state a cent to keep him any longer."

Mr. Nobes then rose, and with both hands on his revolvers ordered the men to leave the car and they went.

Our informant says that Middleton was lying in one of the upper bunks of the sleeping car and heard every word of the conversation that transpired. As soon as the men left, Mr. Nobes called the conductor and asked where he could secrete the prisoner until the next station was passed. The director's car, the last car on the train, was given to Mr. Nobes and his prisoner. Into this car Middleton was hurried, the doors locked and windows closed, the lights extinguished and Nobes and his prisoner left alone.

Upon the arrival of the train at the next station, it was boarded by a large number of men who walked through the cars, scanning everybody very closely. Failing to find the man they wanted, they asked the trainmen if Warden Nobes and Middleton were on the train. They answered, "No," that they got off the train at Sidney. This seemed to satisfy them and they left the train. Our informant is confident that if the last gang could have laid hands on Middleton that night, he would now be in the home of his forefathers.[3]

Upon being received at the Nebraska State Penitentiary, Middleton was interviewed, and among other information gave his age as twenty-eight, which was correct, his birthplace, Mississippi, which was not, and stated that he had a wife and mother. He did not admit having a father, which would indicate that he did not consider J. B. Riley as his father.

Middleton would serve less than four years of his five-year sentence. During that time he was reported to be the most tractable prisoner in the penitentiary. Tom Richardson reminisced about those days:

Doc only had to serve three years and nine months; he got out on good behavior. I was the only one that would write to him, and I was the only one that sent him a cent to buy tobacco. By God, I saved up nickels and Bill Young had a post office and a little store on the island there; and my dad didn't know—my dad says, "I don't want anybody writin' to the penitentiary." And, by god, I was writin' to him and Bill Young was takin' the letters and promised to say nothin' about it. And Jack wrote to me, and says, "Tom, if you can spare a few nickels, they don't furnish any chewin' tobacco here." And he was there quite a while then; and I kept thinkin' about it, and, by god, I was stuck on him, Jesus, everybody was stuck on him; and so I talked with Bill Young —I knew I didn't dare let my dad know I was writin' to the penitentiary—so Bill Young says, "Write to him if you want to, and bring the letters here." And Jack says, "If you want to do somethin' for me, they don't furnish chewin' tobacco here," and he says, "A dollar and a quarter,"—I forget, I saved up my nickels, and Mary give me some money, and I sent him money to buy his chewin tobacco from that on till he got out.

They put him on the stone pile first; well, he was shot, you know, and he wasn't very stout yet; and then, you see, his personality went a long ways, and he got a talk with the warden, and the warden told Billy, that run a knittin' machine upstairs, makin' shirts, says, "Take him up there." So they took him up there and put him to runnin' a machine, by god, no work at all. So him and Billy got to be friends, you know, he was that kind of a feller; and Billy come to him one mornin' and says, "Doc, your time's up," and he took him to a store. He took his prison clothes off and bought him a new blue suit of clothes and a pair of boots and kind of cowboy lookin' hat. Billy asked, "Where do you want to go?" And Jack told him he wanted to go to Pueblo, Colorado, and Billy says, "I'm gonna take money right outa my pocket and buy a ticket so you won't have to beat your way."

According to the official records of the Nebraska State Penitentiary, Doc Middleton was discharged from the prison June 18, 1883.[4] The following week the *Lincoln State Journal* carried this item:

The notorious desperado who figured so conspicuously in Western Nebraska life five years ago, and who was finally captured by Llewellyn's party and sent to the penitentiary, was discharged from the institution last week. His destination is unknown, but he informed the prison officials that he was going to a new country where the name of Middleton was unknown and where he would have an opportunity of leading a new life among strangers. During his long confinement in prison, he behaved himself like a man and conformed to the rules of the prison to the letter, not receiving one black mark. A few days before his discharge, while at work at one of the shops, and intently reflecting on the few days more of prison life, he put one of his fingers too near the buzz saw, cutting it off. The prison physician attended to the finger and the next day Middleton reported to the warden that he was ready for some light work. He was told that he might go to the hospital if he chose but he answered that his services belonged to the State and he was ready to put in the time faithfully.

I have heard more than one explanation of the matter of the missing finger, but the above is undoubtedly the correct version. To resume Richardson's narration:

Well, as soon as he got to Pueblo—he was there only two hours, and stockmen was comin' in, lookin' for men to work —and he could give 'em a story about ridin', don't you see, and everything—and he went right out there to work at $75 a month the last of June, and stayed right there till February, and saved his money up pretty darn good.

But I was goin' to tell you, he wrote to me, and so I got the letter, and he told me—wrote to me not to mention a thing of the past—you know he didn't know about these other charges—as he had me address the letters "D. C. Cherry," that's the way I addressed letters to him till February, '84; I wrote to him right along and signed his name "D. C. Cherry."

13

Doc Middleton's Return

Why did Middleton not return to the Niobrara and to his wife immediately upon his release from prison? Probably because Doc knew that he had lost his wife. Mary did not wait for her husband as she thought she would. She held on for perhaps two years, but began to think of it as being futile, and in this she was influenced by her father, Henry Richardson. It was "common knowledge" along the Niobrara that she divorced Middleton and married Sam Morris. However, no record of such a divorce or a marriage exists. The truth of the matter was that these people thought the fact of Middleton's being in the penitentiary automatically gave her a divorce.[1] While it was true that a long enough enforced separation would be grounds for a divorce, it would not constitute an actual divorce.

As to the matter of her marriage to Sam Morris, according to Tom Richardson, "Cap" Tarbell performed the marriage ceremony as he had also obtained the divorce for Mary. As Tom said: "I don't know; I thought Tarbell took care of it. First thing we knew, they were married and living over at Warner's." Jim Warner was Sam Morris' brother-in-law. Sam and Mary stayed at Warner's for a time and then took a homestead out north of the river toward the flats.

Many other changes had occurred during Middleton's absence. For one thing, his stepfather had died. In the spring of 1880, during Doc's first year in the penitentiary, J. B. Riley moved his family to Mason County, Texas, and located about ten miles west of the town on Little Bluff Creek, a tributary of the Llano River. He registered brand and ear marks for cattle at Mason although he did not sell his place in Gillespie and Blanco Counties. He died on or about September 20, 1880, from what was diagnosed as colic but could have been a gall bladder infection or acute appendicitis. He was buried in the Mason cemetery, in an unmarked grave.

The Riley family scattered, the girls marrying and the boys buying land and selling it and then buying more land, and always moving farther west; most of this occurred before Middleton returned to the Niobrara-Elkhorn valley region.

Back in the Niobrara area, after the 1879 capture of Middleton, there were rumors abroad and reports in the newspapers that William Llewellyn had every intention of returning to the region to take into custody some parties who had befriended the Middleton gang; but they remained rumors and nothing more. These parties were never mentioned by name in his reports to the Department of Justice, and no record of prosecutions has been found. In the U.S. District Court records for Nebraska and Dakota there are a few indictments during this period against parties for milling in government timber and for some lesser offenses, but any connection between these and Llewellyn's work is questionable. Llewellyn did make a request to go to Washington to confer in person with the department, but this was denied on the ground that communication could be carried on by letter and that there was no justification for his absence from duties on the frontier. He continued to operate as an agent for the Department of Justice for more than a year after Middleton's incarceration but was finally dismissed by the department. His dismissal had been left to the discretion of H. J. Campbell, U.S. District Attorney for Dakota Territory. However, Llewellyn, not realizing he had been dismissed, continued on his frontier job for two months until he finally received a letter of reprimand from the department. Eventually his claims were paid and he went to New Mexico where he took a position as agent for the Mescalero and Jicarilla Apaches. He spent most of the balance of his life in New Mexico.[2]

Life was becoming more tranquil along the Niobrara. Several of the outlaws had come to an untimely end, and several others were in prison. Nothing further is known of Holt, Bryant, and Shebley; apparently they drifted to other parts.

Theft of Indian stock largely came to a stop, but few stolen horses were ever restored to the Indians; nor, it appears, did they receive adequate compensation, probably none at all. During 1878 a depredations claim was submitted to the government, asking payment of damages in the amount of over $10,000 to be paid in goods and stock for 665 head of horses stolen from the Spotted Tail Indians by whites.[3] This would include those taken during the winter of 1877-78 while the Indians were at the old Ponca Agency and would be in part Middleton's work. By 1883 the claim had not yet been paid. Two or three times as many horses were stolen after the date of the filing of this first claim, but as far as is known no claims for them were filed.

In the fall of 1879 the first political organization of this unorganized territory was accomplished. This 60-by-170-mile area or portions of it had been designated variously and vaguely as "Doc Middleton's Country," "Sioux County," or simply "unorganized territory." Now the region comprising most of present-day Rock, Brown, and Keya Paha Counties, Nebraska, was organized as Long Pine Precinct, and the area west of it as Creighton Precinct, and attached to Holt County for judicial purposes.

The Carns Post Office was established in 1879. This was in the region of the Morris ferry though not exactly at that site at first. Albert Belmer and T. J. Lee were early postmasters and the post office was located in their respective homes. In later years it was at the site of the crossing and the commercial center there became known as Carns. At first the spelling was Carnes, but later the "e" was dropped.

In 1880 Fort Niobrara was built, at about the confluence of the Niobrara River and the Minnechaduza Creek. This brought about increasing traffic up through the country and contributed toward settlement and development.

After John Morris rebuilt his toll bridge in 1880, the community was known for the next few years as Morris Bridge,[4] and eventually, as mentioned, after location of the post office at the site, it was known as Carns.

"Cap" Tarbell became prominent there. There was the hint of a romantic attachment between Tarbell and Mrs. Rebecca Slack, a sister of Mrs. John Morris. Tarbell and Mrs. Slack both homesteaded in the region. Tarbell built a store and hotel and Mrs. Slack operated the hotel.

The hard winter of 1880-81 practically wiped out the cattle ranches and brought extreme hardship to the settlers. Afterward there began a strong tide of immigration into the country. In this region there was no conflict between the rancher and the settler as there had been in other areas for the reason that by the time the large scale immigration of settlers began the ranchers were gone.

The railroad built from Wisner to Oakdale in 1879, the year of Middleton's capture; in 1880 six more miles were built to Neligh. In 1881, another big year, the line reached Long Pine, a distance of ninety-eight miles. By 1884 the rails had reached the new town of Valentine near Fort Niobrara.[5]

In 1883 Brown County was organized, comprising slightly more than the area in the former Long Pine Precinct and approximately, though not exactly, present Rock, Brown, and Keya Paha Counties.

The Richardsons moved into the house on their claim in the fall of 1879. This was about a mile upriver from Jake Haptonstall's house where they had been living and was on the bench of land immediately above the river bottom near the Morris crossing. For the next few years their lot improved substantially, as did that of many of the other settlers, as the country developed.

Doc Middleton's two young companions, Kid Wade and Black Bill, were not at liberty for long after Doc's capture. The Kid was caught stealing horses, and in the fall of 1879 was convicted in Woodbury County, Iowa. In the same term of court there Black Bill and one Bill Clark were convicted of another horse theft. Each young man was sentenced to a three-year term, and the three were received at the men's Reformatory in Anamosa, Iowa on November

25, 1879. Kid Wade was released on June 7, 1882; the other two had been let out a few days earlier.[6]

The Kid returned to his old haunts and was soon back at his old ways. In the fall of 1883 Wade and a few accomplices, principally Billy Morris (no relation to John Morris) and Andrew Culbertson, stole six horses from Henry Richardson and two from Rev. Clifton near Morris Bridge. Needless to say, this caused a furor. Stealing had been going on, not like in the Middleton days, but sneak-thievery from settlers. The new county had been formed, but the principal offices had not yet been filled by permanent officers; so the settlers met and formed a vigilante committee which they named The Niobrara Mutual Protective Association. This was composed principally of settlers in the vicinity of Morris Bridge. It was drawn up by A. J. Burnham, an attorney, who was home-steading in the area, with a constitution and by-laws, and eighteen men signed the articles. Another committee was formed farther north toward the Keya Paha, in the region of Sullivan's ranch, and another in Holt County around Paddock.

Henry Richardson and his son, Tom, were very active in this work; they spent most of the winter riding, recovering horses, and taking suspects into custody. The records at Ainsworth show that proceedings were instituted against Kid Wade, William Morris, Andrew Culbertson, and several others for aiding and abetting. Eventually, Morris and Culbertson were convicted and sentenced to terms in the Nebraska State Penitentiary.

John Wade, father of the Kid, disappeared in the fall of 1883 and was not found until the following spring. He had been shot and buried in a shallow grave. There were disappearances in Holt County and some hangings. Over toward the Keya Paha, a man named Murphy was hanged, presumably by the Sullivan group. There were many prosecutions in Holt County, more than a few unsuccessful.

Kid Wade was finally captured in Iowa by the Holt County group, brought back to Paddock, and turned over to Henry Richardson and two other men of the group from Morris Bridge. They brought the Kid back to their own community and to Long Pine for the purpose of eliciting information from him. Later he fell into the hands of the sheriff of Holt County who had appeared with a warrant, and on the night of February 6, 1884, he was taken from the sheriff at gun point by a party of masked men and hanged near the little village of Bassett.

The vigilante committees began to fall out of favor with the public; where at first they were supported in the press, now they were being criticized. They themselves were brought to court on occasion. So, feeling that the point of diminishing returns had been reached, they disbanded. A great many changes had taken place after Middleton's departure from the region. The country was settling up. Law and order was coming. This would never be "Doc Middleton's country" again. Nevertheless, he did come back. This is Tom Richardson's description of Middleton's return:

And then, he come over to Valentine—got with Jess Donaldson, throwed right in with him. They went down to Stuart, Nebraska, from Valentine and was in Gould's drug store; and that Gould was a kind of a—furnishin' old man Morris with whiskey—he was a little crooked. Gould and somebody else had a drug store at Stuart.

So they goes down to Stuart on a visit, you know. Well, Jess carried a six-shooter all the time, so they got in this drug store, and somebody jumped onto Middleton and went to roastin' him, you know. Well, by god, Jack, he commenced, "Well, now, looka here," he says, "I'm a free man, and I don't want no more trouble." And, by god, while he was a talkin', Jess Donaldson just walked up and hit this feller a belt in the face, and jumped back and jerked the gun out that quick, and, by god, say, that feller got outa there.

So, then, they goes back to Valentine, when they got around to it. He didn't get up there on the river, to Morris' there, for a long time. He wrote and had me and Bob Wilcox go over to Bassett when the train come down to get him, and I led a horse over there, and the train come down from Valentine and he wasn't on—he never come—made that trip to Bassett and led a horse over there for him to ride, with a saddle on, to bring him over, by god.

Well, he finally got down to Stuart, and he come up there in a one-horse buggy; nobody ever saw him in a buggy before, but that's the way he come, just about a year after he got outa prison. He come up there in a one-horse buggy, and Dug Robison throwed right in with him; just went all over that country with him in that buggy; all the neighbors, the Morrises, the Warners, old John Morris' mother—ohh, she cried and carried on when they shot him, you know, got him —they took him right there, you know. She was stuck on him, and when he come back, five years that June, by god, she took him and hugged him and kissed him—and he told Rene and me, says, "Old Lady Morris smokes a pipe; I got a good old smoky kiss from her." He could tell it pretty good.

They had a dance at Old Man Morris', and supper was over at Mrs. Slack's shack, you know—had to go over there to eat; and I went down there with him; he hadn't been back in that country very long—he'd been out of prison quite a while—and he had on a nice suit of clothes; he was dressed up; so I takes him down to the dance, and really I was proud of him.

Lottie Beals was there and says, "Introduce me to him and I'll dance with him." I took him right in there to people from everywhere and I introduced him around and by god there wasn't any of 'em turned him down.

Middleton was, of course, a stranger to many by now; it was a changed country he had come back to.

And god, how he could play the fiddle—and he danced around a time or two, and first thing I knew he was up there playin' the fiddle; he talked to 'em, and they just handed him the fiddle and he got up there and played for two or three sets. Now, by god, it was wonderful—he wasn't in no practice to play—I heard him say to these fellers, "Boys, I'll tell you, I've been cooped up for a while," and, by god, he played good time. He was very popular there that night; god, anybody would of danced with him.

And Rene, it wasn't long before she run off with him; her and her stepmother didn't get along as good as Mary and her stepmother did. Rene had a temper; god, she was good lookin', and a nice dancer—she danced with them boys on the river but she wouldn't go with 'em; they wasn't worth nothin'—they was just loafers. My god, when Middleton come back there, ohhh boy.

On Sunday night, June 1, 1884, Doc Middleton and Rene Richardson eloped and on June 2nd, Monday, they were married at Neligh, Nebraska. He was now thirty-three years old and she had not yet turned sixteen. This was his third marriage: He had married first the Overstreet girl, as James Riley; then Mary Richardson, as James M. Sheppard; and he married Rene Richardson as D. C. Middleton. To resume Tom Richardson's account:

He come to our place like he did everywhere, till pretty soon my dad come to me one day and he says, "Do you know that son-of-a-bitch is hangin' around here after Rene?" Well, Rene wasn't sixteen till September, but she was growthy, you know; she was the same as an eighteen-year-old girl, and god, I didn't know, I thought he was comin' to visit with us. And Rene went out to where Mary and Sam was, stayed out there a few days, and he got on to it, and we found out that he was out there all night, all night out there.

Sam took a homestead out there right north about two miles on the flats, but there were gulches on each side—oh, he got a nice piece of ground there, and there was a spring right there, too, but he sold it to some newcomer, he give it away pretty near.

Middleton didn't dare to come—that is, Rene told him, you know, what my dad had to say, but he didn't come, till—he was down to Stuart, and in the pool hall, I think, so some stranger come from somewhere, and he put up a job with him; and you see, my dad was wantin' to sell out, when he could prove up; you know he could prove, did prove up, before "Cap" Tarbell—he was land commissioner.[7]

And then, of course, he was talkin'—my dad talked a lot, and he wanted to sell out; well, Middleton heard that, so here he brings this son-of-a-bitch up there on Sunday mornin' and introduced him and said that he was from Missouri or somewhere, and he wanted to buy a place up there; and my dad went—we was buildin' fence down there and Middleton helped me with that fence. It was on Sunday and we had company, a coupla—Mattie May and Eva—was there and we was gonna have dinner, you know, so—but we was workin' on that cross fence, so he quit and went with this feller that claimed he wanted to buy a place; showed him the corners all around. Well, he didn't want nothin'; that was an excuse for Middleton to come, don't you see?

Well, he saw Rene, met her right out there with a bucket of water from the well, and there was an old sorghum mill there, settin' right there; then the bench—here's the house on a bench—then it jumps off about thirty feet down that way, then it was bottom ground, you know. Well, this sorghum mill was right there and he saw her there; I know he met her there, I saw him.

And, by god, I took Mattie and Eva home in a wagon, team and wagon, and crossed up at Morris' on that bridge, and I didn't get home till one o'clock, Jesus. Rene slept upstairs, and lots of times, when I would come in late, I'd set down on the foot of the bed there [his sister's bed], just a habit, pullin' off my boots; my bed—there was a curtain up there—my bed was right in there, and you know, at one o'clock I sat down there—come in and sat down and pulled my boots off and went to bed, and never missed her, and she was gone then.

She never took her clothes off at all, you know, and—she was to meet him down at that sorghum mill, which she did —they stopped down there with the buggy, you know, and he come up that hill there, and she throwed her clothes down out the window, and she told me years afterwards she never took her clothes off. Well, what other clothes she had—she never had much—why, she put in a pillow case and dropped it out the window. Well, he whistled—he had a whistle—and, by god, my dad was sound asleep, you know; she went right down the stairs and right out the door, and he was there, so they got in and hiked for Stuart, and the train had to come down.

And do you know, I got up and dressed and went down, and I never looked and I was down there feedin' the horses, and, by god, I met my dad—Jesus Christ, he says, "Tom, do you know that son-of-a-bitch come and stole that child?" Ohhh, Jesus Christ—my god, I'd pulled off my boots that night before, and dressed and went down that mornin', and I never looked around on her bed, and she'd been gone since one o'clock, or before. So that's how that happened.

Well, he got on old Prince and he run him twenty-five miles—you see, if I'd have missed her that night—I'm glad I did because there'd been a hell of a shootin' scrape, my dad and him; I don't know what might have happened, you know.

So he goes to Stuart, and the train had come down and was gone. And I got on a bronc that I was breakin' and, by god, I took after him, and I got down there—you know I rode that bronc twenty-five miles—and so, when he got there, he went upstairs and that feller was in bed asleep, that was with Middleton, and say, he drew a gun on him—course he hadn't done nothin' only claimed he wanted to buy a place when he didn't—but he went up there under the muzzle of a six-shooter and called him all the sons-of-bitches he could think of, you know. He was up there in bed asleep; he'd been up all night with 'em.

And, by god, Stuart was a new town. There was some brush right below the depot there, and, by god, my dad had his mustache and whiskers shaved off, and Charley Green-leaf, who was the first man to run a livery barn in Stuart, he was to—promised to have the horse out back of the livery barn—says, "If I hear you shoot, I'll have this horse out back of the barn"; and my dad was in that brush with a fifty [caliber] needle gun. Well, they telegraphed down and they got the word back, "Middleton is here and married." Well, the

Wedding picture of Doc Middleton and Rene Richardson, Doc's third wife, June 1884. Middleton's daughter, Ruth, said that her father "nearly always had a ring, watch, or stick pin." *W. A. Croley photo.*

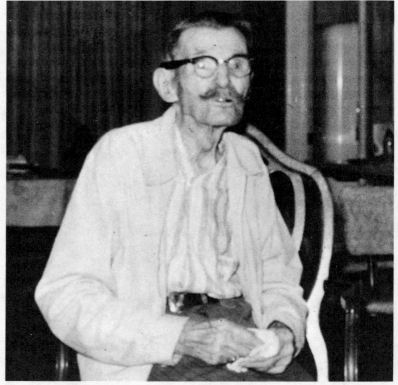

CERTIFICATE OF MARRIAGE.

To the County Judge of _____ County, Nebraska:

This Certifies, That on the _2nd_ _____ day of _June_ _____ A.D. 18_

at _Ardigh_ _____ in said County, according to law and by authority, I de

JOINED IN MARRIAGE Mr. _D C Middleton_ and M_rs Irene Richard_

and there were present as witnesses _Sarah C & Eugene H Emery_ _____

Given under my hand, the _2nd_ _____ day of _June_ _____ A.D. 188_4_

H Emery
Co Judge

Tom Richardson, brother of Mary Richardson and Rene Richardson, brother-in-law to Doc Middleton, 1960. Tom, who provided much valuable information for the Doc Middleton story, died in 1963 at 99 years of age.

train come up that evening, don't you see—by god, if they'd come up that evening, he was in the brush down there, but the train come and they wasn't on it.

And I got down there, and Josh Raver, he was such good friends with us, and he got a hold of my dad, and said, "They're married, what's the use to break 'em up now?" Old Josh talked awful good to him, like a brother, you know, and says, "Henry, just as sure as you shoot him, they'll send you to the pen." It would be premeditated murder; guy'd go to the pen for life. Well, I never was so happy in my life, as when I got him—me on that damn bronc—I never was so happy in my life as when I got my dad headed for home.

So, we let it go; that was the end of it. Rented the place to old John Morris, and sold everything we had to the new-comers, and was no time till we left there in two covered wagons.

It was true that the Richardsons left the country very shortly after the elopement, and it appears to have been years before Rene saw her people again. The Richardsons traveled around the country for a year or two and settled near Custer, Dakota. They sold their land about 1887; Tom came down to take payment, and at that time Sam and Mary moved to Custer.

This article appeared in the July 3, 1884, issue of the *Fremont Daily Herald:*

Doc Middleton and bride returned to O'Neill last week. A grand ball was given in the evening in honor of the arrival of the distinguished couple. Let him steal a few more horses and they will want to send him to Congress.

Doc and his bride lived in Stuart for a few months, and he ran a shooting gallery there. He also did some work breaking horses, as related in Mr. Richardson's narration:

This Bill Smith and Walter Mixer was buyin' horses to leave

the country, and a hundred head of cattle, and he got in with
them down there at Stuart, and helped break some horses
to ride, you know, and work, so they could get ready to
leave the country, and Smith was around buyin' these year-
lin's, you know, so he got quite a job there. And I was in
town, and, by golly, he come out there, led a roan mare out
there; and the neighbor women—Jim Skirving had a store
and she was his wife—neighbor women was watchin' 'em
out there. Mixer and Middleton was breakin' these horses to
ride, you know, and he was makin' money there.

And I stayed all night down there at Raver's—took some
posts down, so I was around there—so he come out with
that roan mare with the saddle on, and, by god, he had his
six-shooter on, and he stepped on that mare, and Jesus
Christ, she'd never been rode before, you know. "Well, he
got her some way, and watched her, and he went on there
slicker than a whistle, you know, caught his stirrup, and gee
god, she went to buckin', and when she was buckin' her best,
he jerked his six-shooter out and shot twice; by god, now,
he could ride, and that mare had her head down between
her forelegs, just a buckin' for gods sake, and Mrs. Skirving
hollered to the other woman, says to the other woman,
"How'd you like to take a ride like that?" And, by god, he
just bucked that mare around there and circled her around
till he about wore her out, but he was helpin' to break horses
to work and all, and helped there quite a while, till Smith
got ready to leave the country.

During Middleton's comparatively brief time back in the country, those few months of 1884, a few more legends grew; these
were the kind of folk tales which were heard so plentifully in the
Niobrara-Elkhorn region, even down to the present day. One man
observed:

He was stayin at Carberry's; some local citizens stopped by
that way, simply to have a look at him; they talked, and
Middleton was agreeable and joking as usual. He looked over

their horses and observed, "You fellows are driving a better grade of horses than you used to back in the days when
I was in the horse business." And their reply was, "If we
had had anything better, you probably would have stolen it."

Another man told a story of being picked up when a youth of
about sixteen years, and taken a few miles in a two-wheeled cart
drawn by one horse, driven by Doc Middleton; he was bearded,
wore a sombrero, and had a rifle strapped across the back of the
seat. Nothing was said as to where he had been or where he was
going, just this chance encounter, but it was an incident in the
youth's life to remember.

Middleton was the overnight guest at this or that settler's home,
and he was the same dashing figure as formerly: the children
would gaze upon him in awe—better dressed than most, of distinguished appearance, and wearing two pearl handled six-shooters.

A story is told of his recovering some horses which had been
stolen by thieves of the Kid Wade type; he worked behind the
scene, and the horses showed up back in their stable.

Someone insulted Middleton during this time in Stuart, and
there was a terrific fight, this time with fists. Almost nothing is
known of this matter except that it happened. By the fall of 1884
the Middletons had left Stuart.

The following items from the *Fremont Herald* show that the
Middletons were moving around a lot during the rest of the year;
they also show that Doc was still a newsworthy personality:

October 30, 1884: Doc Middleton has started a shooting
gallery at Blair, Nebraska.

November 20, 1884: Doc Middleton is about to start a
saloon at Valentine. We are afraid he hasn't thoroughly
reformed.

December 11, 1884: The famous Doc Middleton left Valentine on the first, to start a saloon at Gordon. As the settlers
have said, they will not tolerate a saloon. Trouble is looked
for.

The followers of Rev. Scamahorn, founder of Gordon, did not favor the establishment of a saloon in Gordon, but Middleton did establish a saloon there, and received only one of several liquor licenses issued. The railroad was coming, and Gordon became a boom town. This would be the home of the Middletons for the next several years, with the exception of what appear to have been temporary ventures, in one instance down to Whitman and in another into show business.

14

Gordon, Nebraska

Gordon was a tent colony through 1884 and into the next year, and this was the way the Middletons first saw it. Doc ran his saloon in the tent town before the building of the town began.

However primitive this town in 1884, it had a newspaper, *The Gordon Press*. In January 1885 Middleton had an open letter published in which he admitted having stolen some Indian ponies but insisted that he had never stolen from the cattlemen and settlers.[1]

The building of the town really began in the spring of 1885, and twenty or twenty-five business buildings were built that year. The railroad came by in mid-year. The village of Gordon was organized in the fall of 1885. R. E. Boyle, an old-timer with whom I talked and who had been a resident of Gordon for seventy years at the time of the interview, remembered Middleton's saloon on the east side of Main Street, between 1st and 2nd Streets.

On April 16, 1885, a daughter, Lulu B., was born to Doc and his child wife.

Sheridan County was being formed; during 1885 some sort of temporary county government seems to have been established, and John Riggs, a Texan, who had been foreman for Hunter and Evans, became the first sheriff. Riggs lived in Rushville, the county seat;

deputies were needed at Gordon and Hay Springs, and Middleton was made deputy sheriff at Gordon. There appears among the first records of Sheridan County a bond for Doc Middleton as deputy sheriff. Newspapers of the time carried an occasional item about Middleton being in this town or that on official business. He served through 1886, and after the election in the fall appears to have disappeared from the law-keeping scene, as there is no further mention of him in the records as deputy sheriff.

During this time Doc Middleton appeared on occasion with Buffalo Bill's Wild West Show. From *Buffalo Bill: King of the Old West,* by Elizabeth Jane Leonard and Julia Cody Goodman, comes the following:

> In mid-April [1885] the Wild West assembled again at St. Louis. The show was larger than ever before: 240 people were in the company, including three more women—two cowgirls and another shooting star—a bunch of new cowboys, [and] the notorious bandit Doc Middleton.[2]

From *The Lives and Legends of Buffalo Bill,* by Don Russell, comes this account:

> The 1886 program was not all shooting. American Horse, the younger of that name, headed the Indians. Doc Middleton, the Nebraska bandit whom Sheriff Con Groner had pursued, was there along with his pursuer.[3]

These dates cannot be completely reconciled with other information about Middleton's activities at this time, but his daughter did tell me about her father's being with the Show, though she could not furnish precise dates. The Leonard-Goodman reference places Doc in St. Louis not more than a week after the birth of Lulu B.; though this is certainly possible, one does wonder if he would have left Rene at the time of or a few days after the birth of their first child. In any case, we can presume that Middleton did indeed go with Cody's Wild West show, even if we cannot pinpoint the dates.

It will be recalled that Charley Fugate was sent to the penitentiary from Lincoln County, Nebraska on charges of theft and of
shooting at Sheriff Con Groner; he received two terms of ten years
each, but on June 22, 1885 Fugate received a pardon from the
governor. There was a time during 1886 when the town of Buffalo
Gap (South Dakota) was the terminus of the F.E.&M.V. Railroad. The town soon became a typical Western boom town of
tough characters: desperadoes, gamblers, dance hall rounders—in
fact, more bad men than decent men. There were continual rounds
of holdups, robberies, shootings until finally the businessmen held
a secret meeting to decide how to handle the situation. They concluded to employ a city marshal, and for this purpose chose a
nervy young cowboy by the name of Archie Riordan. The tough
element accepted the challenge and decided to put the marshal
out of business. They chose Charley Fugate, and the plan was to
shoot up the dance hall and in the general disturbance kill the
marshal. Riordan, however, was informed of the plot, and when
the fighting commenced, walked in, and as Fugate made a draw
for his gun, Riordan fired first, killing Fugate. Riordan killed
another man or two in the course of his duties as town marshal,
and it was said that Fugate was buried on the same hill as the
other desperadoes.

After this killing, the word gradually got out that Charley Fugate
was Doc Middleton's half-brother, William Riley, but this is not
widely known even to the present day.

From certain members of the Riley family came the information, or legend, that William went to Africa on a big game hunt
with his employer; this story had been handed down through one
branch of the family.

On February 2, 1887 a son, David Wesley, was born to the
Middletons; on May 23, 1889 Joseph William Middleton was born.

From several sources I heard that Doc Middleton filed on a
homestead and that he went out on the homestead and proved up.
However, the records of the Land Office show that while he did
file on the SW ¼, Sec. 8, Twp. 32, R. 41, November 1, 1887, this
filing was cancelled by relinquishment February 18, 1888, about
three-and-a-half months after the filing. Thus, he sold his relin-

quishment, somewhat in the same way as J. B. Riley had done in Texas.

As 1890 drew to a close, we find Doc Middleton pushing his luck with the law for all he was worth. Capt. James H. Cook told an amusing story:

> During the winter of 1890-91, just prior to the time when United States soldiers wiped out nearly all of Big Foot's band of Sioux, in what has been called the "Battle of Wounded Knee" and many soldiers were encamped in and about the Pine Ridge Indian agency and reservation in South Dakota, I walked out of the headquarters Scouts tent early one morning with a couple of the Indian scouts, and, to my surprise met Doc Middleton, who had just tied his team to the post of a barbed wire fence nearby. His team was hitched to a light spring wagon, which contained some rather large wooden boxes. After greeting Doc in my usual manner I asked him what he was up to now.
>
> His reply was that he had driven over from the town of Gordon, Nebr., in order to "transact a little business with the soldiers at the Agency." He said,—"Come with me and take a look at my chickens." I walked over to his wagon with him and he pulled out of one of the boxes a very nicely dressed, fat fowl. Holding it close to me, he exposed a view of a half pint bottle of liquor, which was enclosed in the chicken. I asked him if he knew what a great risk he was running in bringing whiskey on an Indian reservation, especially at a time when war at any moment was imminent. He replied that he was ready to take his chances. He evidently did not get into trouble in disposing of his load of chickens, as I met him a few hours later, and he told me he had sold out and was going after another load. Evidently I knew little or nothing about the demand for *dressed fowls* at Pine Ridge, and was very glad when I discovered that I did the right thing when I did not report to officials the arrival of that whiskey. Some of those highest up evidently were fond of chickens stuffed with an appetizer.[4]

The "war" did come soon, and at the end of December 1890 most of Big Foot's band were slaughtered by the military. Taking advantage of the resulting chaotic situation, Middleton ran off thirty-five or forty head of Indian ponies and headed southeast with them. It has been said that in some way a couple of horses belonging to whites got in with this bunch. However this may be, John Riggs, by then ex-sheriff, Henry Chamberlain, and a few others formed a posse and set out in pursuit. They overtook Middleton on the Snake River and dispossessed him of the horses.[5]

On June 1, 1890 Lulu B. Middleton had died at the age of five years. She was buried in the Gordon cemetery, and there is a little stone marker at her grave still today.

Here we resume Tom Richardson's narration:

> They had a little girl; I heard that. I had no trouble hearin' from 'em; but I got with this surveyin' party, and way up from home, up there in that god-forsaken country—and I wrote to Rene, and god, she answered it right back, and the little girl had died, and ohhh, Rene was a grievin' awful, and she had the envelope blacked all around the border. So then don't you see, Rene and I, we got to writin', you know; and Mary then lived in Custer, so when I got home, I was with the surveyin' party a year and a half, and I got home third day of August, 1891, and when I was in town, I would go down and see Mary, and she had two or three kids, and a cute little boy, and I was makin' a little money, you see, and when I went to Custer, if I was goin' to stay all night, I would go and see Mary, and I'd give the kids some money —you know, every time I went there I'd give 'em a dollar apiece, you know, and I'd give Mary some money; so I went down one evening, and I went in, and there sat a woman—my god, you know, Rene bred after my mother, had black hair, and she could sit on it, it was so long—oh, the greatest head of hair a woman ever had, and Rene the same way—and there set a woman with the greatest bunch of black hair, all hangin' down here you know—she was sittin' there talkin' to Mary, and, by god, I looked, and Mary

was bawlin' so she couldn't speak, and she kept motionin', you know—course Rene saw me, you know, and I didn't know for a little while—I didn't no more know who that woman was than nothin'—so I got to see her right there that night.

This, then, was the first time that Tom Richardson had seen Rene for about seven years, and it may have been the first time that Rene and Mary had seen each other for about the same length of time.

The next episode in Doc Middleton's life has been so little known that I did not immediately learn the details. One historian reported that Middleton was killed in a shooting scrape in 1891, giving no information as to where the shooting occurred. Obviously, this was not true, but there was some basis for the story. None of the people who remained when I was doing my research, who knew Middleton best, had any knowledge of it. One obscure mention of about two lines was finally found and a lead gained. The place was Covington, Nebraska, across the Missouri River from Sioux City, Iowa. The time was the early morning hours of March 25, 1891.

Gambling and other forms of vice had flourished in Sioux City till shortly before this 1891 date, when a clean-up had taken place. Then the proprietors of many of the gambling houses and disorderly places moved across the river to Covington and set up in business there, and this river town soon became a hellhole.

If the reader should wonder what Middleton would be doing so far from home in such a place, remember that he was a gambler by profession as much as he was a saloon keeper at this time. He ran games in his own saloons, and when not in business for himself, ran gambling concessions in other saloons for a percentage.

Furthermore, he would on occasion be gone from home for rather extended periods of time on "business," which may very well have been gambling. The 19th century was not the late 20th century, and on returning home men did not always report to their families where they had been and what they had been doing.

L-R: Doc Middleton and friend in front of The Maverick Bank in Gordon.

Gravestone of
Lulu B. Middleton (1885-1890),
first child of
Doc and Rene Middleton.
Gordon cemetery.

Doc Middleton,
early 1890s.
*Courtesy Nebraska State
Historical Society.*

Doc Middleton at the Swigert, Herbert & Hummel Livery barn on Main Street, Gordon, 1892. Doc is right of center, in white shirt. *Courtesy Nebraska State Historical Society.*

A record of birth dates of Doc Middleton and family written on Doc's stationery.

He may have been considering going into business at Covington and while there had a try at the gaming tables. It would be strange if he did not.

Finally, as to the expense of traveling, it was known that Middleton had a knack for getting free rides on the trains. He was always something of a celebrity, and the conductors would let him ride for nothing.

Two men named Courtright and Owens had run an elaborate gambling establishment in the Palace Exchange on Fourth Street in Sioux City. This had been seized by the police, and when it was released to them, they moved to Covington and opened in part of a building called The White House, the other part being a saloon. A man named Wilson was running the crap game.

John Peyson, ex-mayor of Covington and operator of a saloon elsewhere in the town, was in the gambling house of Courtright and Owens gambling on the night of March 24. Peyson's wife had gone to Le Mars to attend the funeral of a relative, and he had decided to have a time of it.

Peyson was drinking and losing heavily—about $200 lost at craps. Middleton was a participant in the game. According to the *North Nebraska Eagle,* Peyson accused Doc Middleton of "doing" him; he and Middleton had words which were followed by blows; Wilson separated them, and Peyson left the house, but in a short time returned, accompanied by his bartender, Sam Brown, who was armed. Peyson went at Wilson, and Middleton took a hand, with the intention of helping Wilson. At this instant, Brown pulled his revolver and fired. The *Sioux City Journal* gave this account:

> Tuesday night the games were all running and the house was losing heavily, but not all the players were winning. Among the losers was John Peyson, the former mayor of Covington and at present proprietor of a saloon in that place. Peyson had been bucking the crap game and had lost about $200. A hackman, called "Frenchy," was at the table and it was his turn to throw the dice. He threw them and Peyson bet $5 that he was right—that is to say that "Frenchy" would throw nine again before he threw a seven. Unfortunately for

Peyson he threw seven first and the money was lost. This
riled him and he declared that the game was not square.
Wilson was in charge and he tried to pacify Peyson, but
Peyson seemed to want trouble. Leaving the house, he went
to his own saloon, procured a revolver and ordered Sam
Brown, or Brownie, to close up and come over to The White
House and see that he got a fair shake.

It was three o'clock when the two entered the gambling
room. Peyson advanced upon Wilson and accused him of
cheating him out of his money. The players saw that there
was going to be trouble and there was a general exodus
toward the bar room in the other half of the building. Wilson,
still trying to pacify Peyson, passed through the narrow hall,
followed by his accuser, and just as the latter emerged from
the passage, someone hit Peyson. Peyson then drew his
revolver and made for Wilson, who hastened to get out of
his way. Then there was a wild time, the particulars of
which are told differently by each of the eye witnesses. In
the melee, a shot was fired by Brown, it is believed. The
ball passed through Ed Owen's coat sleeve and struck Doc
Middleton in the right side, just below the shoulder blade.
A moment later, Peyson was knocked senseless by a blow
on the head, but who it was struck him is not known, but
Ed Owens is accused of doing it.

Peyson was conveyed to his home in Covington where Dr.
Allen of South Sioux City was called to attend him. He
found a slight fracture of the skull, which, while serious
enough, he did not deem fatal. When seen by a reporter this
afternoon, Peyson seemed very downcast and was making
preparations for the worst. A will was drawn up and the
priest summoned, but in the evening he was reported as
considerably improved.

Middleton was taken to his room in the Wise block in
Sioux City, where Dr. Conniff dressed his wound. The bullet
was found to have entered from behind, passed through the
ribs and lodged somewhere in the cavity but just where
could not be ascertained. When seen by a reporter yester-

day afternoon, Doc was feeling cheerful and declared that he had never felt better in his life and the only danger he anticipated was that blood poisoning might set in if the bullet could not be extracted. His account of the row was substantially as here given. He said he did not know he was shot until he felt a sharp, burning sensation in his back, and putting his hand to the spot, found that he was bleeding profusely.

County Attorney J. J. McAllister of Dakota County seemed determined to prosecute Owens and Middleton, and to protect Peyson and Brown, although there were plenty of witnesses to testify that Peyson and Brown were the aggressors. To continue from the March 26th *Journal:*

In the afternoon, Sheriff Ryan came over from Covington and had Ed Owens placed under arrest. He was taken before Justice Foley and gave bonds of $2500 pending extradition proceedings. Up to last night Brown had not been arrested, Middleton persisting in the assertion that the shooting was accidental. At one time he told a Journal reporter that the pistol fell to the floor and went off, but the nature of the wound makes the statement impossible. When Ed Owens was questioned about the affair, he told a story materially the same as that already given, adding that when the row began, he skipped up into the room above and shutting the door placed a plank against it. He remained until he heard someone cry out in the room below, and thinking somebody was assaulting his crippled partner, Courtright, he rushed downstairs to defend him. When the row was over, he and Sheeny Phillips walked down to the river bank to the iron bridge where they crossed the river and came to Sioux City.

The following day this appeared in the *Sioux City Journal:*

No move was made yesterday in regard to the fracas in Covington Wednesday morning. Both of the wounded men

are getting along nicely. John Peyson's injury seems to have
been greatly overestimated. A Sioux City surgeon said to a
Journal man yesterday that the ex-mayor's skull was intact
and the wound on the scalp was but trifling. He also suggested that the patient's injury had been exaggerated in order
to force a settlement from Owens at a high figure. If such is
the case, John might have spared his friends the anguish, for
Owens not only refused to scare, but asserts that he can
positively prove that he did not strike the blow at all. He also
hints that Peyson cherishes a lingering recollection of the
power days when he reigned as mayor. One thing seems pretty
certain, John will not die just yet.

Doc Middleton is getting along comfortably. He talked
very cheerfully on every point except the question of who it
was that fired the shot which hit him in the side. He thinks
he will be around again in a day or two.

One notable result of the row is the suppression of open
gambling in Covington. Last night a few games were being
conducted on the quiet, but apparently more for the amuse-
ment of the old timers than for the edification of the tender-
feet. "Beefsteak Bob," after a brief exile for his supposed
connection with the firing of the houses of prostitution, is
again to be seen about his old time haunts, but seems to stand
in some danger of being forever ostracised as a hoodoo.

This is from the April 2, 1891 issue of the *North Nebraska
Eagle:*

Owens, the man who performed the polka act on John
Peyson's head last week, skipped to Sioux City immediately
after and refused Sheriff Ryan's request to come over to this
side of the creek, even though Ryan agreed to pay all expenses. County Attorney McAllister here took a hand and
prepared what he supposed were the necessary papers for a
requisition, and sent them to Lincoln with Sheriff Ryan.
Ryan returned Saturday morning, mad as a March hare, and
without the requisition, the same having been refused upon

the advice of the Attorney General for defects in the papers. Mac stamped the earth and said that the attorney general did not know enough to last him over night, but it was no go; Mac fixed the paper and sent it off by mail this time, and the end is not yet. "How long, oh Lord, how long?"

An open letter from the editor of the *Eagle* to the county attorney hinted at incompetence in office and political fixing in this and other cases:

Take the disgraceful affair at Covington last week, an account of which was published; it is generally understood that the parties in the affair desire it to be hushed up and refuse to make complaints against the aggressors. Why don't you do it? It is a serious charge, assault with intent to kill. You were in Covington the next day, "investigating," perhaps? You know the parties, and you know who were present; you know it can be proven if anything can be proven, that John Peyson started the row and went there armed for that purpose. Is there any partisanship in his immunity from arrest? Gambling is carried on openly in Covington; John Peyson, one of your political friends, knows it now if he didn't a week ago. Why don't you make arrests and use him as a witness? Why was your application for a requisition for Owens returned by Governor Boyd? Why did you seek to arrest Owens for slugging Peyson when Peyson provoked the fight? Covington and Dakota County are proclaimed to all the world as more wicked than Sodom—has your course for three months been satisfactory to your own conscience, if you have any?

And on April 9, 1891:

Doc Middleton and Ed Owens, the Sioux Cityites who figured in the scrap in Covington a few weeks ago, have been put under $500 and $1500 bonds, respectively, to appear before Squire Williams of Covington on the 22nd inst., to answer to a charge of assault with intent at murder. What's the matter with County Attorney McAllister swearing out a complaint against John Peyson and his bartender on the same charge?

Nothing further has been learned concerning the affair; even the succeeding copies of the two newspapers reveal no additional information.[6]

15

Chadron-Chicago
Cowboy Horse Race

Doc Middleton recovered from the wound received in the Covington affair and returned home.

Within the next two years the Middletons moved to Chadron,
Nebraska. The exact date is uncertain, but by 1893 they were
living in Chadron and there they made their home for several years.
While Middleton's life never became entirely commonplace, there
were rather extended periods of comparative calm when he did not
attract sufficient notice to provide a complete record of his doings
in the newspapers; but he was something of a showman, and the
great horse race from Chadron to Chicago in 1893 gave him another chance for the limelight.

In 1893 John G. Maher, a remarkable man, was county clerk and
clerk of the court of Dawes County and correspondent for several
eastern newspapers. He was the perpetrator of numerous hoaxes,
such as The Petrified Man, The Alkali Lake Monster, and others;
sometimes he created considerable excitement, and, of course, each
time he sent news releases to the eastern newspapers. It was never
his intention that anyone should be hurt by these schemes, nor was
he motivated by any hope of financial gain. He simply had a flair
for the practical joke; he liked to astonish the eastern readers, and

175

his hoaxes usually resulted in some publicity for western Nebraska.

Maher sent the first stories out of Chadron regarding the horse race months before any plans for such a race had been considered. The public little suspected that these first releases on the race were only a joke, so hundreds of newspapers over the nation, as well as some in Europe, picked up the stories, and letters began pouring into Chadron for additional information about the race. Maher did not realize that the people of Chadron would get behind the stories and make the race a reality, but the people in this new town were live wires and took steps to make the race one unexcelled in history. Therefore, what began as a casual hoax was suddenly becoming a real, important event.[1]

A meeting was held in March 1893, and a committee was formed to establish the rules, select the route, and solicit funds. The rules were: riders to use not more than two horses (ride one and lead the other, and alternate); horses to be western bred and raised; riders to use western cowboy stock saddle, weighing at least thirty-five pounds; rider and saddle to weigh not less than 150 pounds; entries to close June 1, 1893; race to start June 13, 1893 at 8:00 A.M. from the Blaine Hotel in Chadron; destination, Chicago; riders to register at designated checkpoints along the route; entrance fee, $25; prize, $1,000.

Harvey Weir was made corresponding secretary of the race committee; he made a request of Buffalo Bill Cody that his tent at the Wild West show, then playing next to the recently opened World's Columbian Exposition in Chicago, be made the finishing line. Cody gladly accepted this proposal and offered a purse of $500 in his name as an additional prize.

Dr. G. P. Waller was designated judge at the finish, and several days before the race began he went to Chicago to make the necessary arrangements. Weir was named judge at the registration points for the riders: Chadron, Long Pine, O'Neill, and Wausa in Nebraska; Sioux City, Galva, Ft. Dodge, Iowa Falls, Waterloo, Manchester, and Dubuque in Iowa; Freeport, De Kalb, and Chicago in Illinois.

For a time it looked as if the humane societies would prevent this race being held. George Thorndike Angell of Boston offered

"$100 in money or a gold medal costing that amount, to the man or woman who shall do most to prevent this terrible race which if accomplished will be, in view of all the humane people of the world, both Christian and heathen, a national disgrace."[2]

Concern on the part of the humane societies was occasioned by eastern peoples' misjudging the western horseman and the western saddle horse and by the highly colored literature which was circulated about this affair. For example, it was thought that the element which would comprise the racers would be the daredevil kind, insuring either victory in the race or death to the horse. As the *Chadron Citizen* calmly observed: "The newspaper correspondents made the most of the chance in an extravagant burlesque style well understood by western people, but taken as 'gospel truth' by uninitiated eastern ones."[3] Certainly a few of the names of the men lent themselves to an "extravagant burlesque style." For instance, by mid-May one Chadron newspaper's "list of Racers" stood at twenty-five and some of the monikers clearly connoted daredevils: Cockeyed Bill, Dynamite Jack, Rattlesnake Pete, Snake Creek Tom.[4] Nor did one have to go very far east for extravagant style. The *St. Louis Post-Dispatch* claimed criminal records for a number of the contestants, and Doc Middleton was highlighted as "one of the boldest all-around bad men in the Black Hills district." The whole bunch of riders was, as the newspaper concluded, "one of the most daring and famous bands which ever threw the leather on a broncho for a jaunt together, and nearly everyone on the list has a reputation all through the West in the line of riding, fighting, and general bravery."[5] In other words, sensational language was easily used and just as easily misinterpreted by humanitarians unfamiliar with a genuine western horseman or a western plains horse.

George T. Angell was president of the American Humane Education Society, president of the Massachusetts Society for the Prevention of Cruelty to Animals, and president of the Parent American Band of Mercy. Under this authority he circulated an open letter to sympathetic organizations throughout the United States and to all the newspapers in the country:

. . . *Some three hundred cowboys* were proposing to start from

Chadron, Nebraska, at sunrise on May 15, for a . . . race of *over seven hundred miles* to the Nebraska building at *"The Chicago World's Fair"*—the first arriving to receive a purse of $1500 and the second a purse of $500.

. . . If these *semi barbarians* were to pass through Massachusetts we . . . could take care of all of them without difficulty, but as it was we had written to our friend *John J. Shortall, Esq.,* president of *"The Illinois Humane Society,"* who would unquestionably do all in his power to prevent this proposed outrage.

But letters now coming to us (two by last mail) lead us to say that the race seems to be fully determined upon, that the time of starting is fixed at about June 25th (*perhaps the hottest part of the summer*), and that each rider is allowed *only two horses for over seven hundred miles.*

Under these circumstances we do most earnestly pray all of *the about ten thousand American editors who will receive marked copies of this paper,* and all *our Western Humane Societies,* and all humane citizens, to prevent, by *the power of the press and the enforcement of laws,* this disgrace to American civilization so that if the race is begun, no rider shall ever be permitted to enter Chicago having ridden *two horses night and day, under whip and spur, over seven hundred miles* to win these purses.

And we do most earnestly ask all our *"Band of Mercy"* members and all humane people who may reside in any city or town through which these men, if they succeed in starting, may attempt to pass, to receive them everywhere *with hisses* and *cries of "shame!"*

In behalf of the dumb beasts whom it is proposed to ride in this terrible race, I earnestly pray the assistance of all who are able in any way to assist in saving them from the torture and our country from this disgrace.[6]

On June 14, 1893, Governor John P. Altgeld of Illinois issued a proclamation calling upon "all officers upon whom devolve the execution of the laws as well as all good citizens to see to it that no violation of our law takes place. . . ."[7] The law the governor referred to was Illinois' cruelty-to-animals law.[8] Although Altgeld officially welcomed the racers to the state, it was clear that he did not expect them to be able to meet Illinois' terms:

> We will welcome the so-called "cowboys" into our state and bid them come in all their glory and have a thoroughly enjoyable time while among us, but we cannot permit the laws of Illinois to be trampled under foot as a matter of sport.[9]

While the humane societies prepared their fight, the plans for the race moved steadily on. A handsome revolver was offered as a prize by the Colt Firearms Company; the gun was described as follows: "Ivory handle, blue steel barrel, gold plated cylinder, and upon the handle is carved a steer's head."

Montgomery Ward of Chicago wrote to the Chadron committee indicating their intention to give one of their best saddles to the man giving the most meritorious performance.

Lowenthal Brothers of Chadron presented Middleton with a handsome saddle blanket and a white Stetson hat, the former being valued at $25 and the latter at $12. Both were made to order; on the blanket was worked in gold silk, "Lowenthal Brothers, Chadron Nebraska Rider," and on the sweatband of the hat was printed in silver, "Doc Middleton, Lowenthal Brothers' Rider to the World's Fair."[10]

Middleton was presented a riding bridle by H. D. Mead, a harness maker, with compliments. The bridle was constructed so as to leave no stitches showing on the surface, except a few which held in position on the front a silver plate on which was the following inscription: "From H. D. Mead, to Doc Middleton, World's Fair Cowboy Race, June 13, 1893." Another rider, C. W. Smith, was presented with a riding bridle by Mead, quite similar to the one presented to Middleton.

Of the two dozen aspirants who had announced themselves by mid-May as participants in the race, two were Sioux Indians—He Dog and Spotted Wolf—and one was a woman—Emma Hutchinson. Miss Hutchinson was reported to be coming, but the mysterious lady never arrived in Chadron. Interest had been keen, however. For example, the *Dawes County Journal* read as follows. May 26th: "Emma Hutchinson is on her way, having left Denver a week earlier." June 9th: "The lady rider, Emma Hutchinson, was reported to be within twelve miles of Chadron, having passed through Crawford last Friday. [She] is now keeping in the shade till Tuesday.; she will then transform herself into a clothespin and travel eastward." This was, of course, a sarcastic reference to a woman straddling a horse, a practice frowned upon in those days. June 16: "Before the race the question 'Where is Emma Hutchinson?' was worn threadbare and is still asked. Miss Hutchinson failed to appear." For years afterward also the issue was worn threadbare. Some magazine articles have had "her" being unmasked, revealed to be a man, and then run out of town. We will likely never know the truth about Emma Hutchinson.

The two Sioux dropped out before mid-June, as did a total of twenty of the mid-May list.[11] Of those early entrants, only Doc Middleton and four others actually began the race. In the final analysis, this was the register of the riders, horses, and the horses' owners, as printed in the Chadron newspaper:[12]

Emmett Albright, riding Outlaw and Joe Bush, owned by P. G. Cooper of Crawford, Nebraska.

John Berry, riding Poison and Sandy, owned by Jack Hale of Sturgis, South Dakota.

Joe Campbell of Denver, Colorado, riding Boom-de-aye (only one horse).

Dave Douglas, riding Wide Awake and Monte Cristo, owned by Mike Elmore of Hemingford, Nebraska.

Joe B. Gillespie of Coxville, Nebraska, riding Billy Mack and Billy Schafer.

George Jones, riding Romeo and George, owned by Abe Jones of Whitewood, South Dakota.

Doc Middleton of Chadron, Nebraska, riding Geronimo and Bay Jimmie.

Charles W. Smith of Hot Springs, South Dakota, riding Dynamite and Red Wing.

James Stephens of Ness City, Kansas, riding General Grant and Nick.

Smith's horses were protested, it being the belief that they were Iowa horses, but it was shown that they were western.

However, a more serious protest was made against John Berry, who at the last minute became a rider in the race. He had been on the committee that laid out the route, and when he was on that committee, it was not known that he intended to ride. The route was kept secret until the last; thus, Berry had advance information on the route and had had time to study it thoroughly. Also, it was claimed that he was riding blooded horses, and it was one of the rules of the race that the horses were to be western saddle horses. Berry was therefore not recognized by the Chadron group as being in the race. Nonetheless he rode.

Paul Fontaine, secretary, and W. W. Tatro, agent, with the National Humane Society at Minneapolis, arrived in Chadron the morning the race started and made their investigations. A meeting was held at the Blaine Hotel, and Mr. Fontaine made every effort to dissuade the riders from making the race, but he was unable to convince the nine cowboys or the Chadron committee who had arranged the race. An agreement was made, however, that Fontaine and Tatro would watch the race and inspect the horses at the registering stations and see for themselves that the horses' health and comfort were taken care of in every possible manner.

The following appeared in the *O'Neill Frontier* of June 15, 1893, a dispatch from Chadron:

> Great excitement prevails here and much interest is taken in the Chadron-Chicago Cowboy Race. Heavy betting is being done all around and the Chadron people feel confident of their man, the famous Doc Middleton, winning the race.
>
> These humane cranks that protest against the cruelty of the race do not know much about the broncho of the great West. A gentleman from the East remarked to the writer the other day that everything possible should be done to stop the terrible race. "Just think," he said, "of keeping a horse on a

dead run to Chicago." Such a deluded tenderfoot should never cross the Missouri River. In the old Keystone State, when people want to make a trip of twenty miles, they think about it long before, and when the time of starting comes, get up in the night, take all day for the trip and rest a week before returning. A Western man would think nothing of making the round trip in half a day.

To illustrate what Eastern people think of this great West, I will give here what occurred on the depot platform in Chadron after a train had steamed into the depot. When the train had stopped, a number of doctors with their wives stepped from the fetid atmosphere of a palace car to enjoy the refreshing breeze that was blowing from the southwest.

A general handshaking was participated in with the cowboys who had gathered on the platform to meet the train. Presently one young lady with a screeching voice and with an air becoming a Parisenne mesdame, remarked, "How I would like to see that Doc Middleton; the man that kills men; the famous desperado, outlaw and train robber!"

In a very modest manner, a rather tall, slender man with a long black beard, wearing a cowboy hat and dressed in a neat black suit, stepped up to the lady, saying. "Madam, if you wish to see Doc Middleton, I am that man." The lady's pocket handkerchief was in great demand; her face took on the color of a fine cherry, and in the common vernacular of today, she "stepped off the roost."

It is plain to see how Eastern people underestimate the humanity and morality of Westerners. A horse that is kept in good condition is not abused, and it stands to reason that the man who will win the race, in this case where both horses have to be taken along together, will be the man who keeps his horses in first class traveling condition.

Every Nebraskan should take an interest in the race. Should Doc Middleton win, Colonel Wm. F. Cody and Doc Middleton will be the most popular things at the Fair. Eastern people are giving very little credit to the cowboy and his steed, and it will soon be manifest that they have been judging the cowboy of the plains and the great West by a wrong standard.

W. B. Lower

Doc Middleton, aged forty-three, was older than any of the riders except Joe Gillespie, and was favored to win, though C. W. Smith also had a strong following. At fifty-eight years of age, Gillespie was by far the oldest rider; and also the heaviest, weighing 185 pounds, though he was, as one newspaper later commented, "a light rider."

Now all was ready. Each rider was given a map of the route, the gun was fired by J. O. Hartzell, and the race was started from the Blaine Hotel in Chadron, at 5:34 P.M., June 13, 1893.

The general feeling around Chadron was that 50 miles a day would be a good average and would win the race. Middleton said that he thought a pace of 50-60 miles a day would win it. Of course, the distance between Chadron and Chicago must be determined. Before the race, the humane society articles referred to the mileage as "over 700 miles." After the race, the Chicago newspapers totaled it as slightly over 1,000 miles. John Berry estimated "that the crooks in the roads followed . . . make the distance . . . fully a thousand miles."[13] Some years later a Nebraska source claimed the distance was 1,400 miles,[14] and in 1955 two authors shortened it to 500 miles.[15] Ed Lemmon pegged it at *exactly* 1,000 miles; as a matter of fact, that was why *Chadron* was chosen, he said, because it was precisely 1,000 miles from Chicago.[16] In any case, the figure "1,000" is so nice, round, and dramatic that it is the one that has been most used for eighty years. On this basis some writers have calculated the winner's average speed at about 75 miles a day. However, it is impossible to understand how the mileage could have added up to 1,000—except for the handiness of the figure. A careful computation of the route traveled results in a total mileage of 850 miles. Using this figure, we see that Middleton's estimate was not too far off, for the first rider into Chicago actually averaged 62.2 miles a day, and the second and third arrivals averaged 61.6 miles a day. The *New York Times* reported of the early western Nebraska stretch: "During the heat of the day the riders have made four miles an hour, but at night they are nearly doubling that pace." [17] Toward the end of the race, in Illinois, it was reported that John Berry was "riding about five miles an hour." [18]

> Apropos of the feverish interest in the cowboy race all along the line, comes a story from Valentine: an old gentleman who keeps a stable of refreshment for itinerant bronchos became so excited as the time approached for the racers to appear that he could do little but scan the Western horizon and re-hash Doc Middleton's exploits. A fellow townsman, well known to the old gentleman, dressed himself in a slicker, a slouch hat and a brigandish look, mounted a weary-looking horse, hired a small boy to shout, "Doc Middleton is coming!," and presented himself at the aforementioned hostelry, asking in a cowboy tone of voice for hay, grain and humane treatment for his horse. The poor old man tumbled into the trap at once. "Certainly, sir, certainly, sir; we've got 'em for you, sir; been looking for you, sir; come right in and your horse shall be cared for, sir," bowing and smiling till the fellow ably assisted by the bystanders, fairly roared with laughter. The true Doc Middleton was received with cautious enthusiasm. [19]

The riders arrived at Wood Lake, Nebraska, not a check point, in the following order early in the morning of June 16, 1893; first, Gillespie; second, Middleton; third, Stephens; fourth, Albright. All horses were in fine condition. Jones, Douglas, and Campbell were considerably in the rear and Smith and Berry not heard from.

The same day, during the noon hour, Middleton, Gillespie, Stephens, and Albright arrived at Ainsworth, Nebraska. Douglas and Campbell were near Wood Lake, while Smith and Berry had not shown up at any point since leaving Gordon. Jones was not heard from.

Middleton, Gillespie, and Stephens registered at Long Pine on that Friday afternoon (June 16) at 4:45, three days after the race began. Albright arrived shortly afterward, and the next morning Smith, Jones, Douglas, and Berry registered. No mention of Campbell.

A large crowd of people gathered to greet the boys at O'Neill Saturday afternoon, at which time it was thought they would arrive, and they were not disappointed. At 1:30 Jas Stephens rode in and registered, followed closely by Joe Gillespie and Doc Middleton. They immediately stabled their steeds, saw that they were properly taken care of, and then took dinner at the Hotel Evans. Doc Middleton was greeted by a number of his old acquaintances who seemed anxious that he should win. The rest of the riders straggled in from 6 o'clock until Sunday morning, Joe Campbell being the last to register. He is riding but one horse. Dave Douglas, riding Mike Elmore's horses, was taken sick at Atkinson and abandoned the race. Mr. Elmore went up Saturday evening and rode the team to O'Neill Sunday morning, where he purchased a buggy and set of harness and started a man out to drive them through. His is a fine team and he is determined they shall make the trip by some hook or crook [—though, of course, not hoping to win anything].[20]

Humane representatives Fontaine and Tatro were at O'Neill to inspect the horses. The *O'Neill Frontier* had this to say in its regular "No Man's Column":

Their intentions are no doubt good, we think they are, but they have been over-zealous in this instance and made themselves laughing stock of the west. The diminutiveness of their bump of conception is lamentable: they have but little idea of this great west, and underestimate the people who inhabitate it. This is clearly shown by dubbing the riders "semi-barbarians" and even intimating that they would ride "two horses night and day, under whip and spur, over 700 miles." This . . . will appear most ludicrous to those of our readers who saw the 300—which were nine—cowboys ride into O'Neill last week. The horses were in excellent condition and showed little evidence of having been "ridden both night and day, under whip and spur," while, instead of the riders being "semi-barbarians" they were as quiet, and perhaps as humane as Mr. Angell himself [President of the American Humane Education Society].

The humane interference has evoked little sympathy in the west, and instead of the boys being received "with hisses and cries of shame" they have been greeted by brass bands and escorted through the different towns along their route in a manner that would have flattered a Roman conqueror.

The humane society could have made more friends and alleviated the sufferings of more over-burdened animals by confining their efforts within the boundaries of their respective cities, administering to the poor horses which are daily goaded almost beyond endurance on their streets.

While the cowboys were in the city last Saturday "No Man" was witness to a little incident that might not be out of place to mention in connection with the great hue and cry raised by the humane societies over the race. The notorious "semi-barbarian," Doc Middleton, was having one of his horses shod and the humane gentleman, Mr. Tatro, was superintending the work, when a poor, blind beggar was guided into the shop by a small boy who handed each individual of the party a printed appeal for aid, which read something like this: "Stranger, I know not who you be, nor whether charitably inclined; but in the name of humanity, I appeal to your charity. Buy this ballet of me and remember that he that giveth to the poor lendeth to the Lord."

Doc Middleton, by the humane people called "semi-barbarian," with generosity which is characteristic of all typical westerners, donated to the weary and unfortunate wayfarer, while the humane gentleman from Minneapolis who proudly boasts of belonging to a society that has a reserve fund of $3,000,000 for the prevention of cruelty to animals had not a cent for the mitigation of the sorrow and suffering of a fellow mortal. The scribe witnessed this scene with regret and turned away with the thought that the world must be a hoodoo.[21]

Wausa, Nebraska was the next check point. Gillespie was the

first to register there, at 3:31 P.M. on Sunday, the 18th. Stephens, or Rattlesnake Pete, was second, and Doc Middleton a close third.

One of Middleton's horses, Geronimo, had been growing lame and at Coleridge, Nebraska had to be abandoned; Doc proceeded to Sioux City on Bay Jimmie.

Excitement ran high at the towns along the route. The following from Sioux City, for example, will show the amount of enthusiasm manifested in that section:

> There were many amusing occurrences in connection with the excitement over the expected arrival of the cowboy racers. The question was, "Have the cowboys arrived yet?" There was no reliable information to be had but it was the general belief that the police knew about the movements of the riders and of course everyone went there with the same question. The police told all comers that the cowboys had just arrived and were at that moment at the livery barn just around the corner, and away the crowd would go.

As early as a full twenty-four hours before the actual arrival of the first riders at Sioux City, a crowd was waiting at the old levee on the river front. Excitement ran high when three riders were seen to board the ferry boat *Vint Stillings* on the opposite shore (that is, on the Nebraska side); the boat crossed to the Iowa side, the captain making an incessant din with the whistle. When the landing was made, the riders dashed through the crowd of people on shore, who wide-eyed and gaping gazed on whom they took to be the cowboy riders; however, it was an anticlimax, for the riders were not the long looked-for cowboys, but only a reporter and two citizens of Sioux City returning from a day's fishing at Crystal Lake.

About 9:00 P.M., the day before the first arrivals, the people of Covington got up a demonstration on their own account for the benefit of the crowd on the Iowa side, and they brought every man on the streets of Sioux City to the river front. The Covingtonites discharged firearms, waved lights, and filled the air with resounding cries, "Hurrah for Doc Middleton!" and "Bring the ferry boat!" It was soon learned that the display was a hoax, and the watchers returned to town, disappointed for the second time. Up to midnight there were people on the river front, straining their eyes to get the first glimpse of the racers. It was reported at 2 o'clock in the morning that two of the cowboys had actually arrived at South Sioux City, but it was still premature.

At 8:05 P.M. Tuesday, a week after the start, Middleton, Gillespie, and Stephens arrived at Sioux City. The ladies strewed Middleton with flowers and pulled hairs from the horse's tail for souvenirs until he had to ask them to stop; but Doc, always something of a showman, played up to the attention he was getting. However, it was soon to be the end of the trail for Middleton; one horse had been abandoned and the other was growing lame. The *O'Neill Frontier* carried a one-sentence conclusion: "Middleton's horses played out at Sioux City and he is no longer in the race."[22] Nevertheless, Doc pushed on. The *Omaha Daily Bee* recorded his registering at Fort Dodge on June 23rd, at Waterloo on June 24th, and at Manchester on June 25th. Was the O'Neill newspaper wrong? Did Doc not drop out of the race at Sioux City? Tom Richardson said of Middleton and Geronimo—"strained a tendon and had to leave that one horse." Tom continued: "He went clear through on one horse [Bay Jimmie]; he didn't expect to win, but he was figurin' on gettin' in [again] with Buffalo Bill's Wild West show." At Sioux City Middleton probably gave up the race unofficially, knowing his horse could not carry him through a winner, but kept on riding at a reduced pace because he did want to get to the Fair. We note that Doc was in Manchester on June 25th. Later that day he reached Earlville, ten miles closer to Chicago. Then we read that "Middleton left Earlville at 5 o'clock p.m., and at 10:45 had not appeared at Dyersville, Dubuque county, seven miles beyond. He has probably laid up for the night."[23] Just as likely he by-passed Dyersville, because he soon arrived in Dubuque, thirty miles from Earlville, but he was not making rapid progress. Finally it happened at Dubuque: "Doc Middleton dropped out of the cowboy race to-day, taking the train for Freeport, where he hopes to catch those ahead of him. His horse gave out entirely."[24] The *Chicago Tribune* reported Middleton in Freeport on June 26th, and the *Chicago Daily News* headlined on page one:[25]

COWBOYS ARE NEAR HERE.
They Expect to End the Wild Race to
the Fair To-morrow
Night.

MIDDLETON THROWS UP THE STRUGGLE

But we read that at midnight on June 26th Middleton and Albright passed through Davis Junction, fourteen miles south of Rockford,[26] and that the next day, June 27th, Doc was in Dixon—"He took the cars for Chicago from here."[27] The route from Freeport to Davis Junction to Dixon to Chicago seems circuitous, and our information about Middleton in Illinois is minimal. However, his arrival in Chicago is dramatically documented with the famous photograph at Buffalo Bill's 1,000-Mile Tree.

But back to the race and the other riders. Stephens, or Rattlesnake Pete, dropped one horse at Sioux City and continued on. All the horses on the road were reported in satisfactory condition by the Humane Society officials. The same could not be said for the riders. A June 20th dispatch out of Moville, Iowa, reported:

> The boys were in good spirits, notwithstanding the fact that Stephens was suffering from a slight hemorrhage of the lungs, caused by the constant jolt of riding in a slow trot. Dr. Dewey gave him some medicine and also a prescription to be filled along the line. They were kept pretty busy answering questions while here.[28]

John Berry came to the front at Iowa Falls and maintained first position as the riders crossed into Illinois, but, as the *Chicago Daily News* reported, "Berry's lead is not disturbing the other riders to any extent as they do not consider him in the race.[29] However, except for the other riders and the folks back in Chadron, the rest of the country did consider Berry in the race, especially when he was the first to arrive at Buffalo Bill's tent on June 27th, Tuesday morning, about eight hours short of exactly two weeks from starting in Chadron. Berry said, "I rode the last 150 miles in twenty-four hours."[30]

Emmett Albright arrived next, and he was credited with second place for a brief time; but it was discovered that he had shipped his horse part of the way, and he was denied the honor.[31]

At 1:30 P.M. the same day Gillespie arrived; he and his horse were in excellent condition. About fifteen minutes later Smith arrived. He and Gillespie had been together until the last few miles when Old Joe urged his horse on and left Smith behind. Jones arrived in Chicago the next morning, Wednesday, June 28th. Stephens and Campbell came in the following morning.

Buffalo Bill Cody recognized John Berry as the winner and awarded second place to Gillespie. The Chadron group still considered Berry ineligible and gave first place to Gillespie. The purses were awarded as follows:

Buffalo Bill's purse of $500: John Berry, $175; Joe Gillespie, $50; C. W. Smith, $75; George Jones, $75; James Stephens, $50; Doc Middleton, Emmett Albright, and Joe Campbell, $25 each.

Chadron's purse of $1,000: Joe Gillespie, $200; C. W. Smith, $200; George Jones and James Stephens, $187.50 each; Doc Middleton, Emmett Albright, and Joe Campbell, $75 each.

The Colt revolver went to Gillespie and the Montgomery Ward saddle was awarded to Berry.[32]

The distribution of the prize monies may appear a bit puzzling; for example, third-place Smith got more of Colonel Cody's purse than second-place Gillespie. The complex distribution roots in the fact that as the race drew to a close there were quarrels among the riders about who had ridden "square." Bandied about were charges of horses being shipped by rail, of riders riding in buggies, and of attempted doping of horses. They were unable to settle the wrangle among themselves, though they did agree on one thing:

> "Doc" Middleton is the one they all would like to have seen win, but when his horse failed him it was a scramble with the others.[33]

With the issue of who won unresolved, the riders and owners turned to Paul Fontaine and made him referee. At the end of the race they

Doc Middleton at finish line of the Chadron-Chicago horse race, June 1893. *Louis W. Friesleben photo. Courtesy Nebraska State Historical Society.*

Just before the horse race began, June 13, 1893, in Chadron.
Doc Middleton is center above, with beard.
Foss & Eaton photo, from *Harper's Weekly,* July 1, 1893, photo entitled
"The Cowboys' Nine-Hundred-Mile Race from Chadron, Nebraska, to Chicago."

Doc Middleton, Chicago, June 1893. *Louis W. Friesleben photo.*

had a much improved opinion of the Humane Society officials. Tatro and Fontaine had made some good suggestions about treatment of the horses, and the riders had heeded them, realizing their merit. A much better understanding between the two groups had been achieved. Tatro himself said of the race and its participants:

> It started in foolishness and was foolish business all through, but it has been an educator of the people, showing them that the so-called cowboys are not a set of horned animals, all wild brutal men, and the Humane Society discovered that it was wrong in supposing that the riders would treat their animals badly. It considers the race a big success in every way.

Fontaine ended up dividing the purses among the contestants not just in terms of who crossed the finish line first and second, but also in terms of general sportsmanship, how the rider treated his horse, and so forth.

Doc Middleton, John Berry, and Harvey Weir arrived back in Chadron on Friday, July 7, 1893.

16

Family

The Middletons stayed at Chadron for several years, until about the turn of the century. During part of this time they were neighbors of A. E. Sheldon, the Nebraska historian, and he described Middleton as wearing a Mormon beard and having the air of a traveling Methodist minister. [1]

Doc always kept the hope of cashing in on the Middleton legend, and newspaper accounts of the period, of which there were quite a few, gave his plans for a "Middleton Wild West Show." But the show never materialized. Undaunted, Middleton maintained high ambitions. The press reported:

> Doc Middleton of Chadron, the famous cowboy, is going to take to the lecture field.

> Doc Middleton, the old time terror of Elkhorn valley who is now a resident of Chadron and who was recently converted and joined the church, has begun negotiations to go on a lecturing tour in conjunction with Frank James, the ex-bandit. They propose to first tour the country and then visit England. Doc thinks there are millions in it. We presume he had aban-

doned his wild west show project.[2]

So far as is known, the lecturing venture went the way of the Wild West Show project.

In the meantime the Middleton family was growing. On October 24, 1894, a daughter, Ruth Irene, was born to the Middletons in Chadron.

Tom Richardson tells of a meeting between him and his wife, Mary, and Doc and Rene:

> We went to Mary's folks in Iowa and then came back home by Omaha and the Omaha Exposition [Trans-Mississippi and International Exposition, June 1 to October 31, 1898], and we got to Omaha from Iowa, and I was on Farnum Street, a main street, one morning, and my wife was in the hotel, and I was down there for somethin', I don't know, and I got up —come up Farnum Street, and I looked up, and, by god, here come a man with hair way down over his shoulders, and whiskers, good god, whiskers down around here [indicating his waist], and, by god, it was Middleton! He'd just come out of the Diamond Saloon, and we met; I knew who it was—I heard he had long hair—he was goin' to go with the Wild West Show; well, he didn't pay no 'tention to me till as close as here to the wall.
>
> And he was goin' back home and he'd go up on the same train, and ohhh, my god, my wife, she got a glimpse of him, and she said, "I don't want to meet that man." He stayed back in the smoker; he knew she didn't want to meet him. And so Chadron was where they lived, and we was runnin' along up there, and I told Doc—I was back there visitin' with him all the time—so I told him then I would like to see Rene; so we stopped somewhere and he sent a message to the depot agent at Chadron, and when the train got there, Rene was there; and there was the first time she ever saw my wife; and ohh, my wife, she just loved her right from the start—and the conductor held the train for a little while for us, I'll say ten minutes, 'cause we was visitin' out there. The agent was out

there, and they liked Middleton, you know, and so we visited
pretty lively—the train wasn't goin' to stay long, and the conductor, he walked around there and the agent was around
there, and Middleton got off, with his long hair and whiskers,
and he just stood around there; well pretty soon the conductor told us they'd have to go. That's the first time I saw Rene
since 1884.

We recall that earlier (supra, p. 167) Tom Richardson said he had
seen Rene for the first time since 1884 during an 1891 visit at the
home of his other sister, Mary (Doc's former wife, then Sam Morris'
wife). But let us also recall that Mr. Richardson was ninety-eight
at the time of the interview; we can grant him a lapse or two in
chronology.
    Tom went ahead to tell of further visits with his sister:

And Rene, Rene come after we saw her down there like I tell
you; why her and the boys come up here, and I was down
there—my wife liked her awful well—and them meanest
damn kids you ever saw, and Rene and her two boys—they
was comical devils—they was just doin' somthin'—you
know, Willie was the youngest—and Rene would get after
them; she had a pine stick, and she'd go in the bedroom—
and they'd go to bed, and they'd just raise the devil in there,
and she'd go and talk to 'em, you know—"You lay down
there and go to sleep!" and then she'd get back there visitin',
and she looked in there and there was Wesley layin' down
with his heels up like this, you know, and she took this
great long pine stick, and, by god, she got a work in on him
there, and she hurt him—and they went to sleep—but she
had to whip 'em to sleep pretty near every night.
    Well, then, after that quite a while, one night we heard
some people out there at the fence corner—they had missed
the road, comin' 'round here, and Middleton and Rene and
them two darn boys, and Ruth was born then, the whole
bunch was over, stuck in the corner of the fence—well, they
stayed there with us a couple of days, and then went to

Custer to the rodeo—and, soon as he got in there, Middleton got right around there with George Campbell, you know —he got in, and he win some forty dollars, by god—he was around there and this George Campbell throwed in with him, and he got into a game some way, and, by god, when he come outa there, they come back down to my house— they took my new wagon and left their damned old wagon, took the new wagon uptown—come back down to leave my wagon, and he come back down with forty dollars more than he went up with.

And I seen Doc and George Campbell together, and here come a feller from Deadwood that used to be in Custer, and played in the poker game, and, by god, he was playin' in a stud poker game and he pulled a leather wallet out, you know, and opened it up, and, by god, he had two or three hundred dollars in there—he'd take that out, take some money out, you know—get some more chips—and the next day, I seen Doc and George Campbell, and George says, "Say, we been talkin' about that feller that's got that wallet and," he says, "I tell Doc we can take that money away from that son-of-a-bitch." By god, they was out there talkin' it over, how they was goin' to rob that feller, you know—but they never tried it.

But Middleton was dealin' stud poker—Middleton got to dealin' poker and you know, by god, he'd take the rakeoff —you know, he'd run his fingers down over a stack that high, you know—they throwed down a big hand, why they had to give up so much, according to how big a hand showed down, for the table, for the house, you know, and he got half of it, and, by god, he run his four fingers down over a stack that high, and oh, they was drinkin' and talkin' and hell, they didn't know.

So, they got back down there to leave the wagon, and went back down.

The following newspaper item indicates that Middleton might have lived in Crawford for a time, though I have found no other evidence of it:

> Doc Middleton, the famous cowboy, scout and ranger, was in Crawford recently, looking after a dwelling for his family. He expressed himself as becoming civilized, and moved to Crawford so as to give his children the benefit of school. While in town, he had his long black hair and whiskers shaved and he is a stranger to his most intimate friends.[3]

Sometime near the turn of the century, the Middletons moved to Oelrichs, South Dakota for a few months. The daughter, Ruth, had a faint recollection of their living there, on the second floor of a building on the main street, but this is all that is known of it.

After a brief stay there, they moved to Ardmore, South Dakota. This would be their last move. On June 26, 1900, a son, their last child, was born to Doc and Rene Middleton; they named him Henry Thomas. At about this time Rene's father, Henry Richardson, died at Custer.

To return to the Rileys in Texas. In 1887 Nancy Riley and her children disposed of the remainder of the J. B. Riley homestead on Williamson Creek in Blanco and Gillespie Counties to Gustave Schuman;[4] some had previously been sold to William Schuman. The descendants of the Schumans are still in possession of the property. Also in 1887 John Shepherd, becoming restless for the old days on the trail, left his farm in the care of a hired man and went to New Mexico with a trail herd. On his return he found that the hired man had burned the barn down; a lawsuit proved futile.[5] In 1890 or 1891 John left home for good. He took the stock and left his wife in possession of the land. They had a son, Sid, born in 1875, and a daughter, Jessie, born in 1885. He appears to have taken Sid with him and left Jessie with her mother. I talked with Jessie, and she had a faint memory of visiting her great-grandparents, Joel and Mary Cherry, when she was about five years old. Tom Riley and his mother, Nancy, had taken Jessie with them in a wagon to visit the Cherrys, and her recollection of them was of their sitting side by side on the front

Doc Middleton and family, late summer 1899. L-R: Doc, Joseph William, Ruth Irene, David Wesley, Rene.

Joseph Riley
and his wife Lydia.
Joe was a son of
J. B. and Nancy Riley,
brother or half-brother to
James M. Riley (Doc Middleton).

Thomas Riley,
son of J. B. and Nancy Riley,
brother or half-brother to
James M. Riley (Doc Middleton).

Nancy Cherry Riley, mother of James M. Riley (Doc Middleton), when she was about seventy. Only known photo of her.

Doc Middleton's mother, Nancy Cherry Riley, died here. This is a 1960 photo of the Eldorado, Texas house that Tom Riley built about 1900, where he lived with his mother, Nancy Riley, and his sisters, Emma and Dora. The latter, the last survivor of the trio, died in 1953.

porch, smoking their clay pipes.[6]

By 1891 both of Doc Middleton's grandparents, Joel and Mary Cherry, had died.[7] They had lived to be about ninety years old.

In 1889 Margaret, whose husband, Zachary Light, had been found shot to death in the early '80s, married Ambrocio Belez, a Basque, at the old Vereins Kirche in Fredericksburg, Texas.[8] Her two children were in a convent for a time, but it appears that she and her new husband took them when they went to Spain to live. At least this is what was said of their plans, though nothing further is known, except that many years later Margaret was living in Mexico.[9] I have been unable to locate her descendants.

In 1891 Nancy Riley was living in Noxville, Kimble County, Texas. Tom, Dora, and Emma were living with her. That same year Andrew was killed in Duncan, Arizona when he was thrown from a bucking horse and struck his head on a rock. Also in 1891 Nancy applied for a pension on J. B. Riley's Mexican War record.[10] The following year a pension of $8 a month was granted and made retroactive to 1887, the date of enactment of the Pension Act. This gave Nancy Riley several hundred dollars, probably the most money she ever saw in her life.

Did Doc Middleton ever return to Texas and visit his mother? There is a story among the Riley descendants that "Uncle James" did come to visit, perhaps during the 1890s, and that he shocked his mother by telling her that he had enlarged and framed pictures of his three wives hanging over the head of his bed.[11]

Joe Riley, after leaving Mason County, moved on west, settling for a time west of Fort McKavett. He worked for ranchers, did some freighting, and carried mail from Kerrville to Bulls Head on the Nueces. He and his family eventually moved on and settled near Eldorado in Schleicher County, acquiring a section of land. Here they made their home the rest of their lives.

For a few years, perhaps during the late 1890s, Nancy Riley, Tom, Dora, and Emma moved to Bandera County to be near daughter Nancy and her husband. About the turn of the century, Tom made his appearance at Eldorado, looking for work, and decided to settle there. He built a house and brought his mother and sisters there.

People at Eldorado with whom I talked remembered Nancy Riley. Claude Riley, son of Joe, remembered his grandmother well; he described her as being small and dark and giving the appearance of perhaps having some Indian blood. She was always jolly and always had some little gift for her grandchildren. He said she would have had to be jolly and good-natured to rear fourteen children. By this time Nancy Riley was nearing seventy years of age. She had seen a lot of living, many years of hardship and toil, suffering and sorrow.

Tom, Dora, Emma, and their mother made a home in the house Tom built. Whoever could get work would take it; sometimes this involved living away from home for a while. Sometimes all of them would be working; sometimes some would work and others would stay and keep the home. They and the Joe Riley family were known as the finest of people but poor and having to work hard for a living. Tom's most intimate friends did not know that he had ever had a wife. Miss Dora and Miss Emma, as they were known at Eldorado, never married.[12]

Nancy Riley died in 1907 and was buried in a now-unmarked grave in the Eldorado cemetery.[13]

17

Ardmore, South Dakota

Doc Middleton's first real estate transaction in Ardmore took place in 1903 when he bought Lots 12 and 13, Block 9 at a cost of $200. In 1906 he bought Lot 2, Block 10 for $350 and Lot 14, Block 9 for $50. It is said that Doc built a saloon on one of the lots, one became his family's residence, and the rest rental property.

Archie Riordan, the ex-marshal of Buffalo Gap who had shot Charley Fugate (William Riley), was in the bottling business in Hot Springs by this time. He supplied Middleton with soft drinks for his saloon and commented favorably on Middleton's business integrity.

I talked with Howard Dodd of Ardmore; he told a very brief story of Doc's taking a shot at a man with a 30-30 rifle in his saloon and then shooting out one of his own front windows as the man went out the door and made a sharp right turn.

Herman Moritz told a story of a big man, weighing perhaps a hundred pounds more than Middleton, in a surly mood, coming back of the bar and making for old Doc. Doc warned him to stay out from behind the bar, but the man kept on coming, whereupon Doc grabbed a hammer and struck the giant several blows in the face with it; but he kept coming, grappled with Middleton, and both went to the floor. Mr. Moritz ran up, grabbed the giant by the shirt collar, and tugged; the shirt ripped and came off in tatters, and the man, for some reason, got up and ran out, and the saloon was deserted except for Mr. Moritz and Doc.

Another story was told of an incident which took place in Crawford. Doc would go there, spend the day, and come back on the train in the evening. On one of these occasions, he bought a sack of potatoes from a Dutchman there. On his next trip to Crawford, he accused the Dutchman of putting all the little potatoes in the bottom of the sack and the big ones on top. The accused man said, "You iss a liar." "Don't call me a liar!" Doc replied. The man swung and connected with Middleton's jaw, dropping him in a sitting position on the sidewalk, and breaking a pint bottle of whiskey Doc had in his hip pocket. Doc said, "Goddamn you, I spent the last dollar I had for that bottle! I'm going to get up and whip you!" He did just that.

Another story is told of Middleton's being in a fight with a man perhaps half his age; Doc, by this time old and gray, was getting the worst of it. The crowd interfered, and Doc admonished them, "You keep that man off me or I'll kill him!"

And so it goes. The stories are very brief, but they are what one heard when asking about the old days when Middleton ran a saloon there. Many more such short stories could be related in a similar vein, but these serve to convey what Doc was like in those days.

According to another oldtimer, Doc was good to his family and provided well for them. He might steal coal off a gondola car, he said, but the railroad company was considered fair game.

According to Middleton's own daughter, he never punished his children; he would talk to them, reason with them. Their mother, on the other hand, used to discipline them. Doc, however, was moody and morose on occasion. Sometimes he would come home in a temper, get his gun, and get off a few practice shots.

To a large extent, the family was accepted socially, on the same basis as anyone else. There were those who looked askance at Doc, or at any saloon keeper for that matter. Some feared Middleton to a certain extent; he was no one to trifle with. But by and large, he was quite well liked. The following story, told by Tom Richardson, illustrates, among other things, just how well liked Doc was.

George Swett got to runnin' a saloon up there, and Middleton quit runnin' a saloon, but he sold whiskey. He got whiskey in boxes that big and he sold it; but George Swett and another fella was really runnin' a saloon in Ardmore, and they was playin' poker in there, and that John was into the game. And they got into a fight, and Middleton was gettin' old then you know; and they clinched, and Doc told me all about that fight, and he says, "He throwed me, and then he kicked me and broke two ribs." He throwed him and then he kicked him and broke two ribs.

Well, then they separated them, and Middleton went outa the house with his ribs broke—said he felt them break, just as plain—and this John set down and went to playin' again. Doc went right to his house and got a Winchester—and George Swett told me this, and, by god, he come in there with that Winchester and George said, "I knew I didn't have a second to lose." And this John was lookin' at his cards, and, by god, there he come—and Swett got around there and hit the lower side of the gun so hard he hurt his wrist, and the bullet went up in there in that building—anyway, they took the gun away from him, and he come that near killin' that feller. And if he'd a—that was premeditated—he'd a went back to the pen for life.

And there wasn't nothin' done about this; so it went by. And Wesley and Willie was growin' up, young men, see; and it went along, for I don't know how many years; and Wesley was married, and was tendin' bar for $50 a month down there at Crawford, and lived there.

Anyhow, this John dropped in there at Crawford, and Wesley and Bill got out a lookin' for him; he got down to Crawford on some business, and he carried a pair of steel knucks in his pocket and had a gun on, a little gun—and Wesley got the man who owned the saloon where he was tending bar to let him off for a while, and him and Bill went a lookin' for this fella; and they come around right in front of this saloon here, and they saw him comin'—Bill told me this, and Bill wanted to take him, and Wesley said, "No." They told me Bill was a harder man to whip than Wesley, but I never believed it—and Bill says, "I'll take the son-of-a-bitch," and Wesley says, "No, I'll take him,"—and Joe Garvey told me a lot of stuff you know—well they met, and the first thing, this John hit Wesley right square on the nose, and Jesus Christ, Wesley got to fightin', you know—and this fella never offered to use them knucks or gun or nothin'— and here they come outa the saloon door, don't you see? A lot of 'em knew Wesley, and knew about the fella breaking' Doc's two ribs — a lot of 'em knew this — and I think five years had went by.

Well, by god, Wesley got him down, and they wouldn't pull him off of him, and he beat that John until the . . . . Well, this old man told me that, way after it happened, when I went down to Crawford one time. He saw it, and I had Bill's word for it, but I didn't know for sure, and, by god, this old man told me the same damn story; he says, "We wouldn't have pulled Wesley off of him if he'd a beat him to death." I don't know how he come to quit beatin' him, but he beat him till the . . .

So, then, when the fight was over, they had him arrested for disturbin' the peace, and it cost him $50 and costs, and he went back to Ardmore all beat up, and was fined $50 and the costs; just got a *hell* of a beatin' down there; just got a *hell* of a head on him; and then they had him arrested for disturbin' the peace; well god dammit, the *boys* disturbed the peace, but they was all for Wesley and agin this feller. Well, that's how that deal come out.[1]

Morose and moody though Middleton often was, no one remembered his ever deliberately provoking a quarrel. In his later years at Ardmore, Middleton did on occasion get drunk, though he had not drunk to excess in his earlier years.

The years went by. The younger generation of Middletons was

Doc Middleton,
about 1900.

Doc Middleton
ran a saloon in this building,
Ardmore, South Dakota.
A 1955 photo.

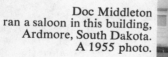

R-L: Doc Middleton; Chippy Lampson, rancher, hunter, traveler; unnamed roundup cook, at Agate, Nebraska. James H. Cook used this
picture in his 1923 book *Fifty Years on the Old Frontier* (p. 230) and
dated it "about 1900." Middleton's daughter, Ruth, when shown the
photo in 1969, said, "I think this date 1900 is wrong"; but since she
could not date it more precisely, perhaps the "about 1900" must stand.

R-L rear: Doc Middleton; A. H. (Bert) Hardy, saddlemaker at Hyannis, Nebraska and famous rifle and pistol shot. L-R front: Rex Burgess; Billy Binder, champion roper, bronc rider, and showman; Doc Williams. Hyannis, August 1902. *Courtesy Harry E. Chrisman, Denver.*

L-R: Doc Middleton, Truman P. Moody, John N. Bruer, 1909, Crawford, Nebraska. Moody and Bruer, friends of Middleton, once backed him in a saloon venture. *Courtesy Nebraska State Historical Society*.

Doc Middleton,
1909, Crawford, Nebraska.

L-R, rear seat: Doc Middleton, clerk, John N. Bruer. L-R, front seat: driver and James Dahlman, who was running for governor of Nebraska in the fall of 1910 when this picture was taken in his 1908 Franklin campaign automobile. Dahlman lost the election, his defeat attributed to active opposition by William Jennings Bryan.

Middleton family reunion, Thanksgiving Day 1910. L-R, front: Vera, Mrs. Wesley Middleton's daughter by a previous marriage; Doc Middleton; Rene, Doc's wife; Henry, Doc's youngest son. L-R, rear: William, Doc's middle son; Ruth, Doc's daughter; Bert, Wes' wife; Wesley, Doc's oldest son.

growing up. Then on November 11, 1911, in a hospital at Hot Springs, Rene died.[2] She was forty-three years old. For details of her death and funeral we return to Tom Richardson's account:

> I was unloadin' a load of corn, and one of the neighbors come over and told me. Dr. Walker phoned out to Custer; course they got my wife on the phone, and he told her that Mrs. Middleton died of heart failure; well, hell, the nurse told her, and Middleton got there in time and she [nurse] told him that they had her [Rene] dead as a doornail on the table there for three hours and a half. You know, they operated on her before for gall stones and left one in; and, by gosh, it growed and made a fuzzy growth and hurt her; and Walker says, "Don't need to have nobody come; it's an operation, but you can be back home in a week." Yeah. Well, he got in there and it's so big it wouldn't come out through the gall bladder, you know—couldn't get it—too big—well, he had her there, the nurse told her, three hours and a half, and finally just took gall bladder and all away from her, and she died the next morning.
>
> Middleton got there on a water train, and then got around up there, and he was right in there with her when she died, he told me. And that night I slept with him in that rooming house, and he dozed—he slept—but he just groaned all night long; by god, I didn't sleep a wink. We had the funeral at Ardmore and buried her down at Crawford.

I have many times wished to be able to reproduce the pathos in Tom Richardson's story as he told it, but when it comes out in hard, cold print a certain quality is lacking.

> I got down to Hot Springs; Rene was dead and in the morgue. Wesley wanted to see me, and he says, "Tom, I'll tell you—," and they [Wesley and his wife] was wearin' diamonds, and, by god, he said he was broke; Rene's casket was there in that morgue and it was $183, and he says, "We're goin' to have to ask you to pay that bill." And I

went down there and took a look at Rene in her casket in this morgue, and I wrote out a check for $183. And they had these four little houses down there in Ardmore, you know—somebody got possession of those places, you know, and Ruth told me, and Bill told me, that all they ever got out of these four outfits was a nice tombstone there at the lot.[3]

We buried Rene down at Crawford, where Wesley lived, but we had the funeral at Ardmore. We took the casket off the train and had the funeral and him [Doc] and me walked side by side up to where her casket was; and Ruth had stayed with a neighbor there, so I went to get her and met her; when we got to the door and she saw her mother's casket, she fainted dead away, and 'twas quite a while before she came to.

Well, after the funeral we loaded the casket for Crawford; and they had the grave dug down there; and the neighbor women had a good supper at Wesley's house, and we buried her that afternoon. And when they—that fellow who tended to the funeral—middle-aged man—was all ready to let Rene down in the grave, and Wesley—ohhh, god, they was all cryin', Willie and Wesley, and Willie's wife—and Wesley asked him if we could get to see her again, and that fella, he was awful good; he had to open the outside—what you call it, you know—and take the top off the coffin, the casket, you know, and turn it up, and we all got a good look at Rene, and ohhh, my god, they just cried—we just all cried, that's all, we just all cried; and then he set her down there and closed the outside box, you know, and let her down. Then we was done.

Then we all went to Wesley's home, don't you see, and there the supper was all ready for us, you know; and I stayed there all night, and took the train the next morning back for home at Custer.

It appears that Tom Richardson and Doc Middleton met only once after that, and this was the occasion:

I come to Edgemont and had to lay over to get on the train

next morning for Custer, you know, the Deadwood Coach, and I was layin' over, and I went in a saloon and there Middleton stood there, and he'd hit a man, and he was drowzy drunk—and he'd a never known me at all, and I looked at him a while—and this man he had hit was drunk, and they had him over there, three or four men around him, and Middleton was leanin' up agin the bar and I went up to him and spoke to him so he would know me—and he began to talk about the tombstone that they'd got for Rene down there, you know, and this tombstone peddler—I forget his name, seems like it was McMillan, or some such a name. And the administrator—they paid McMillan, the tombstone man, for the tombstone. That outfit that put out the tombstones, they wrote me a letter and hadn't got no pay yet, and says, "We're askin' you to pay off D. C. Middleton's note." Course I never answered nothin', but this feller [the administrator], then they got after this feller, and he paid McMillan for the tombstone.

On December 15, 1911, Middleton petitioned for letters of administration of the estate of Irene Middleton and for letters of guardianship of the minor children. It was several years before the final settlement of the estate.[4] In the meantime, Ruth kept house for her father for a while at his home in Ardmore. Oldtimers remember this, but nothing further is known.

18

Douglas, Wyoming

And now came Doc Middleton's last boom town. The town of Douglas, Wyoming, and the little village of Orin nearby, became the scene of a great deal of activity duing the year 1913, with the building of a new railroad line. The following appeared in the February 6, 1913 issue of the *Bill Barlow's Budget:*

> The Colorado and Southern are now within three miles of Orin with the laying of the new 85 pound steel. The C. B. & Q., according to the Denver Post, have also let contracts for the grading between Powder River and Orin Junction.

In another month the job was developing: contractors arrived in Douglas, contracts and subcontracts were let, labor camps were established. Soon there was not a vacant house in Douglas. With this boom, here was the ideal situation for the operation of a saloon. During the summer, Middleton investigated the possibilities and in August received a letter from H. A. Gillespie stating that a building owned by him at Orin was available for rent. It was suggested that Doc come out and get acquainted and familiarize himself with the local situation. On October 4, 1913, Middleton leased the building for a year, and he and his son Wesley began operating a saloon. They bought their beer and liquor from the firm of Wiker & Son, dealers, at Douglas.

This place of Middleton's has been described as a "blind pig"— an illegally operating saloon. In 1919 Wyoming adopted prohibition as a state, before the 18th Amendment became national law later that year, but in 1913 local option prevailed. However, what about unincorporated villages such as Orin? There was misunderstanding about whether a license was necessary in such a situation, and the chances are that Doc, along with many others, was not entirely clear about the law. The following from the *Laramie Republican* gives a fairly straightforward picture of matters:

> Blind Pigs news items from all over the state relating to troubles in blind pigs seem to be frequent. Not long since, there was one that furnished occasion for a squeal near Sheridan. Another was found doing business at Orin Junction. Sixteen men were held up and robbed in one at Gebo, and the Republican was given direct information last summer, that liquor could be bought at Centennial without going to any considerable exertion. These institutions are the fruits of "dry" territory, where the sentiment is not rigidly against the sale of liquor. If the people of a community are decidedly in opposition to the sale of liquor, they will see that the law is enforced. If they are inclined to wink at the violation of the law, then its enforcement is out of the question.
>
> Blind Pigs are more objectionable in some ways than open saloons, although, generally speaking, the sale of liquor is reduced in the aggregate by making the territory "dry," even where the sentiment favors the selling of liquor. There are some who would sneak around into a bootleg joint and take a drink on the sly, who would not openly go into a licensed saloon and take a drink, and those same people, generally, drink more than they would in the open.
>
> Every effort should be made to enforce the law. Let the "blind pigs" be driven from the state. *There are certainly enough unincorporated towns in Wyoming to do all the liquor*

business that is demanded.[1]

Sheriff Peyton of Converse County counted eighteen drunken men on the streets of Douglas one Sunday and could not learn where they got their liquor. Three men were taken before the county attorney on Monday following; they stated that they bought whiskey in saloons but were unable to name the person who handed it out to them, as the whiskey was passed through a canvas curtain separating the saloon from an eating place in the rear. Complaints were commonly heard of liquor being sold in saloons having lunch counters in them.

Various means were taken to circumvent the law. The elder Mr. Wiker was chairman of the board of county commissioners, and he was criticized editorially in the newspapers because the board of commissioners had passed a resolution instructing the sheriff and county attorney to enforce the law where liquor was sold without a license, but at the same time the firm of Wiker & Son was selling liquor to unlicensed places.

The Middletons operated for ten days, selling more beer and whiskey than any two saloons in Douglas. Then there occurred an incident which was not of their doing and was beyond their control but which brought the spotlight of attention to their place.

An old ex-sailor by the name of George Spencer had been hanging around Douglas for some time, gathering beer bottles and junk and exchanging them for liquor, and then had begun frequenting the place at Orin. Also at Orin was a one-armed sheep herder by the name of H. L. Plunkett. On the 16th of October Spencer had gone out to the toilet behind Middleton's saloon, and upon attempting to enter the place, had found the sheep herder, Plunkett, there. Spencer, who was of a quarrelsome disposition, was enraged at Plunkett's presence and kicked him several times. Plunkett drew a knife and jabbed it into Spencer's abdomen, and when Spencer grappled with the one-armed man and attempted to take the knife from him, he received two deep gashes in his right wrist.

Dr. A. H. Cantril and Sheriff Peyton were summoned by telephone; Plunkett was arrested and lodged in jail in Douglas awaiting the result of the wounds inflicted on Spencer by him. Spencer was treated at Orin and then was taken to a hospital in Douglas, his wound being such as to let the entrails protrude, but an examination failed to show that they were cut or punctured; he eventually recovered.

Because of the cutting scrape and the publicity given his place, Doc Middleton was arrested on Friday, the day after the knifing, when in Douglas on business. He was charged with selling liquor illegally. He waived examination and was bound over to the district court in the sum of $500. Wesley Wiker and H. A. Gillespie were his bondsmen.

At Orin, beer and whiskey continued to be available, notwithstanding the fact that Middleton was under bond to answer in district court and his place was closed. Meanwhile the county attorney was preparing his case, and it appeared certain that Middleton would be convicted of illegal selling of liquor.

On December 9th the case was called in the District Court of the Sixth Judicial District, Converse County, State of Wyoming, Judge Charles E. Winter presiding. Middleton was represented by John Stansbury while the prosecution was handled by County Attorney Miller.

Stansbury made a brief talk, asking clemency for his client, stating that others were likewise guilty and offering extenuating circumstances on other grounds. County Attorney Miller called attention to the fact that the owner of the building had been fined for a like offense and that Middleton knew of it and was entitled to no leniency. The county attorney further stated that because of prominent citizens patronizing the place it was next to impossible for the authorities to secure evidence for a conviction. When Middleton was asked how he wished to plead, he answered "Guilty," and his plea was so recorded by the court. Judge Winter then pronounced sentence: a fine of $150 and costs; the costs came to less than $50, making a total of less than $200.

About 1960 I talked at length with Wesley Wiker, one of the bondsmen and the younger member of the firm of Wiker & Son, dealers in liquor, Middleton's supplier. Mr. Wiker told me that Doc was unable to raise the money to pay the fine and costs, for

Wesley Middleton had taken the bankroll with him. Some days went by; Wiker and Gillespie became uneasy, thinking that Doc might simply go back home, and they would be out their $500. They went to Doc and asked to be released from the bond, and Doc willingly released them; he accompanied them to the sheriff and was placed in custody. Doc was lodged in jail in Douglas pending payment of the fine and costs. It would seem that these men, having contributed to Middleton's plight, could have stayed by him a bit better. Of course, they could not foresee the tragic result.

These newspaper articles tell the story as it progressed from bad to worse. *Douglas Enterprise,* December 17, 1913:

> D. C. Middleton was yesterday removed to the pest house from the county jail and is quite ill with erysipelas contracted in that institution. A nurse is in attendance, County Physician Keller attending to the medical needs of the patient. Joseph Kelly, who was removed from the Arlington Hotel, Tuesday morning of last week, had been in jail and either contracted the same disease there or infected the jail, for he died from erysipelas and other causes. Mr. Middleton is a man in the sixties, and having been fined for selling liquor at Orin, and unable to pay the fine, it would seem that his troubles are multiplying. Three other prisoners were yesterday removed to the court room, and will be kept there while the jail is being disinfected by the County Physician. All clothing belonging to the prisoners has been fumigated and it is hoped that no other cases will develop, but the conditions are no credit to the county. The jail, containing but two cells and a corridor, precludes the use of the cells along, the prisoners being permitted to use the cells and corridor, in order to receive some degree of comfort, but the building has outlived its usefullness and is a disgrace to the community.

Harrison Sun, December 26, 1913:

> Doc Middleton, the once noted Doc, is having plenty of

trouble of his own at present. He was arrested and thrown in jail at Douglas, Wyoming for running a saloon contrary to law, and while in jail, contracted erysipelas, which is going very hard with him. His two sons were sent for, and are with him, and his chances for getting well are not very encouraging.

Well, old Doc has seen more fun (such as it was) and excitement in the 60 or 65 years he has lived than most men would, should they live to be a thousand years old.

Mr. Wiker told me that he had been instrumental in sending for one of the sons and had met him at the train and walked with him to the pest house, which was a small building with only two rooms on the hill near the cemetery. They walked up to the pest house in the dusk of evening, found Doc alone and unattended and the place dark; one of them struck a match and lighted a kerosene lamp, and Doc's eyes were swollen so nearly shut that he could not see. Mr. Wiker told a touching story of old Doc's embracing his son and weeping like a child.

Douglas Enterprise, December 31, 1913:

D. C. Middleton died on Saturday [December 27, 1913] after a week's illness with erysipelas and pneumonia, the latter developing a few days before, but because of his advanced age and general condition was unable to rally. Funeral services were held on Monday by Rev. W. W. Whitman, after which the remains were interred in Park cemetery temporarily, at the county's expense, it being the intention of his sons to remove the body to Nebraska in the spring.

Doc Middleton was about 63 years old and had resided at Ardmore, S. Dak., for many years. Surviving him are a daughter, 18 years of age, at Ardmore, a son, 13 years, attending a convent at Alliance, Nebr., Wesley and William residing at Alliance, the latter arriving here Sunday in response to a telegram telling them of the death of their father.

Doc Middleton sleeps in an unmarked grave in Douglas Park

Cemetery. His body was not moved in the spring as contemplated, and when I first visited the grave, no stone had been placed there. Nearly fifty years had passed.

It has been said that Middleton was buried in a potter's field, but this is not true; while it is true that he was buried at county expense, a friend donated space. He was buried on December 29, 1913 in Section 3, Block 2, Lot 3, Space 2. A marker should be placed there.

The following appeared in the *Douglas Enterprise* for January 7, 1914:

> The West has lost one of its more picturesque and most interesting characters in the death of Doc Middleton, which occurred Sunday morning at Douglas, Wyoming, after a siege of erysipelas, to which pneumonia was added as a final and fatal complication.
>
> Mr. Middleton was 64 years of age [actually Doc would have been 63 in February 1914], and came to the West in the early days when the Indians roamed the prairies and the Iron Horse had not yet penetrated the wilderness beyond the Missouri.
>
> He was rated a desperado in those days and many are the stories existent of his fights with Indians, his stealing of horses and fights with the authorities. He is reported to have killed several men but never served time for any of these except for the slaying of a colored trooper from Fort Robinson. Mr. Middleton had a legion of friends, however, on account of his reckless daring and his kind treatment of those who were on good terms with him. In recognition of his experiences in the old pioneer days, now practically past, Mr. Middleton was invited each year to come to Cheyenne and drive the big stage coach in the performance during the annual Frontier Show. He was thus a familiar figure at this great exhibition and his place will be hard to fill in the years to come, as the genuine old-timers are nearly all passed from the stage of life.
>
> Mr. Middleton is survived by his sons, Wes Middleton and William Middleton of this city, Harry Middleton, who is

attending St. Agnes Academy, and Miss Ruth Middleton of Ardmore. His sons went out to see him a week ago while his condition was not considered serious. Pneumonia set in and his life thread soon parted.

Doc Middleton's burial place, foreground.

19

Obituary

This lengthy obituary appeared in the *Omaha World-Herald* (reprinted in the *Alliance Times-Herald* for January 13, 1914). It contains some inaccuracies. Several are of the kind that sometimes creep in where facts and stories are transmitted a number of times; others are deliberate tall tales told by Middleton himself. Some of the assertions can be neither confirmed nor denied by my evidence, but the sentiments expressed as to Middleton's personal qualities are considered correct. I have decided to use the article in its entirety and to footnote only occasionally for correction and clarification.

> David C. Middleton is dead. He died the other day at Douglas, Wyoming.
> There's nothing out of the ordinary in the foregoing paragraph to attract more than passing notice, is there? And yet, wrapped up in this brief statement, lies the pipe-line that reaches far back into early Nebraska history, as well as other Western neighboring states. For the David C. Middleton referred to is no other than Doc Middleton, a man who had, years ago, cut over a score of notches in his pistol handle;

a notch for each human life he took—some in defense and others in attack.[1] And yet, after all, it is said by old plainsmen that, with his many years of roughing it, Doc Middleton never took advantage of any man and never killed a man except in self-defense or to protect his own life or his property.

And so Doc Middleton is no more. He died keeping his resolve that he would never permit his history to be written, although many tempting offers were made by Eastern publishers. Had his real history been written it would have run red with blood and pathos through many a page, and would have been perhaps the most startling book issued, relating to cattle rustling days on the frontier.[2]

Doc Middleton was first known as a cowboy in Arizona,[3] and for several years rode the range with many of the old time rough riders of the Northwest, that now have all passed away. He was an expert with both rifle and revolver, and in his younger days was one of the best rope men in the country. To make a cast and catch a steer running at full speed while he rode a broncho was only sport and he rarely made a miss.

It was during the early '70's that Middleton sprang into prominence in Western Nebraska, where he had "Hoo-Doo's," the mission of the members being to get rid of the vigilantes when they began to worry the members of the "Hoo-Doo" gang.[4] In the gang were many of the pioneer cattle rustlers and bad men in general, but none of them had the bravery that Doc Middleton had. He was absolutely fearless and openly declared that if the vigilantes did not clean up his "gang," that the vigilantes would be wiped out, and it is claimed by Western men that over fifty[5] of the "committee" came up missing, either being killed in quarrels or caught on the plains. How many of these deaths can be laid at the door of Middleton, no one but he ever knew and all that he would say about it was, "I played a fair game throughout and never took a life unless forced to do so."

Middleton was a quiet appearing man with a spare frame. His eyes were piercing black, and were never known to flinch, even when staring death directly in the face at the point of a six-gun. There were times when he had his getaway on his cow-pony, but that was different; he was racing for his life and always kept his followers busy dodging the bullets that he sent back along the trail.

It was in the middle '70's when the late Major John B. Furay and W. H. H. Llewellyn, the latter now a prominent figure in the politics of New Mexico, were special agents of the Treasury Department, that word came that the Middleton gang was running off livestock from the ranges of the Niobrara. The special government officers went after Middleton and after considerable time, located him, and by a ruse, captured him, they having gained his friendship in some manner. Accompanying the government officers was Captain Hazen, a gun fighter of note and endurance.[6] He was with the party when the capture was made and received from the revolver of Middleton three or four bullet holes in his body. Middleton was ironed and brought to Omaha and placed in jail, and Hazen was taken to the old hospital, then operated by Dr. Mercer in Omaha where he was treated and recovered. When the case against Middleton was called, evidence was lacking and he was finally released and returned to the Western part of the state. Before he left Omaha, Middleton said to Major Furay, "Hazen can come back up our way if he wants to, and we will not molest him. His hide is too tough for our bullets."

The vigilantes continued to be the bane of life for Doc Middleton and his followers, who were accused of rustling at every opportunity. The nearest the intrepid leader of the gang, so far as was ever known, came to admitting that he had rustled, was when he said to an old friend at Rushville, "I have come to the conclusion the rustling don't pay very big dividends, and I am going to live straight hereafter if they will let me alone."

In the old days, it used to be a common occurrence for a gang of rustlers to locate a herd on the range and cut out a hundred or more fine steers and drive them away to some secreted place where the red hot branding iron would soon change the existing brand into another brand. Then as soon as the wound healed the cattle would be shipped or driven out of the country with comparative safety. Young stuff that had not yet been branded was easy prey and were driven off at every opportunity and branded by the rustling gangs as their own. Middleton was accused of being the foremost leader in this class of work and tradition has it that he accumulated a fortune by rustling, but if this was so, the proof was lacking when the cases were called.[7]

There is one thing about Doc Middleton that does not apply to all men by any means. He never deserted a friend in need, and never refused, as long as he had a cent, to come to the rescue of any desiring person. Old cowmen often tell of times without number, when he had ridden long distances to the home of some ranchman, to carry provisions to him and his family and that ranchman not a member of what was known as his "gang." While he was brave to the limit, he would take almost any kind of chance; he was as tender-hearted as a woman and couldn't bear to see anyone in distress. Many is the time, it is said, that he had given his last dollar to help an unfortunate, and then straddled his pony and rode away in the night to sleep rolled in his blanket on the bleak prairie, because he had no money left to pay for a bed in town.

In the early days, there was always gambling of all sorts in the little cow towns of the West. Middleton was an invete-rate gambler and it took a pretty shrewd gamester to outwit him. He had often played poker—the old-fashioned draw poker—from early in the evening to sunrise. Sometimes he would leave the table a big winner and again he would lose all he had and all he could borrow from his friends. At Sidney, one night, it is related, Middleton cleaned up $7,000 in poker at one sitting, and when the game was over, tossed his antagonist a bundle of bills which contained about a thousand dollars, with this advice, "You better learn how to play cards before you again tackle Doc Middleton or any of his pals."⁸ The recipient of the gift afterward told the keeper of the gambling joint that he had decided to shoot himself and that Middleton had saved his life. He was a tenderfoot from the East and sought to get rich at the expense of one of the best poker players in the West, with the usual result.

Not long ago, Doc Middleton was interviewed on his past and asked to give his ideas of the value of the vigilance committees which were so largely responsible for ridding the western part of Nebraska of cattle rustlers and horse thieves, over a quarter of a century ago. The old man, for he had grown old and grizzled, replied, "I don't now, and never did believe in vigilance committees. It has been the history of the West that such organizations are a blood-thirsty, hanging gang, ever anxious to kill anybody and everybody they can who crosses their path or interferes with them in any manner, right or wrong. I ought to know, for I had considerable experience with those fellows in the old days. I have seen them commit the most cold-blooded crimes imaginable. For instance, I recall that I saw them, under the guise of law and order, although most of the crowd were rotten to the core and they knew it—take poor little Kid Wade out and hang him because he was suspected of knowing who rustled a few cattle. The fact was that in that very crowd were several men who did the rustling.⁹

"At another time, I saw them hang a man, and because his wife entered complaint against the crowd, naming some of them she recognized, they visited her home at night and killed her and her two little children. I was not present when the woman was killed but I saw the man hanged and an old friend of mine told me he was with the crowd when they killed the woman and children. He was forced to be present but took no hand in the crime.¹⁰

"I will never forget the time one fall that a vigilance committee got after me on a framed-up charge of stealing a cow that I had bought and paid for in good hard cash. I was in a little western town out in Nebraska when I got the tip that the bunch was after me. I saddled my horse, placed a fresh supply of ammunition in my saddle bags and taking my rifle and Colt revolver, started into the Sand Hills. As I left town, I saw a dozen or so men after me, riding fast, and I knew in a moment that the race was on in earnest. To make a long story short, I'll say that for twenty miles they followed me and pumped lead whenever they got close enough, and all for an old cow that I had not stolen and which was not worth $10 anyway. Just the same I had the satisfaction of emptying several saddles along the trail, and I never got a scratch. They were a rotten bunch of shooters.[11]

"I made my escape and surrendered to the sheriff at Sidney. I gave up my arms and was placed in the jail for safety and to wait till my claim that I had bought the cow had been investigated. The members of the committee came to the little jail, poked their rifles through the bars and wanted the sheriff to let them kill me in cold blood, but he stood his ground and they went away. It was then that I swore that if I lived to get my hands on my guns again, I would either get that bunch of cowards or see that they were got, and I did. In a few days, the man I had bought the old cow from, showed up and I was released.

"As soon as I was free again, I got the boys who were my friends, together, and we marked our men. Some of us got every one of the bunch, including a sheriff who stood in with them. Kid Scott shot him and scalped him and for a time carried the scalp with him as a trophy." [12]

Doc Middleton had been in jail more than once. At one time he served eight months for killing the man who cut away his right thumb and part of his hand. The fight was in a saloon and Middleton was attacked without warning; he was cut and slashed in several places and was fast losing ground and soon would have been finished when he managed to draw his revolver and shot his antagonist dead.[13]

At Sidney one time, a crowd of soldiers decided to clean Middleton up; one of the party picked up a quarrel with him and the others sided in; Middleton was getting the worst of it when he drew his revolver and killed the soldier and then opened fire on the other soldiers taking part, seriously or mortally wounding every one of them.[14] He was able to prove that he was not the aggressor and was not punished.

It would take pages of the average newspaper to tell all the exploits of this old Westerner who went to sleep the other day out in Douglas, Wyoming. True, he had his faults, but he also had his virtues. There are but few of these old fellows left and in a very few years they will live only in memory, just as the deeds credited to them will only live.

Of late, he had lived at various places in the West, including Buffalo Gap, Hot Springs, Deadwood, in South Dakota; Hemingford, Rushville and other Nebraska towns, where he operated as a rule a saloon or gambling house.[15] Of late years he had drunk liquor, but during his earlier years when he was making history, he never touched a drop of anything stronger than black coffee.

In 1893, when the Exposition was held in Chicago, Doc Middleton was one of the cowboys that started to ride from Chadron, Nebraska to Chicago on horseback, and was safely ahead of the other contestants when his horse sprained its shoulder and he had to abandon the race, which he undoubtedly would have won. He went on to Chicago on the train, where he spent three weeks with Buffalo Bill's Wild West show. Up to recent years he used to visit Omaha, where he was well-known. His friendship, as the years passed, seemed to grow stronger than ever for old cowmen, as he used to call them. He never missed an opportunity to attend all the cowboy carnivals and cattlemen's conventions of the West, where he attracted much attention, for most everyone who had had to do with the West during the past three decades and over, had heard of Doc Middleton. While his past record stood out against him, that he had reformed, so far as rustling was concerned, weighed in his favor, and he was always met as Western men meet, on an equality.

Said an old cowboy at the stockyards, "Peace to the ashes of the old range-rider; may his long sleep be free from worry as were his sleeps out on the prairie of Western

Nebraska."

Thus the tumultous life of James Riley, alias Doc Middleton, had come to an end. He had been born in obscurity, had been reared in hardship and poverty, and had died in adverse circumstances. His life, while not especially long, had not been uneventful. While he had been in serious trouble several times, he had his excellent qualities. He was generous to a fault, kind and gentle, yet it was never safe to trifle with him. While he had taken several lives, he could not be considered vicious. He had the courage to live his life according to the dictates of his code without always counting the cost. The great majority of his offenses had been against the Indians, and this had had the tacit approval of the whites, a fact of which we, the whites, cannot be proud. To the conservative element, Middleton's life would appear to have had little purpose. He did nothing toward the advancement of civilization on the frontier and probably regretted seeing settled society come. Yet the story of the West would not be complete without him, and a place in history, at least a small niche, belongs to him.

Epilogue

It will be remembered that Doc had been made administrator of his wife's estate. This estate was still pending at the time of his death. After Middleton's death, Warren Milham was made administrator *de bonis non*. Documents were filed in February and March, 1914. At the time of filing of these papers, the address of all four heirs was Alliance, Nebraska.

There was an indebtedness of $683.50, owed to the Ardmore State Bank, on bar fixtures. This debt was acquired in 1909, at 10%. There were unpaid taxes as well as bills. There were expenses incidental to the Irene Middleton estate as far as the matter had progressed. The matter dragged on until 1916.

Milham was adjudged insane and R. F. Drennan was made administrator. By now the value of the property was reappraised downward; either the values in Ardmore had declined or had been estimated too high previously. Finally, in 1918, the estate was closed. Total receipts for real estate appear to have been $370, and total claims against the estate came to exactly $370, leaving a balance of nothing.

Ruth had married Zeno Herz and was living at Ottumwa, Iowa, and had taken Henry with her. Ruth and her husband completed

Henry's upbringing and education. They all eventually moved to Kansas City, Missouri where Henry Middleton became a pharmacist. He was married but had no children. He died in Kansas City at about the age of sixty years, leaving a widow. Ruth and her husband reared several fine children, and at the time of this writing were living on the outskirts of Kansas City.

Bill Middleton married and had a daughter, but little is known of him. During the 1930s, a slightly built, middle-aged man made his appearance in various towns along Highway 20 in Nebraska, riding a saddle horse and leading another; he stated that his name was Bill Middleton and that he was a son of Doc Middleton. Nothing further is known of this matter.

Wesley Middleton married a woman who had a daughter by a previous marriage and had no children of his own. Thus the Middleton name died in one generation. The following from the narration of Tom Richardson tells something of the career of Wes Middleton. He was running a saloon in Hot Springs, in partnership with another man, and making good money.

> He was makin' a hundred dollars a day, and I told Wesley to spend half of it and put the other in the bank for god's sake; I says, "So you'll get a nest egg; something to stand on." I explained to him that he'd have credit and everything. And ohhh, they sold out, he and his partners; he left Hot Springs with $4,000 and headed somewhere up in North Dakota, a gambling outfit, and went up there and lost it, and drifted around to Sheridan, Wyoming, and went to work by the month, day, or week, or somethin' in a saloon.
>
> And he wrote me for $4,000 [somebody wanted to sell a business and Wes wanted to buy it] to buy—you know, they wanted to sell out; they wanted $15,000, $4,000 or $5,000 down; well I never answered the letter at all.
>
> So, while they had money, he had bought her [wife] $1,200 worth of jewelry, a diamond ring, and a watch and chain, and bracelet, or wristwatch—no, it was a watch and chain—and down to Crawford, at Rene's funeral—it was pawned at Sheridan, Wyoming, for $300, that $1,200 worth of jewelry

—and Wesley's wife told—he was tendin' bar for $50 a month down there—she told me, "We can't never redeem it," and says, "If you want to redeem it for $300, you can redeem it and give it to your wife." Well, if I'd redeemed it, I'd of give it back to her, see, and I never paid no attention to it at all. So they lost that $1,200 worth of jewelry. I was makin' money and I was goin' to buy us a diamond ring apiece; and my wife says, "Why, I wouldn't of wore a thing of it." You know, my wife had bad hands; salt rheum or somethin' in her hands, and she says, "I wouldn't wear a diamond ring if you'd buy it." So, I never bought one for myself. I wouldn't buy one for myself, see, I wouldn't wear one myself and my wife not have one.

So, then Wesley, he got up to Casper during prohibition, and, by god, and Bill was worth money. Bill Dudley was a retired lawyer, and he knew Middleton; and he kept track of Wesley's affairs, and when he'd see me, he'd tell me; and he said, "Wesley now is worth a hundred thousand dollars." And he had a ranch and cattle, and he had a man and his wife out there runnin' that ranch, and he had a home in Casper, and he had town property around Casper that would have been worth money.

By god, he wouldn't quit; he went up into that big timber country like I tell you, with a load of liquor, and sold it and got away with it; but they got his number, and then, by god, he goes back again and they got him, and he was in the pen eighteen months. [This matter has been described to me by other informants as involving running liquor across the Canadian border; they say that Wesley served time at McNeil Island, but I have found no record of this.]

So, then you know, he come back down to Cheyenne where Bill was; Bill had a rooming house; it was full every night, and I was there about a week, takin' up a room that they could rent, you know; and there's where I got so well acquainted with Bill's wife. And Wesley took me to dinner down there; Wesley's wife was sick there in bed, and Wesley took me to dinner, and they furnished me a room and fed me an' everything. . . .

[Later] Wesley's wife had died; and this widow woman lost her husband—he was a ranchman, he had had ranches and cattle—and she sold out and bought a rooming house in some town and a big one in Cheyenne, and she thought she was goin' to get Wesley—Wesley was a fine lookin' feller, you know; he always looked like he'd just come outa a band box. And Wesley told Willie he never had any 'tention of marryin' her. And she had them two rooming houses and $40,000 and a Cadillac car, and, by god, she had a chauffeur come there with the car, you know, and they'd drive around—and they'd been out that night and they got in about 12 o'clock and was eatin' a lunch—Wesley had had a little trouble with his head about two weeks before, but the doctor done something, I don't know—well, right there at lunch, he fell over right there, with brain hemorrhage, and I saw where Wesley is buried; they just got a little space there.

As mentioned, Nancy Riley had died in 1907 at the home in Eldorado. Miss Dora, Miss Emma, and Tom continued on. It was an easy matter to find people who had known them for many years.

John acquired a farm near Camargo, Oklahoma. He married and had a daughter.[1] The marriage did not last and they were at odds over custody of the child. One would have the daughter for a while and then the other. John took her to New Mexico and searched for a lost mine he had heard of but without success. About 1917 John and the daughter went to Texas and visited relatives; they visited Joe and family and Tom and the Misses Dora and Emma.

In 1919 Joe Riley died. He had been out hunting on his ranch and failed to come home. He was found dead, apparently of a heart attack.

Soon after this John's daughter went to Wichita Falls, Texas, and was married. John sometimes stayed with her, sometimes with Sid at Elk City, Oklahoma, and sometimes with Jessie near there. In 1928 John petitioned the Pension Commissioner in Oklahoma City for a pension on his Confederate service. He was awarded the pension.

I had a long conversation with a man in Eldorado who had known the Rileys for years. He had nothing but good to say: "They were the finest kind of people, but they had to work awful hard." Tom was reticent; his friend had no inkling that Tom had ever had a wife. He said, "I knew Tom intimately, and never once did he give me the slightest clue to that."

Tom was a familiar figure around Eldorado with his team of golden sorrels and camp wagon. He would go out on the prairies when not otherwise employed and trap, staying for weeks at a time. In 1934 Tom Riley died at about the age of seventy-six and was buried in the Eldorado cemetery in the Riley lot.

Miss Dora and Miss Emma continued on alone. Miss Emma died in 1946 and was buried in the Riley lot in the Eldorado cemetery. There are no headstones for Nancy Riley or her children, but I identified Miss Emma's grave from a temporary marker placed there by the funeral home.

John Shepherd, who almost outlived them all, was a remarkable man; he never got old, he enjoyed life, he lived it to the fullest. In his 80s, and even 90s, he was still going to square dances, swinging the ladies as he had done sixty years earlier at Fort Zarah, as described in his letters. His children and grandchildren feared for him, lest he should fall and break his bones, but it was useless to try to restrain him. When he played cards, it was in dead earnest, and he never tired. He would play into the small hours of the morning, as long as he had an opponent. He has been remembered as one of the kindliest of men.

A Wichita Falls newspaper of about 1940 showed a picture of John, with his Van Dyke beard and sombrero hat, with this caption:

> Tall and straight, despite the burden of almost a hundred years, John Shepherd, Confederate veteran, is shown with his daughter, Mrs. Loreatha Henry, as the two came to Wichita Falls Wednesday to see "Gone With the Wind."

However, the movie "Gone With the Wind," with the romantic

John D. Shepherd (in buggy), Doc Middleton's half-brother, with friends in Oklahoma, about 1900.

John D. Shepherd holding cake for his 100th birthday, with daughter Loreatha Henry and grandson Robert F. Harvey, Jr.

setting of wealthy aristocracy of the deep South, represented little of the memories of Mr. Shepherd. The Texas phase of the war had much more of the frontier aspect.

It was finally necessary that John enter an institution, and he was near his hundredth birthday admitted to the Confederate home at Ardmore, Oklahoma. An article from the *Hammon Advocate,* Hammon, Oklahoma, December 18, 1947, reads in part:

> John Shepherd, who was born on the Texas frontier, celebrated his 101st birthday in the Confederate Hospital in Ardmore.
>
> Loss of eyesight, rather than infirmities of the body caused his hospitalization, he wishes it understood. Members of his family, who spent the day with him on his birthday, found him active, and ready with stories of Indians, buffalo hunts, the Civil War and cattle drives in the late '60s and '70s.

In April of 1949 John Shepherd died at the age of 102 years and five months. On his death certificate the name of John Shepherd is given as his father and Rebecca Cherry as his mother, presumably on information given by himself. (We know that Nancy Cherry was his mother.) He was buried at Wichita Falls, Texas. I visited the grave in the early 1960s; again, after a lapse of over ten years, there was no monument at his grave—only a temporary marker of the type placed by funeral homes. John was one of the last of the Confederate veterans, and his record entitled him to a Confederate marker; through my efforts and those of his Texas relatives, a nice marker has been placed, furnished by the U.S. Army's Memorial Division.

John at one time wrote a pamphlet about the Chisholm Trail in an effort to clear up some misunderstanding about it.[2] His picture hung on the wall of the Old Trail Drivers Association's Memorial Hall in San Antonio, Texas. His life story is one of the most remarkable that I encountered in the preparation of this work.

Miss Dora, the last of the Rileys, died in San Angelo, Texas, in 1953 and is buried in the Riley lot in the Eldorado cemetery. She had been living for some years on an old age pension.

Thus, it can be seen that I lacked only a few years of meeting some of the members of Doc Middleton's family. What stories they might have told!

A

APPENDIX

Researching Doc Middleton

Reader, have you ever aspired to write a book? If you entertain such an ambition, think well before you undertake it unless you have several factors clearly in your favor. It is a monumental task. How did I, a rancher, many years out of school and untrained in this kind of endeavor, happen to embark upon a project which has been, as of this writing, twenty years in maturing? Why did I tackle the researching of a man's life forty years after his death and seventy-five or more years after the period of his greatest notoriety?

In 1953 some articles about Doc Middleton appeared in the local newspaper. I had grown up in "Doc Middleton's Country" along the Niobrara River and had heard many bits and pieces of folk-lore about him. Also, as a child of perhaps ten or twelve years, I had read a short story of Middleton's career and could still recall the account of his several imprisonments and the rather desolate ending of a colorful life. I determined in 1953 to learn more about Doc Middleton. A couple of years earlier I had joined the Nebraska State Historical Society, so I started there. Thinking that they would have the Middleton story more or less in entirety, I wrote to Lincoln and inquired and was surprised to find that the story had not been written. Well, then *I* would write it. I would offer it for publication in the local newspaper where I had seen the recent Middleton articles. It was not my intention to write a book. I would have settled for less if there had been a comfortable place to stop, but as it developed there seemed to be no intermediate ground. After getting in, the trail kept leading further, and so I raised my sights a few times.

I began by searching for that article from my childhood. I remembered that it had appeared on the back page of a weekly newspaper or perhaps in a farm magazine. I never found it. The archivist at the State Historical Society then put me in touch with their Middleton material; it was meager enough, yet it was a start. As I learned much later, when James Riley left Texas a fugitive, his stepfather had told him to tell no one where he was from and to make no friends. James certainly did not take the latter counsel, but he followed the first advice so well that he need have little worry about his friends. He simply took another name—D. C. Middleton —and so effectively left "James Riley" and Texas behind that neither his Nebraska and Wyoming contemporaries nor researchers for generations to come would know for certain the details of Doc's background. Of course I was one of those researchers stumped by Middleton's covering his trail so well. In addition to changing his name, Doc burned Texas letters, threw out red herrings to anybody who asked about his past, and later threatened anyone who attempted to write his story. Even in his own lifetime, Middleton was said to be from Arizona, Illinois, Mississippi, Missouri, Ohio, and Texas.

Initial data from the Historical Society had contained the place, time, and circumstances of Middleton's death, some folktales, and the *Nebraska History* article by Captain James H. Cook. It did not take long to determine that the year 1876 was crucial in this story; Cook had Middleton coming up the trail from Texas that year with a cattle drive. However, books were of little help in my researching specific information about Doc. They made no great contribution to the Middleton story. They unraveled no mysteries about his origin or anything else, and the material in any given book was usually only a line-or-two mention or just another of the myriad of anecdotes on Middleton. Even down to the present day

writers are still recycling the same old tales about Doc. In at least
one case, the very same article was reused verbatim; "Doc Middleton—Horsethief or Lawman?" was published in 1968, and five
years later was run again in the same magazine. But back to my
own research. I scoured the newspapers of Nebraska and Wyoming for the years 1876-1879 and began to make real progress. A
major breakthrough was finding the letter from J. B. Riley of
Martinsburg, Texas to D. C. Middleton (infra, pp. 36-37). From
newspaper items and other data it had become apparent to me that
Doc Middleton had previously been known as James Riley. This
letter was key proof. It also centered the research on Gillespie
County, Texas. A check with the Texas prison system revealed that
James Riley had been incarcerated at Huntsville, and the list of
fugitives of the Texas Rangers noted James Riley of Blanco County,
which adjoins Gillespie County. One diverting item was the persistent newspaper reporting that Middleton was a fugitive from
Texas on a murder charge. James Riley's record at Huntsville indicated that his crime was theft, so I could not be sure I was on the
right trail.

Acting upon a report that many dime novels had been written
about Doc Middleton, I searched the list of the thousands of Beadle
and Adams novels but found nothing containing Middleton's name.
From leads found in newspapers, I tracked down in the National
Archives the reports of Special Agent W. H. H. Llewellyn to the
U.S. Department of Justice. These proved to be another important
breakthrough in my research, for they had never been used before
by anyone doing work on Middleton. Of course, I used Texas census schedules and the records of Blanco, Gillespie, and other counties. The old Spanish Archives in Texas also proved valuable; these
records are handwritten and were read to me by a translator while
I took notes.

By now it was clear that this would be no short article. The
Nebraska end of Doc's story was coming clear, but there remained
the perplexing problem of learning definitively about Middleton's
ancestry and childhood. I had, over a period of two or three years,
worked out everything I could, but the trail went cold with Gillespie and Mason Counties. I was stalemated.

About five years passed. I continued my ranching. I went over my Middleton research data many times, trying to discover something I had overlooked. Finally it dawned on me that J. B. Riley might have served in the Mexican War and if so there might be some genealogical material in a pension record. Another breakthrough, perhaps the most important of the entire project. Here was Nancy Riley's maiden name, the date and place of her marriage to J. B. Riley, the statement that this was her only marriage, the date and place of her husband's death, and the date and place (Eldorado, Texas) of Nancy Riley's death. This led to my first contact with Riley descendants. Among others, I contacted Claude Riley in Odessa, Texas; he was Joe Riley's son, and he was the one who said that "Uncle Jim" had changed his name to Doc Middleton. Another two years were required to work out new leads, locate other Texas relatives, and obtain the letters, pictures, and data which were so important. I interviewed several family descendants and collected from them dozens of old letters saved for three-quarters of a century.

By now about ten years had gone by. It had become obvious to my friends and neighbors that I was working on some kind of literary project, but I had revealed very little because I had hoped to surprise them. At this point I made the announcement and thenceforth answered a host of questions about the progress of the book.

Another contribution of major significance was the interviews with Tom Richardson, Doc Middleton's brother-in-law. Tom had written a manuscript of his own, but it dealt mainly with the Richardson family and only in passing with Doc. However, Tom knew a lot about Doc and about "Doc Middleton's Country." Tom had been fifteen years old when he arrived on the Niobrara; he was ninety-eight when I interviewed him, but sharp of mind and wit. For the better part of three days he talked into my tape recorder, with my asking questions occasionally. I transcribed these valuable reminiscences and indexed the material; the 50,000-word result is part of the author's collection but will go later to the Nebraska State Historical Society.

Middleton himself is supposed to have left a manuscript of his life, but I was never able to find what became of it, except to hear that his son once offered it for sale; there were no takers and it was never published. Such a document would have been a bonanza, though we could not have mined it uncritically because old Doc was not above a little exaggeration here and there.

It was now time to do something with all my data. As in the building of a log house when the real work begins after the logs have been laid up, so in writing a book the real work commences after the research has been completed. Where the finding and collecting of data had been interesting, even exciting at times, now there was nothing but hard work. Reader, you have nothing until you have a manuscript, and there is one way to get one: write it yourself. I wore out one typewriter just researching Doc Middleton. I traded for another and began writing. When you have produced a manuscript of a hundred thousand words, you may have typed a million. Perhaps two years were required to finish my manuscript, and within another year I had a contract with Alan Swallow of Denver. However, the untimely death of Mr. Swallow caused several years' delay, but another contract was made with the new Swallow Press. It was, in many respects, a fruitful delay, for the book is a better one now: documentation, more illustrations, and other refinements were added.

A sigh of relief? Not really. During the years of research, I collected much data as a by-product of the Middleton story. I found myself enlarging my scope and gathering material for two more books, both about the early-day Niobrara River country. So much work remains to be done.

Acclaim I neither sought nor expected. The greatest satisfaction comes from the feeling that something of our colorful past has been preserved. So it is with a feeling of humility that I bring this work to my loyal friends who have borne with me throughout the years, never doubting its eventual publication. That alone is adequate reward.

To a host of friends and acquaintances I made along the way I happily owe many debts and thanks for their help in making this a better book than it otherwise would have been. I name only a few here who especially went out of their way in my behalf: Donald F. Danker, then archivist and historian at the Nebraska State Historical Society; Llerena Friend at the Barker State Texas History Center in Austin; Edythe L. George and Will Robinson at the South Dakota State Historical Society; Lola M. Homsher and Reta Ridings at the Wyoming State Historical Society; Dorman H. Winfrey at the Texas State Archives; Ray C. Wisdom at the General Land Office in Austin, Texas. And of course I acknowledge with deep appreciation the contributions of Doc Middleton's descendants who were so cooperative.

B

APPENDIX

Doc Middleton's Ancestors

Chapter 2 sketches the immediate family surrounding the birth and growing up of James Riley (later Doc Middleton). The paragraphs below expand on the background of the Riley and Cherry families and nod toward relevant political events affecting their lives in Texas. A few sentences here are repetitious of Chapter 2, but by and large the attempt is simply to broaden the context a bit for understanding Doc Middleton's ancestors.

In 1803 came the Louisiana Purchase. Because the western boundary of the Louisiana Territory was vague and uncertain, it was not determined whether or not Texas was included. Because of this uncertainty, there were several armed invasions from the United States by soldiers of fortune during the early part of the nineteeth century. Then in 1819 the boundary question was finally resolved. The United States bought Florida from Spain and relinquished claim to Texas as part of the payment.

Spain, now in a friendlier mood, welcomed settlers from the United States. The land terms were generous beyond imagination. Each settler wishing to raise cattle could receive a square league or *sitio* of land (4,428 acres); each who wished to farm could receive a *labor* of land (177 acres). If the settler wished to both

farm and ranch he could receive both claims, totaling over 4,600
acres. The impressario or colonizer who induced settlers to come
could receive a grant of 23,040 acres for himself for each hundred
families he brought in under these terms. The impressario was permitted to charge his colonists 12½¢ per acre for administrative expenses and defense. The settlers were to learn the Spanish language
and to become Spanish subjects. Schools would be taught in Spanish. Also, the settlers were to embrace the Catholic faith.

Compare this with the land policy of the United States at that
time; it would be about forty years before the U.S. would enact a
homestead law giving a settler 160 acres of land. While there had
been a preemption law since 1801, it at first excluded the average
settler because he was financially unable to make the minimum
purchase. In 1820, however, the minimum sales was reduced to 80
acres and the price reduced from $2.00 to $1.25 per acre; and in
1832 the minimum sale was reduced to 40 acres.

However, much of the U.S. public domain was handled in about
this fashion: the government, after the Indian title had been extinguished, would sell the land in large tracts to companies of
wealthy citizens, who would then become land proprietors and sell
the land to settlers at a handsome profit. Interest was high and
conditions hard. The country got settled and civilization advanced,
but the settler's lot was a hard one and the proprietors got rich. If
some hardy souls decided to precede civilization into the Indians'
country and squat on land, they not only ran the risk of Indian
attacks but of having civilization eventually overtake them, resulting
in the land being sold out from under them, with the proprietor
getting the advantage of any improvements, such as clearing.

In 1821 Mexico gained her independence from Spain and continued the policy of granting land to "North Americans." The colonists were to have a measure of self-government, and an agreement was drawn up in 1824 defining their rights. The settlers came
at an increasing pace for several more years. Many came from
southern states and brought their slaves with them. In 1829 Mexico
abolished slavery. This was only one of the causes of conflict between the colonists and the Mexican officials. The Americans did
not become Mexicans, but preserved their own institutions and

looked toward complete self-government. These were hardy, self-reliant people, the product of several generations of the freedom of the frontier. By 1831 there were 20,000 Americans in Texas.

At this point James Riley arrived with his family. "Jaime Riley," his wife, and their five children arrived in Nacogdoches on October 27, 1834, and on March 19, 1835 he received title to one square league of land in David G. Burnet's colony in Leon County. The land was about 10 miles south, 10° west from Centerville.[1] Also found in the Spanish archives was a character reference stating that Riley was of good moral character, etc.

From descendants of Riley we learn that James Riley first settled on the "other side of the Trinity in Angelina County and stayed there one year, then moved to Leon County."[2]

James Riley was born in 1796, probably in Georgia. In the census reports of 1850, 1860, and 1870 he was twice listed as from Georgia and once from Kentucky. Indications are that he was brought as a child from Georgia up through Tennessee and Kentucky to Indiana and Illinois and that other Rileys took the same route of migration during perhaps a generation of time. Of the five children he brought to Texas, the names of four are known, all born in Illinois: James B., known throughout his life as J. B. Riley, born in 1826; Paulian, birth year not known; Thomas, born about 1830; and Nancy, born in 1832.

Some claim that James Riley was a second cousin of James Whitcomb Riley and that he, James Riley, and the father of the poet enjoyed an old swimmin' hole in South Carolina during their boyhood.[3]

Texas became an independent republic in 1836. For the next several years the land policy of Texas was as follows: Texas recognized valid titles issued by Spain and Mexico, but all vacant lands became the property of the Republic. Heads of families living in Texas on the day of the declaration of independence were entitled to a league and a *labor* of land; single men, one-third of a league. In the case of immigrants, after the declaration and before October 1837, heads of families could receive 1,280 acres; single men, 640 acres. Between October 1, 1837 and January 1, 1842, heads of families could receive 640 acres; single men, 320 acres.

In 1841 Joel Cherry and his family arrived from Tennessee. Since he arrived between the last two mentioned dates, he was entitled to receive 640 acres. He was issued Certificate No. 627 and located a tract of 438 acres on the headwaters of Lilly's Creek in Titus County 24 miles south and 45° east of Mount Pleasant.[4]

Joel Cherry was born in 1799 in Tennessee. His wife, Mary Thrasher, was born in 1802 in South Carolina. They were married August 20, 1823. At the time of their arrival in Texas, the Cherrys had at least seven children: Rebecca, about fifteen, Martha, thirteen, James, eleven, Nancy, nine, a son about six, who seems not to have reached maturity, Joseph, three, and Robert, an infant.[5]

Meanwhile, down in Leon County, three more children had been born to the James Riley family: Isabella, Lewisa Jane, and the youngest, David Crockett, born in 1839.[6]

James Riley served as a Minute Man in Thomas Green's Company of Rangers in 1841.[7]

On December 29, 1845, Texas was admitted to the United States as the twenty-eighth state.

John Coffee Hays, better known as Jack Hays, came to Texas in the late 1830s as a surveyor. He later distinguished himself with the Texas Rangers. In 1846 came the Mexican War. In early 1847 Governor J. Pickney Henderson of Texas received word that 10,000 Indians had come into Texas and were along the Rio Grande and that some of them were within eighty miles of Austin. The numbers seem to have been greatly exaggerated, but one can see why the governor might apply to Washington for assistance. At the same time, Hays had made a trip to Washington seeking permission to raise a company of frontiersmen for a shorter term than the regular army enlistment. His objective, in contrast to that of the governor, was to aid in the war in Mexico. There seemed to be some confusion; however, Hays got his company. His regiment of Texas Mounted Volunteers was enlisted for six months. The command left San Antonio May 14, 1847, planning to cross the Rio Grande at Laredo and join General Taylor.

James B. Riley was in this group, in James Gillespie's company.

General Taylor's courier met the regiment at the Nueces River with the order that the men were to be enlisted for the full term, or be returned and discharged. The men did not care for the longer enlistment, so were marched back to San Antonio and discharged. Eventually, they were paid. To quote from records of the Treasury Department:

James B. Riley is mustered as a private, 21 years old, enlisted as a recruit April 25, 1847 at San Antonio, Texas, period not stated, and mustered out June 4, 1847 at San Antonio, cause not specified. No remarks concerning him alone appear on the roll. He is given credit on said roll for travel pay and allowance for 250 miles travel to the place of enlistment and for the same distance from place of discharge home, equalling 25 days at 20 miles a day. He was paid as follows: Pay April 25 to June 4, '47, 1 month 10 days, @ $8 per month, $10.66; clothing allowance, same period $4.66; use and risk of horse, same period, $16.40; rations and forage @ 25¢ per diem for both or 12½¢ for either, $1.87; travel pay and allowance, $35, making a total of $68.59. Stop am't due sutler, $3.25; balance $59.34 [?]. Add am't due prior to muster into the service at San Antonio (see affidavit) $6.16; final am't paid $65.50.[8]

It was at this time that Riley received Bounty Land Warrant 47996 (supra, p. 11).

To return to the Joel Cherry family. About the time that Rebecca Cherry married John G. Shepherd, the Cherry family presumably moved to the region of present Burnet County. We noted (supra, p. 9) that between 1844 and 1847 three children were born to John and Rebecca; their names were William, Mary Jane, and Dan. Between 1847 and 1850 two more children, Malvina and Julia, were born to the Shepherds.

As noted earlier (supra, p. 9), about 1850 the Shepherd and Cherry families moved to Bastrop County. Aside from the census, the only mention of the Cherry and Shepherd families found in Bastrop County was found in the records of the Commissioners Court. Under Class 2, Precinct 8, in what seems to be the November 1850 term, concerning a road between Bastrop and Lockhart, Desha Bunton, W. V. Waldrip, "Old Chery," Shepherd, and A.

Murchison were appointed commissioners "to mark out the most practicable route commencing at the ferry to the settlement at Walnut Creek, Lockhart Springs." The ferry mentioned was a ferry across the Colorado River at Bastrop. The town of Bastrop had become something of a commercial center; navigation had begun on the Colorado River, with steamboats arriving at Bastrop with fair success, even going as far as Austin if there was a rise. And a main road to San Antonio from farther to the northeast crossed the Colorado on the ferry.

On August 28, 1851, Nancy Cherry's sister, Martha, married George Bell at Lockhart in Caldwell County. We will recall that James Riley (later Doc Middleton) and Lewis Bell, Martha's and George's son, were sent to prison in 1875 for horse theft (supra, p. 16).

The following pages contain two
genealogical charts about Doc Middleton's family.
(Neither chart is complete
but each is adequate for our purposes here.)
The first begins with James Riley,
who was the father of James B. Riley,
who in turn was the father or step-father of
James M. Riley (Doc Middleton).
The second begins with
Doc's maternal grandparents,
Joel and Mary Cherry.

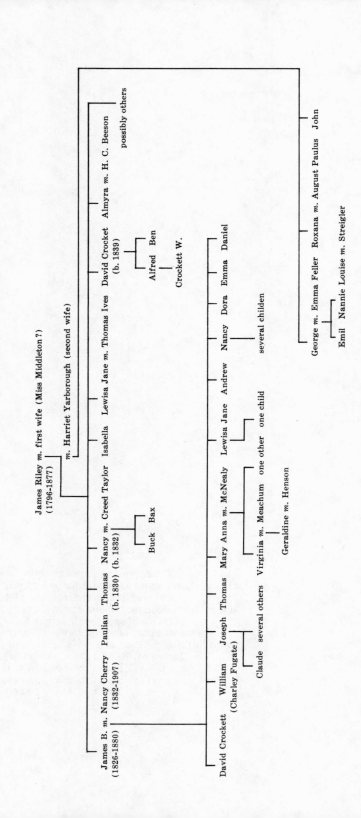

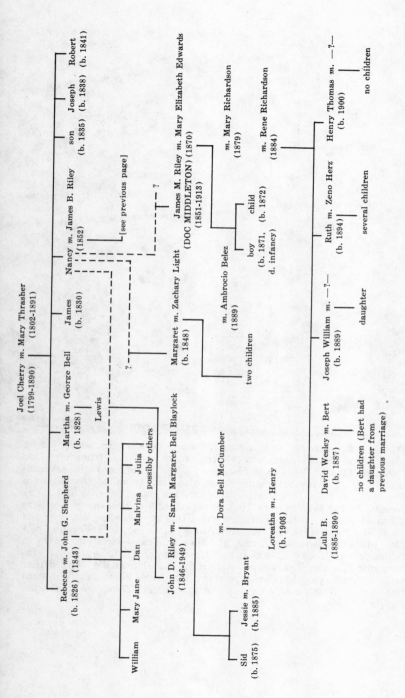

Joel Cherry *m.* Mary Thrasher
(1799-1890)   (1802-1891)

Rebecca *m.* John G. Shepherd
(b. 1826)   (1843)

Martha *m.* George Bell
(b. 1828)

Lewis

Nancy *m.* James B. Riley
(1852)

James
(b. 1830)

son   Joseph   Robert
(b. 1835) (b. 1838) (b. 1841)

[see previous page]

?

?

?

William

Mary Jane

Dan

Malvina

Julia
possibly others

John D. Riley *m.* Sarah Margaret Bell Blaylock
(1846-1949)

m. Dora Bell McCumber

Margaret *m.* Zachary Light
(b. 1848)

two children

m. Ambrocio Belez
(1889)

boy   child
(b. 1871, (b. 1872)
d. infancy

James M. Riley *m.* Mary Elizabeth Edwards
(DOC MIDDLETON) (1870)
(1851-1913)

m. Mary Richardson
(1879)

m. Rene Richardson
(1884)

Henry Thomas *m.* —?—
(b. 1900)

no children

Ruth *m.* Zeno Herz
(b. 1894)

several children

Joseph William *m.* —?—
(b. 1889)

daughter

David Wesley *m.* Bert
(b. 1887)

Lulu B.
(1885-1890)

no children (Bert had
a daughter from
previous marriage)

Sid
(b. 1875)

Jessie *m.* Bryant
(b. 1885)

Loreatha *m.* Henry
(b. 1903)

– – – – denotes out-of-wedlock union

Doc Middleton is not in this photo, though he has been identified by some as the second man from the left; others identified from left: Doc Howard, fourth; Wild Bill Hickok, fifth; California Jack, seventh; Bloody Dick Seymour, ninth. Some also locate the Metropolitan in Denver, Colorado, on Larimer Street between E and F (14th and 15th) Streets. Joseph G. Rosa, the Hickok expert, doubts that the picture was taken in Denver, but confirms the Wild Bill identification and suggests an 1874-75 date (Hickok was shot August 2, 1876). In 1874 and 1875 Doc Middleton was still James M. Riley in Texas—stealing horses in Gillespie and Cooke Counties, and from July 1875 to April 1876 incarcerated in the Texas state penitentiary at Huntsville. The earlier error in identifying Middleton in this photo likely roots simply in confusion about Doc's past. *Courtesy Western History Department, Denver Public Library.*

C

APPENDIX

Doc Middleton Defends His Name

The only known autobiographical writing by Doc Middleton is the open letter he wrote to the local newspaper when he was living in Gordon, Nebraska. The rarity of an account from Middleton's own hand obliges that it be reprinted in full here. I find it very near the truth, as nearly as the truth can be determined. There are a few discrepancies between Middleton's story here and the results of my research about his life (e.g., Doc's claim that "I never was fugitive from Texas" and his version of how the Tienkens recovered their horses); however, I stand upon the conclusions reached in this book. Except for a few small corrections or clarifications noted in brackets, I have not detailed discrepancies, but leave the judgment of my account and Middleton's to the reader. The *Gordon Press,* January 21, 1885:

Will you allow me the use of space in your paper to contradict some statements that are being made in the newspapers about me, that are false and calculated to do me an injury?

The papers are constantly publishing articles about me that are untrue and I now ask, once and for all, the opportunity to deny some of the untruthful things said of me.

In particular, I desire to deny the statement made in an article published in the Police News in November last.[1] I do not know how one would go to work to put more falsehood into as small a space as that article contained.

The article stated in brief that in 1880 I was the leader of a band of horse thieves; that we drove off whole herds of horses and cattle belonging to stockmen; that I was previously a fugitive from Texas, where I was under indictment for murder; that W. H. Llewellyn was my captor; that he joined the band and was brave as a lion, and much more in the same strain.

The article has been extensively copied into other papers and has been read by nearly everyone in the West. It is a tissue of lies from beginning to end, made up and given to the press by that cowardly braggart, W. H. Llewellyn. In contradicting the statements therein made and in telling the story of my arrest, your readers have my word for it that I will adhere strictly to the truth. I have sowed my wild oats and reaped the harvest and now, having settled down in the determination to be a man among men, I can afford to tell the truth, and I cannot afford to do otherwise. I claim that among those who know me best, my word is as good as that of any man and will not be doubted.

In the first place, I say to Mr. Llewellyn that I never was fugitive from Texas. At the age of 14 I went to work for a stockman and I followed that occupation nearly all my life until I was shut up in prison.

I did not drive off whole herds of cattle and horses belonging to stockmen. The truth is I never, with the exception of the instances which I will name, took any horses whatever from stockmen.

I drove off horses from Tinken Brothers ranch on the Niobrara below the ferry near Atkinson. These men and Tom Buckberry [Thomas H. Berry of Paddock], sheriff of Holt County, had laid in ambush for me at old man Franklin's house for the purpose of capturing me or shooting me. I believed at the time that they intended to kill me and I drove off their horses and went to see them. They did not deny laying in ambush for me, but said they did not intend shooting me and I returned their horses.

It is utterly false that I stole horses from either stockmen or citizens. On these occasions I resorted to a game of bluff to protect myself and made it work. Many of the ranch men, both then and now, were and are my friends. I do not deny that I drove off horses from the Indians. I did do that, but it was not from choice that I did so.

I did this, however, on my own hook. Great stress is laid on the word "gang" in the article referred to, and it is said I was "leader of a gang." This is false. Charlie Fuget is the only man who was ever with me for any length of time and he and I did not run off horses together. Once only I was assisted in capturing a small herd from the Indians, and when Llewellyn says there were always nine or ten men with me, he lies. It is as easy for him to lie now as it was for him to run from the scene of a "little unpleasantness" in 1879; but I am coming to that.

Between the 9th and 12th of July, 1879, W. H. Llewellyn and William Hazen [Lyman P. Hazen] came up where I was stopping and inquired the way to Rosebud Indian Agency. I immediately told them that they were not going there and didn't intend to go there. I told Llewellyn that I had a description of him and that there was no use for him to deny that they were after me.

Llewellyn then said that if I would help them to capture Jack Nolan and Pete Johnson [probably "Little Joe" Johnson] that they would be able to help me and would do so. I told them that I did not know of anything Nolan and Johnson had done that was wrong, but that I had heard that Nolan was broken out of jail and that I would go into Atkinson and see if they were still there, but that I would not assist in their capture. Nolan and Johnson were not associated with me as is stated.

I went to Atkinson with them and then back home.

On Sunday, July 17 [20], 1879, the fight with Llewellyn, Hazen, and Luykens [Billy Lykens] occurred. I see that Llewellyn claims there were nine or ten of me that day, and the way he ran his horse over the hills I have no doubt he thought so. The fact is there were four of us, all told, riding, and Luykens lying in a bunch of willows to shoot me.

I was riding side by side with Llewellyn and a fellow whom I have since learned went by the name of "Kid Wade" was with

Hazen. This man was not associated with me in any manner and I had known him only three or four days.

We rode down a canyon and crossed a little creek when I heard a gun missfire in a clump of willows within 20 or 30 feet of me. I drew my revolver, but could not make out distinctly where the man was in the brush and his gun went off, the bullet whistling past me. My horse jumped from under me, but I landed on my feet. Luykens ran away after firing at me.

Llewellyn never stopped to fire, but ran without that formality. The "brave lion" ran his horse 25 miles to Bassett's ranch, where the animal died a few hours after from fatigue. He rode that day a fine roan mare and I have always been sorry that mare died. Hazen had a much poorer horse, and after shooting a number of times he ran off a short distance and jumped off his horse. Before he could level his rifle across the saddle I had him covered with my revolver.

He said, "Don't shoot." I told him that if he did not move I would not, but that if he moved I would kill him.

I then walked up toward him and began passing around him. Jo appeared to turn his head as he inquired, "Who is all that coming out of the brush?"

I glanced away for an instant, and a bullet from Hazen's rifle went into my side and broke my hip. I then shot Hazen twice and left him for dead, though he afterwards recovered and came to see me in prison and showed me his scars.

As soon as I could get assistance I moved about seven miles northwest and had my tent put up in a deep canyon. My wife and a young fellow who went by the name of "Bill," I do not know his name, were with me in the canyon. Bill told me that he came up there to look for land and I engaged him to help me about moving to the canyon and to stay with me.

When Llewellyn left Bassett's ranch he did not go to Fort Robinson as the article reports, but to Fort Hotsiff [Fort Hartsuff]. Here he got a detail of 14 soldiers who were under the command of Capt. Montgomery, I think. There were also with the expedition George Eisley of Indiana; Smith of Wyoming; Leach of Ogallala; Happy Jack, a scout; the sheriffs of Grand Island and St. Paul, this state; and W. H. Llewellyn. These I remember, but there may have been others.

It is stated in the article in the Police News that my father-in-law was hung up before he would consent to lead these men to the canyon where I was concealed. The old man was not hung up at all, but I have reasons for believing that he voluntarily led them.

They came to the top of the canyon on Sunday, July 24 [27], and immediately began shooting into the tent. No one was hit, but a bullet struck a tree only a few inches from my wife.

I got up and tied my wife's apron about my hips and tried to walk but I fell down and could not walk on account of the wound Hazen gave me a week before. But I crawled on my hands and knees down the canyon some two or three hundred yards.

I rested there a short time and looked back. I could plainly see a number of the men who were busy shooting at the tent. I had my gun and could easily have shot some of them, but did not.

Three men came down and drank water, dipping it out of the creek with their hats. They were within a few feet of me and I could easily have killed them if I had been inclined, but I did not during the entire attack fire a single shot.

I thought the men who drank from the creek so near me would surely see me. Two or three times they seemed to be looking directly at me, but they finally went away.

I then crawled into the creek, which was full of green flags about two feet high. The cool water seemed to revive me and I drew my wounded leg through it and I was getting along very well when in lifting my leg over a little mound I raised myself too high and Happy Jack saw me and shot at me. I was not hurt but saw that I could not escape and gave up.

They then came and took me. George Eisley, I think, was the first one to reach me. Then came Leach and some of the soldiers. Some of these men then carried me to the top of the hill.

Llewellyn burned my tent, bed, and what furniture there was.

I was taken to Wyoming where I was tried and convicted of horse stealing. My sentence was for five years instead of four, but fifteen months before the expiration of my sentence, I was pardoned and all my rights restored.

It is my purpose and wish to so conduct myself in the future as not to be a violator of the laws of my country. All that I ask is to be let alone while I am trying to earn an honest living. I am, I think, not unlike other men in desiring not to be the victim of falsehood, and, I hope I do not beg too much when I ask the newspapers to let up on me now that I have suffered the penalty of the law.

Notes

The sources for the epigrams on p. vi are as follows: Edgar B. Bronson, *Cowboy Life on the Western Plains: The Reminiscenes of a Ranchman,* p. 199; A. J. Leach, *A History of Antelope County Nebraska from Its First Settlement in 1868 to the Close of the Year 1883,* p. 88.

Chapter 1:   Up to Nebraska

1 James H. Cook, *Fifty Years on the Old Frontier,* pp. 81-82; Cook, "Early Days in Ogalalla," *Nebraska History,* vol. 14, no. 2, p. 89.
2 This story was told the author by Robert Ferritor of Custer County, Nebraska.
3 A couple of years or so after the Sidney shooting incident, Middleton sent his account of the affair to the *Yankton Press and Dakotian;* the story was picked up and reprinted in the *Cheyenne Sun* of August 3, 1879. This Middleton account is a curiosity. It was submitted to the *Yankton Press and Dakotian* by R. W. Johnson, a friend of Doc's, but Middleton's name is not mentioned; instead, the name "Jack Hanford" is used throughout.
4 Solomon D. Butcher, *Pioneer History of Custer County,* pp. 121-23. I have added some paragraphing for this quotation here.
5 Harrington O'Reilley, *Fifty Years on the Trail,* p. 277.
   Illustrative of how the telling of the Sidney story later got a little

out of hand is Edgar Beecher Bronson's account in his *The Red-Blooded*:

> When he first came among us, hailing from Llano County, Texas, Doc was as fine a puncher and jolly, good-tempered rangemate as any in the Territory. Sober and industrious, he never drank or gambled. But he had his bit of temper, had Doc, and his chunk of good old Llano nerve. Thus, when a group of carousing soldiers, in a Sidney saloon, one night lit in to beat Doc up with their six-shooters for refusing to drink with them, the inevitable happened in a very few seconds; Doc killed three of them, jumped his horse, and split the wind for the Platte. (p. 85)

6 Donald F. Danker (ed.), *Man of the Plains: Recollections of Luther North, 1856-1882*, p. 263. Luther North said that in 1879 Doc Middleton told Luther's older brother, Joseph, that "the buffalo robe kept him from freezing to death and that this was the reason he never bothered our ranch." One of North's ranch hands, Bax Taylor, had a different reason. He said that he had known Doc in Texas and that Doc had stolen a horse from him; Taylor had vowed to kill Doc and felt this threat kept Middleton away from the North ranch.

7 The original indictment notation read "Dock Hamilton." The "Hamilton" was then scratched out and "Middleton" written in its place. Whether Doc was actually known at that time by the name of Hamilton or whether it was merely a mistake on the part of the clerk is not known. Certainly Doc was not averse to using aliases! On the other hand, the clerk might have made a simple aural error, confusing the sound of "Hamilton" and "Middleton."

CHAPTER 2:   FROM TEXAS

1 Appendix B contains a more detailed account of the Texas families and persons relevant to the Doc Middleton story, but for this chapter I have only sketched in a few of the major characters. Appendix A and Appendix B together also give the reader some sense of the process of my research into Doc's Texas background.

2 Record of this incident was found in "Collections of Bastrop County" in the Texas State Archives at Austin. No mention of the matter was found in the county records at Bastrop.

3 Texas State Archives.

4 This account of John Riley's Civil War service is compiled from the following sources: Records in the Adjutant General's Office of the War Department; the Oklahoma State Archives (he submitted his claim for a Confederate pension in Oklahoma); *Fron-*

NOTES

tier Times, Fall 1958; *Hammon* (Oklahoma) *Advocate,* December 18, 1947; *Fort Worth Star-Telegram,* November 22, 1947; *Wichita Falls Record-News,* November 15, 1935; other newspaper clippings, without names and dates, furnished me by family descendants; Riley letters in my possession; and other letters furnished me by John's daughter, Mrs. Loreatha Henry of Fort Worth, and his granddaughter, Mrs. Velma C. Lynn of Wichita Falls, Texas. It should be noted that John Riley later went under the name John D. Shepherd, as I explain elsewhere.

5 Office of Clerk of District Court, Court House, Fredericksburg, Texas.

6 Riley letters, author's collection.

7 The survey (#571) for this land was made April 18, 1874. William and Joseph assisted in the survey and their signatures appear along with their father's in the General Land Office in Austin. The tract was 10¾ miles north, 62° west from Blanco City, located on both sides of the boundary line between Blanco and Gillespie Counties, on a branch of Williamson Creek, a tributary of the Pedernales River.

8 As told by Henry, Bob, and Ben Harrison to Perry Moody, of Chadron, Nebraska, who told it to the author.

9 Interview by author with Tom Richardson; see Appendix A for details.

10 Letter to author from Mrs. Geraldine Henson, Dallas. Mrs. Henson is a granddaughter of Mary Anna Riley, sister or half-sister of James Riley (Doc Middleton). Mrs. Henson's mother was orphaned when she was a very young child and was reared by Nancy Riley. Consequently, Mrs. Henson has knowledge of the histories of the Cherry and Riley families; also she has the Cherry family Bible.

11 Gillespie County court records, Minute Book D, p. 387. Case #254 referred to young James' theft of the horse; case #355, State of Texas *v.* James Riley and Surety, pertains to the forfeiture of the bail bond.

12 Minute Book D, p. 533.

13 Huntsville Penitentiary records.

14 Gillespie County court records. In these records John Riley is referred to as J. D. Shepherd, but I explain elsewhere why this is the same person.

15 Gillespie County court records. The Moore transaction, e.g., involved Survey #215 on North Grape Creek.

16 No record of this marriage was found, but records probably burned with the Blanco City court house which was destroyed by fire in 1876—as were so many court houses in the 19th century.

17 Information about John's marriage, child, and name change came mainly from Mrs. Geraldine Henson, Dallas, and Mrs. Jessie Shepherd Bryant (daughter of J. D. Shepherd), Clinton, Oklahoma.
18 J. Frank Dobie, "On the Trail in '66," *Frontier Times,* Fall 1958.
19 Ibid.
20 Letter to author from Claude Riley (son of Joe Riley).
21 Interview by author with Claude Riley. After the 1876 drive north, Joe returned to Texas that fall; the following year, 1877, on the 11th of June, he and Lydia Mackey were married in Blanco County, Texas. Her maiden name was Hill; she had been married before and had one child. Joe was nineteen years old and his wife about eighteen when they married.
22 Danker (ed.), *Man of the Plains,* p. 263. Buck Taylor and Bax Taylor were sons of J. B. Riley's sister. If Doc were actually fathered by J. B. Riley, then he would have been a true first cousin to Buck and Bax, but they did not care to claim him.
23 Reference here is to the first wife of James Riley, Sr. In other words, there are suggestions but no proof that the Middleton name became part of the family with James Riley's first marriage. More solid evidence exists that the William Middleton who lived near the Rileys in Leon County (supra, p. 8) was a relative. There exists a letter written to Buck Taylor in 1888 from a friend or relative telling Buck something about his ancestors; the letter refers to Buck's grandfather, James Riley, and to Buck's "Uncle Bill Middleton." (Author's collection) Mrs. Geraldine Henson told me that she was certain the M. in James M. Riley was for Middleton.

CHAPTER 3: NEBRASKA PANHANDLE

1 Bronson's *The Red-Blooded* tells this same story but without naming anyone except Middleton. Harry E. Chrisman's *The Ladder of Rivers: The Story of I. P. (Print) Olive* (p. 204) has Middleton, Scurry, and Baldridge doing the stealing, but since it was Smith who was indicted, we will assume he was involved. (Nothing more is known of Baldridge except that he was later reported killed by Indians while attempting to steal horses from them.)
2 *Cheyenne Daily Leader,* April 8, 1879, relating an event over a year past.
3 Interview by author with Tom Richardson.
4 Though many horses were stolen by Indians from Indians in the West as a whole, this practice was not a major problem in Nebraska during the 1870s and 1880s.
5 *Cheyenne Sun.*

6 *Sidney Telegraph.*
7 Bronson, *Red-Blooded,* pp. 84-85.
8 Martinsburg was near the Blanco-Gillespie county line; the name was later changed to Hye and the post office moved a short distance.
9 Interview by author with Claude Riley.

CHAPTER 4: DOC MIDDLETON'S COUNTRY

1 For more detailed treatments of the Black Hills gold rush, see Donald Jackson, *Custer's Gold: The United States Cavalry Expedition of 1874* (esp. pp. 2n1, 111n13) and Watson Parker, *Gold in the Black Hills* (esp. pp. 22-23, 28-37 on the Gordon party).
2 An 1875 map shows both the "Black Hills and State Boundary Wagon Road" and the ferry; also, a dispatch rider for the Hills recorded his crossing on this ferry in late April of 1875. From these sources we can establish the existence of the route and the ferry at this early date, though later maps do not show them.

   The map, a result of the Wiltse Survey of 1873, is dated August 14, 1875 and labeled Township 33, Range 17, Surveyor General's Office, Plattsmouth, Nebr., Jno. R. Clark, Surveyor General. Copies exist at the Soil and Water Conservation Service, Ainsworth, Nebraska, and in the Land Office records at the Capitol Building, Lincoln, Nebraska.

   H. I. Chapman was the dispatch rider. The *Sioux City Weekly Journal* for June 8, 1875 tells of Chapman's leaving Sioux City on April 10, 1875 with letters and papers for the Gordon party, encamped in their stockade near Harney's Peak. Unknown to Chapman, Capt. John Mix and soldiers of the 2nd Cavalry had on that very day (April 10) dislodged the remaining eighteen members of the Gordon party from the stockade and were escorting them to Fort Laramie. Chapman went up as far as Snake River but could not get across the Niobrara and returned to O'Neill City, where he met Captain Giles who was on his way up to the Niobrara to establish a ferry. Chapman accompanied Giles, assisted him in getting the boat into the water, crossed on it himself, and was on his way toward the Hills. However, cold weather and his inexperience turned Chapman's trip into a disaster; he never reached the Hills, and he almost lost his life. In any case, Chapman had earlier sent word back by a traveler that he had crossed the Niobrara on a ferry. On May 6, 1875 the *Niobrara Pioneer* printed an article about Chapman's journey, but the editor did not believe there was a ferry on the Niobrara and scoffed at Chapman's story.

3 Large freighting firms ran ox trains; Pratte and Ferris, who operated out of Sidney, also opened a branch for this route. Jack Hale, formerly sheriff of Madison County, operated a sizeable bull train with forty-eight yoke of oxen and several wagons; strung out in single file, they were an impressive sight. Lauren Means, who later located on the Niobrara, freighted to the Hills, as did Barrett Scott, well known in the area. Also there were many settlers who did some freighting.

4 *Oakdale Pen and Plow,* May 15, 1879.

5 Although it was out of the question for a few outlaws with no mining or excavation equipment to produce an underground excavation of the magnitude to stable a herd of horses—and a raid on the Sioux would commonly net seventy-five to 125 horses—there was, it seems, one underground corral in the area. Martin Spann, an old-timer in Bassett, Nebraska, with whom I talked, told of a settler he remembered on the Niobrara who was determined that thieves would not get his horses. So he excavated a stable for his few horses and built his house directly in front of the underground area. The only access to his horses was through his living quarters! This may appear more comical than likely, but the man was desperate. I believe the story. Furthermore, it is just possible that this small, personal underground corral was a germ for the later and fantastic tales of Middleton's unique hiding places. I must confess to perhaps being the source for another tall tale of Middleton's underground exploits. Some years ago a writer was poking around the Niobrara asking questions about Doc. I remembered that a scatterbrained kid had long ago told me of an escape tunnel Doc had from Carns, so I casually and jokingly passed the story on. I certainly did not tell it for the truth, and I surely did not expect to see the tale appear later in print as a fact. But it did.

6 *Niobrara Pioneer,* March 31, 1879.

CHAPTER 5: HORSE STEALING

1 Cf., A. J. Leach, *History of Antelope County:* "It is certain that they [Middleton gang] had confederates in Holt and Antelope counties, and men in Boone and Madison counties were strongly suspected of being in league with them. After the gang was broken up it was found that they had confederates as far east as central Iowa." (p. 84)

2 This material is taken basically from an article in the *Niobrara Pioneer* datelined "Paddock, Nebr., June 5, 1878." Captain Henry W. Wessels, Company H, 3rd Cavalry, had been on duty at Camp

Robinson and Sidney Barracks. When the Spotted Tail Sioux were moved from the old agency in western Nebraska to their new location near Niobrara, formerly the Ponca Agency, Capt. Wessels and his company were chosen to escort the Indians. This was done to keep order generally and to protect the Indians from depredations at the hands of whites. During the winter of 1877-78, Capt. Wessels and his command were stationed in a temporary tent camp near the Indians to further discourage molestation of the Indians by white outlaws and to keep order between the Indians and the white settlers across the Niobrara River. On one occasion the military group crossed the river and confiscated liquor and ammunition in the stores at Paddock; on other occasions they pursued the Middleton gang after horse stealing raids.

3 It is my opinion that Ed Smith was Edgar Scurry of Texas.
4 Butcher, *Pioneer History of Custer County,* pp. 123, 126 (paragraphing added).
5 Ibid., p. 127.
6 *Niobrara Pioneer* article datelined "O'Neill City, Nebr., January 20, 1879." Mr. Dutcher is quoted as angrily wondering: "And now I want to know where the Indian agents get their authority to pass out their plundering savages to raid on and run off stock from the pioneer settlers of Northern Nebraska."
7 Leach, *History of Antelope County,* p. 85.
8 Letter to *Niobrara Pioneer,* December 27, 1878.
9 Information about the Tienken family comes from a sixty-five-page typewritten booklet containing the recollections of Henry Tienken, one of the brothers. Copy in author's collection. Referred to hereafter as Tienken memoirs.
10 Leach, *History of Antelope County,* p. 86.
11 Tienken memoirs.

CHAPTER 6: CAPTURES

1 Interview by author with Tom Richardson.
2 This account comes primarily from court records and the *Niobrara Pioneer* for October 18, 1878. Leach in *History of Antelope County* (pp. 87-88) tells the same story, differing slightly only in figures (e.g., size of posse, number of cattle confiscated). The Grand Jury found No Bill against Mason or Morris, and they were finally released from jail on March 24, 1879. Morris then sued Jep Hopkins for $5,500, claiming damages for false imprisonment, lost time, and the confiscation of his two horses. Although Morris was a tough old boot and had what it took to survive there among

that den of outlaws, I am convinced that he was innocent and was wrongly imprisoned for months. He simply was not part of the horse stealing operation, and Mason probably was not either. (For court records see: State of Nebraska v. George Holt et al., March 1879 term, Criminal Docket 1, Case 11, p. 20, Center, Knox County; John Morris v. Jeptha Hopkins and John Bellmer, District Court, Holt County, Civil Case 11, O'Neill.)

3 Tienken memoirs.

4 Richardson interview.

5 *Cheyenne Sun*, March 14, 1879. Little has been written about the beginnings of the "special agents" of the railroads or the "railroad detectives," especially in the West. Henry S. Dewhurst's study, *The Railroad Police*, deals almost exclusively with the twentieth century. "It was around the turn of the century that the establishment of individual railroad police departments . . . really got under way." (p. 23) Dewhurst gives only a nod to the nineteenth century and then mainly to the Civil War period. In a more recent book, *The Western Peace Officer*, Frank R. Prassel has given brief (pp. 138-40) but excellent treatment to the railroad detective in the West during the 1870s and 1880s, citing state legislative action which gave police authority to these special agents. If historians have slighted the work of the nineteenth century railroad police, so did writers at the time. Contemporary newspapers, for example, mentioned the railroad detectives inconspicuously, never with headlines. References to them and their work were usually on a back page, and seldom were names recorded. There is even a hint of confusion about the authority under which these special agents operated; the newspapers sometimes tactfully questioned the legality of such police action, but then generally went ahead to implicitly assume or suggest that it was all right because they seemed to know what they were doing. The railroads are known to have paid good salaries to some detectives, but I suspect that reward money was an important inducement for many agents. It appears that the railroad detectives would on occasion depart from strictly railroad interests and, mounted and armed, take the trail after "horse thieves, stage stoppers, and various outlaws." (infra, p. 68) There is sufficient evidence to identify five of these special agents of the Union Pacific: N. K. Boswell, a sheriff from Laramie; James L. Smith, deputy sheriff from Cheyenne; George Eisley, from Indiana; W. C. Lykens, who prior to his railroad employment was a stock detective for the Wyoming Stock Growers Association; and M. F. Leach (or Leech), who played a role in tracking down the Big Springs train robbers (1877) and was to have a significant part in capturing Doc Middleton.

6 Tienken memoirs. For a good biography of I. P. (Print) Olive, see Harry E. Chrisman, *The Ladder of Rivers;* in chapter XVI Chrisman deals with the deaths of Mitchell and Ketchum.
7 Lincoln County records, North Platte, Nebraska.
8 *Cheyenne Sun,* March 14, 1879.
9 *Niobrara Pioneer,* May 2, 1879; article reprinted from *Omaha Republican.*
10 "Early History of Cheyenne and Kimball Counties," *Nebraska History,* vol. 7, no. 1, p. 15; Butcher (p. 132) uses the name McDonald.
11 Butcher said: "As they entered Sidney they rode through a freighter's camp, when the officers sprang out and shouted: 'Throw up your hands!' At the same moment McDonald jerked away Smith's revolver and pinned his arms to his side. Smith threw himself from his horse, wrenched himself loose from McDonald's grasp, and would have gotten away had an officer not filled him with a load of buckshot which ended his career on the spot." (132)
12 Richardson interview. The Niobrara River in its upper part was often called the Running Water.
13 Leach in *History of Antelope County* (p. 86) says that the incident occurred at the time Fugate was captured at North Platte.
14 *Sidney Telegraph,* May 10, 1879.
15 The story is that Valdez was upstairs in a brothel with a prostitute; Nolan was out on the town with another. When Nolan and his girl came back to the house, she learned that Valdez was upstairs with an Anglo girl. This rankled her, and she dared Nolan to shoot Valdez. Nolan tried to get into the room upstairs, but Valdez held the door; Nolan fired through the door and hit Valdez in the abdomen. Valdez died a few hours later.
16 Butcher, *Pioneer History of Custer County,* p. 108.
17 Ibid., p. 132.

CHAPTER 7: DANCES, CANDY, THREAD, AND THINGS

1 Interview by author with Tom Richardson.
2 Ibid. The Robison family, still living today on the Niobrara, spell the name with only one "n," but because clerks and editors since the 1870s have insisted on spelling it Robinson, legal documents and newspapers (e.g., infra, p. 123) almost always have it that way.
3 Bill Huntington, *Good Men and Salty Cusses.* This incident took place in 1877 or 1878. Huntington also related that his father, Frank Huntington, worked with Middleton on the E. W. Ranch. This is one of the few instances of Middleton as a hired hand. But,

of course, he never dared stay in any one place for very long.

4 In the days of Middleton and Joe Smith the only activities on the Long Pine Creek were ranching and the milling of lumber; there was as yet no identifiable place called Long Pine. Stories such as this stranded immigrant tale exist in a still-strong oral tradition which can today be heard along the Niobrara and Elkhorn Rivers. See also Maurice Frink, *Cow Country Cavalcade*, pp. 92-93.

5 Richardson interview.

6 Ibid.

7 Interview by author with Jim Nightengale of Atkinson, Nebraska. Mr. Nightengale was eighty-five years of age when interviewed and had his information from his father, J. O'D. Nightengale, an early Atkinson settler.

8 This quote and the previous stories since the dream/premonition one are all from the Nightengale interview.

9 The personal diary of M. D. Long was supplied to the author by Dean Selah of Omaha.

10 Leach, *History of Antelope County*, pp. 82-83. Much of the information concerning Middleton in *History of Antelope County* came, as Leach said, from "Lauren Means, who had become quite well acquainted with Middleton while teaming to the Niobrara ranches and to the Black Hills. Afterwards, when Middleton himself was captured, he talked freely of these things." (86)

11 Lewis F. Crawford, *Rekindling Camp Fires*, p. 266-67.

12 John Edward Hicks, *Adventures of a Tramp Printer*, pp. 68, 69, 70, 71.

CHAPTER 8:   SIOUX

1 *Niobrara Pioneer*, December 27, 1878, reprinted from *Chicago Daily Inter Ocean*, December 19, 1878. The immediate background of General Sherman's letter was as follows. A few months earlier, on May 20, 1878, during discussion of the army appropriation bill (H.R. 4867) for the upcoming fiscal year, Representative William Kimmel of Maryland introduced an amendment making it unlawful "to use any part of the land or naval forces of the United States to execute the laws either as a *posse comitatus* or otherwise, except in such cases as may be expressly authorized by act of Congress." Kimmel's rationale rooted in the "dread and detestation" of a standing army, and he argued:

> Under the laws of the several states, the sheriffs have the power to summon the *posse comitatus*. . . . No one, I presume, will attempt to maintain that a sheriff has the right to summon the

Army of the United States as a posse. If . . . the standing Army of the United States can be used as a *posse comitatus* for the execution of the laws, we are living under a military despotism unqualified and absolute, for what is military depotism but the use of troops against the people without due authority of law?
Kimmel's amendment died without vote, but a week later Representative J. Proctor Knott of Kentucky introduced a similar amendment, adding the penalties referred to by General Sherman in his later letter. Knott's amendment passed 120-112 on May 27. In June the Senate debated and passed a similar amendment to the army appropriation bill. For the debates, showing the views of leading Congressmen on the question of the use of the army as a posse comitatus, see *Congressional Record*, 45th Congress, 2nd Session; House: May 20, 1878 (pp. 3579-86, esp. 3582, 3586), May 21 (pp. 3631-35), May 27 (pp. 3845-52); Senate: June 7 (pp. 4239-48), June 8 (pp. 4295-4304).

2   Senator Paddock introduced his bill (S. 1492) on December 12, 1878, submitting as evidence of need of the bill the letter from General Sherman and the letter signed by the following ranchers: W. A. Sharp, W. A. Paxton, B. A. Sheidley & Bros., James Creighton, John A. Creighton, Coe & Carter, and Kountze, Yates & Co. The bill passed the Senate on December 18 and was sent to the House the following day but died with the 45th Congress. Senator Paddock re-introduced his legislation when the 46th Congress convened, but again success eluded him. He was still trying in 1880. In the meantime, the prohibitions and penalties outlined by General Sherman continued in effect. For Senator Paddock's arguments supporting his measure, see *Congressional Record*, 45th Congress, 3rd Session, December 12 and 18, 1878 (pp. 125, 275-76); 46th Congress, 1st Session, April 24 and 25, 1879 (pp. 814, 903-06).

3   The Kid Wade and Black Jack Gang horse thefts from the Sioux are recorded in William Henry Harrison Llewellyn's reports to the U.S. Department of Justice (Record Group 60, Correspondence with Special Agent W. H. H. Llewellyn, Department of Justice, National Archives). Llewellyn was a Special Agent of the Department assigned to find evidence and make cases against horse thieves stealing Indian stock. Subsequent quotations from the Llewellyn file —correspondence to and from him—are not footnoted.

4   Interview by author with Jim Nightengale. This incident is also mentioned in the histories by Butcher (p. 107) and by Leach.

5   *West Point Progress*, April 7, 1881.

6   Llewellyn report for January 1880 identifies Black Hank as Frank Slaven.

7   *Sidney Telegraph*, July 5, 1879; *Chicago Times*, June 10, 1879.

8 Governor Albinus Nance's Correspondence, Nebraska State Historical Society, Lincoln. T. H. Tibbles and his second wife, the former Susette La Flesche (Bright Eyes), daughter of the Omaha chief, Joseph La Flesche (Iron Eyes), were strong champions of the rights of Indians. See, for example, Tibbles' memoirs, *Buckskin and Blanket Days*.

9 Governor Nance's Correspondence.

10 James H. Cook, "Early Days in Ogalalla," *Nebraska History*, vol. 14, no. 2, pp. 90-91.

CHAPTER 9:   MARRIAGE AND PARDON

1 Holt County records at O'Neill, the county seat. At the time this license was issued, O'Neill City had succeeded in winning the county seat from Paddock, but the functions of office continued at Paddock through July 1879.

2 Mrs. Skinner's story first appeared in Frances Sims Fulton's book, *To and Through Nebraska*, published in 1884; her story was reprinted in 1910 in a special issue of the *Long Pine Journal*.

3 Riley family letters indicate that Middleton had written home that he was thinking of going to Canada. One branch of the Riley family even tells a story about Middleton that he did in fact go north and that he married the daughter of a rancher for whom he worked in Canada, but there is no evidence for this at all.

4 Interview by author with Tom Richardson.

5 See note #6 for Chapter 6.

6 Record Group 60, Correspondence with Special Agent W. H. H. Llewellyn, Department of Justice, National Archives. I have found nothing to substantiate Leach's conclusion that "Middleton himself was suspected of having had a hand in robbing a post office, and on this charge . . . Llewellyn and Hazen were instructed to capture him." (*History of Antelope County*, p. 88)

7 This Llewellyn reference is the only time I have run across the "Jack Lyons" alias.

   I earlier noted that I could find no record in Texas of Middleton's being charged with a murder, though in Chapter 2 I did deal with the "legends of three homicides in Texas committed by James M. Riley." (supra, p. 12)

8 The *Omaha Daily Bee*, October 20, 1879, covers the capture of Nolan and Johnson. Files 191 and 192, U.S. District Court for Nebraska, Federal Records Center, Kansas City, Missouri, indicate that they were sentenced by the Hon. E. S. Dundy to terms in the Nebraska State Penitentiary. Llewellyn's reports during the

month of February 1880, and also newspaper clipping he sent to the Department of Justice (received by the Department Februray 28, 1880), deal with the killing of Curly Grimes.

CHAPTER 10: TREACHERY

1 Supra, pp. 30, 34. This is the William C. Lykens who had earlier captured Doc Middleton in December 1877.
2 Mrs. Skinner's account is in Fulton's *To and Through Nebraska,* p. 132. Butcher in *Pioneer History of Custer County* also refers to a signing, but in his account it is the pardon itself that is to be signed:

> They sent him word that they had a pardon for him, signed by the governor, which in order to become effective would have to be signed by Milton [Middleton], with a promise to lead a better life in the future. ... A meeting was had and Milton agreed to sign the document and reform. Hazen and Llewellyn ... and Kid Wade, accompanied by Milton, started to a house to get pen and ink to sign the paper. There was a dense thicket on the road which they had to pass by on their way to the house and the detectives had previously placed a man in this thicket to kill Milton as he passed by, as it did not appear to be a part of their plan to try to take him alive. (pp. 132-33)

It is interesting to note that Butcher refers to Lykens only as "a man in this thicket," explaining that since "he played the part of a murderer and a coward we will not chronicle his name." (p. 133)

Regardless of how many papers were involved, we can assume that at least the fake pardon paper existed. It is my opinion that when Llewellyn went to Lincoln to see the governor and get "something under the seal of the state" (supra, p. 114), he actually wanted a seal or a piece of the governor's stationery on which to forge the pardon; and I think he got it somehow, even if by subterfuge.

3 In an account (see Appendix C) written almost six years after the event, Middleton said: "I was riding side by side with Llewellyn and ... 'Kid Wade' was with Hazen." I am inclined to think that time had distorted Doc's memory on this point, as it had when in the same article he remembered the day as "Sunday, July 17" (instead of Sunday, July 20). Since Llewellyn was chased and fired at by Wade and since it was Hazen and Middleton who exchanged shots at close range, it seems logical to assume that Llewellyn and Wade had been riding together and so had Hazen and Middleton. Hazen, in his account (*Omaha Daily Bee,* July 26, 1879), places

Llewellyn and the Kid about fifty yards in *front* of Doc and himself. These discrepancies are hard to dispose of, but I have concluded that Llewellyn and the Kid were *behind,* as Doc originally said. If they had been in front, then Llewellyn could have easily fled right on down the river to the Skinner place, where, as he said in a later report, he had intended to go after the shooting. However, if he were behind Middleton, then he would logically have fled up through the timber onto the higher ground between the creeks, exactly as he did. This route was unfamiliar to Llewellyn, and he would surely not have taken it unless necessary. As a matter of fact, as he also later admitted in one of his reports, he got lost in a canyon; this was likely caused by his confusion in having to cross the other branch of the Laughing Water which he was not acquainted with.

4 *Cheyenne Daily Leader,* August 5, 1879.
5 *Niobrara Pioneer,* July 25, 1879.
6 Statements by Hazen appeared in the *Omaha Daily Bee,* July 26, 1879 and in the *Oakdale Pen and Plow*, August 7, 1879; there are serious inconsistencies in these two accounts.
7 Bronson, *The Red-Blooded,* pp. 87-88.
8 Fulton, *To and Through Nebraska,* p. 131.
9 Governor A. Nance's Correspondence, Nebraska State Historical Society.

CHAPTER 11: DOC MIDDLETON'S CAPTURE

1 *Yankton Press and Dakotian.*
2 It is interesting to note, from Llewellyn's reports, that this army detail was officially listed as being out searching for deserters. The use of the army to assist civil law officers in making arrests was still illegal (see notes #1 and #2 for Chapter 8)—thus the mislabeling of the unit's mission, a common subterfuge.
3 *Cheyenne Daily Leader,* August 1, 1879.
4 This letter lay in a trunk containing Nancy Riley's belongings until 1962, when it was sent to me by Mrs. Geraldine Henson.
    After her husband was captured, Mary Richardson Middleton went back home to live with her father and stepmother.
5 Governor A. Nance's Correspondence, Nebraska State Historical Society.

CHAPTER 12: PRISON

1 Supra, p. 30. These year-old Wyoming charges, brought before he

became infamous, seem to be the only charges against Middleton. Though Llewellyn's bungled plot did ultimately bring about Doc Middleton's capture, Llewellyn's special investigative services for the Department of Justice do not appear to have resulted in any indictments brought against Middleton in either Nebraska or Dakota Territory. I have searched the records of the U.S. District Courts at Omaha and at Yankton and have found nothing pertaining to Middleton in either jurisdiction. I am convinced from this evidence and from Llewellyn's reports themselves that he never even attempted to develop a federal case against Middleton—this in direct violation of the orders of the Department of Justice that cases were to be made in Federal District Court, and, if in Nebraska, tried at Omaha and, if in Dakota Territory, tried at Yankton. As a matter of fact, after Doc's capture, Llewellyn proposed to the Department that Middleton be taken to Cheyenne, for there, Llewellyn claimed, he would get a longer sentence (three counts carrying fourteen years each, totaling forty-two years), but the Department refused to agree, saying that it did not matter where he would get the longer sentence. However, to Wyoming he went, *because that is where the reward money was.* It is likely that Leach took over after Middleton's capture; he represented the Wyoming interests. And we can assume that with the money involved, Llewellyn did not need a lot of convincing about the wisdom of moving Doc to Cheyenne. Certainly there was Nebraska reward money for Middleton's capture, but it was less. Thirteen Wyoming ranchers had put up $100 each (John Bratt, *Trails of Yesterday*, p. 261. The ranchers are not named, but presumably they were members of the Wyoming Stock Growers Association for which Lykens was detective before joining the Union Pacific Police Force), so we know that there was at least $1,300 in reward money in Wyoming. However, we do not know how much reward money each of the participants got. We do know that the State of Nebraska paid Sheriffs Kilian and Krew $150 each for their part in Middleton's capture. We also have a letter from Hazen to Governor Nance, dated February 12, 1880, from Canon City, Colorado, in which Hazen complains that of all the Middleton rewards he got "only $200 and got the worst of it too." (Governor A. Nance's Correspondence, Nebraska State Historical Society) If Hazen got $200, surely Lykens, Leach, Smith, and Llewellyn would have also been paid, and perhaps more than $200, as Hazen suggests. Some years later Llewellyn was in Topeka, Kansas and gave a story to the newspaper about his captures of outlaws. He said that he got $5,000 cash from the railroad for the killing of Curly Grimes; he claimed to have received $10,000 for the capture of Middleton

(*Rio Grande Republican* [Las Cruces, New Mexico], October 13, 1888, reprinted from *Topeka Capital*), but this seems a considerable exaggeration. It was widely believed that the Union Pacific offered a reward for Middleton's capture. However, I have searched relentlessly to document this and cannot; besides, Doc was never any trouble for the railroad, and it appears logical to conclude that they offered no reward for him.

2   Reprinted in the *Omaha Daily Bee*, September 23, 1879.

3   It was on this trip, the night before arriving at the penitentiary, that Middleton made a special point of thanking one of the North brothers for a kindness shown him in January 1877 (supra, note #6 for Chapter 1):

> When they were taking him to Lincoln to serve his time, they brought him through Columbus. He stayed in Columbus over night under guard, of course, and while at the hotel he sent word to my brother, J. E. North, requesting him to come to the Clother House to see him. My brother was very much surprised at the message, and not a little curious, and went to the hotel.
>
> When he went into the room, Doc said, "I guess you don't know me."
>
> My brother said, "No, he did not," and then Doc told him where he had seen him.
>
> Three years before my brother had made a business trip to the Black Hills in the winter, and the weather was very cold. He went by stage coach from Sidney, Nebraska, and took a big buffalo robe for protection. When the stage coach reached the first station out from Sidney, a man got on to go to Ft. Robinson. The stage was full, and this man was obliged to ride with the driver on the outside. My brother saw that he was not very warmly clad, and had no overcoat, so he gave him the buffalo robe to wrap around him. He wore it until they got to Ft. Robinson, when he returned it to my brother. This man was Doc Middleton. [Danker (ed.), *Man of the Plains*, pp. 262-63]

4   In the 1920s Addison E. Sheldon, editor of *Nebraska History*, made "strenuous efforts . . . to secure an authentic picture of Doc Middleton." Among other sources, Sheldon contacted the Nebraska State Penitentiary; W. T. Fenton, Warden, replied:

> We do not have his photograph, as several years ago there was a fire here which destroyed most of the early records at that time. We do have his record which is as follows: Doc Middleton No. 74, from Laramie County, Wyo. Territory. . . . Age 28; Hgt. 5-9¾; Comp. Fair; Hair, Lt. Br.; Eyes, Brown; Born, Miss.
> [*Nebraska History*, vol. 10 (1927), no. 4, pp. 351-52]

CHAPTER 13:   DOC MIDDLETON'S RETURN

1   In interviews with the author, three long-time residents of the area, Thomas Peacock, Earl Armstrong, and Alexander Dugger, indicated that they knew of these circumstances; they attested to the fact that indeed it was the belief among folk along the Niobrara then that a prison absence was all that was required to dissolve a marriage.

2   The Department of Justice on May 12, 1880 sent a telegram to Llewellyn: "United States Attorney Campbell to continue your employment if he needs you." On September 11, 1880 Campbell informed Llewellyn that his services were no longer required. When he continued to do investigative work for the government, he received his letter of reprimand in November, and his claims for expenses were turned down. However, the whole unfortunate affair was finally blamed on a breakdown in communications, and Llewellyn's claims were allowed, though they were protested as excessive.

   Information about Llewellyn for the period after Middleton's capture and trial comes from his final reports to the Department of Justice, from J. L. Smith-Llewellyn letters (Record Group 75, Letters received 1881-1907, Office of Indian Affairs, National Archives), and from sources listed in a bibliography furnished me by the Museum of New Mexico at Santa Fe.

3   Depredations Claim #2883, Bureau of Indian Affairs, National Archives.

4   Many references will be found to "Morrison's Bridge," but as far as I have determined, these all mean John Morris' crossing, or Morris Bridge.

5   There is always the question of which came first, the railroad or the town. In the case of Valentine the situation was as follows. There was a terrific job getting across the Niobrara here, and a labor camp, a real hellhole, grew up at Thatcher, on the south side of the river. Fort Niobrara was also on the south side, a little distance from Thatcher. However, Thatcher was located in rough sand dunes and was therefore a poor townsite. Valentine began to grow in anticipation of the rails, although in December 1883 there was only one house on the site. But by May 1884 the river had been bridged, and the Thatcher merchants moved to the Valentine site. Within weeks after the railroad reached Valentine, the town had a hardware store, a furniture store, two general stores, a government store for the Indians, a restaurant, a hotel, five saloons, twenty-five houses, and a newspaper.

6   Kid Wade's court case was #407, criminal files, Sioux City, Iowa. At Anamosa, Wade was inmate #638.

I have deduced that Black Bill's real name was James Church. In Llewellyn's reports to Washington, D.C. about these three culprits, and in his descriptions accompanying tintypes of the three that he also sent to Washington (tintypes now at National Archives), he referred only to Kid Wade, Bill Clark, and Black Bill. The court trial files and the reformatory records referred only to Kid Wade, Bill Clark, and James Church, giving no indication that Church used the alias "Black Bill." However, since Wade, Clark, and Church were the only three defendants prosecuted in Sioux City at that time for horse theft and sent to Anamosa, it seems reasonable to conclude that Black Bill and James Church were the same person.

7 The Land Office was never at Carns, but F. W. "Cap" Tarbell was a notary public and could take a claimant's sworn statement.

CHAPTER 14: GORDON, NEBRASKA

1 See Appendix C for full text of this letter by Middleton.
2 Elizabeth Jane Leonard and Julia Cody Goodman, *Buffalo Bill: King of the Old West*, pp. 243-44.
3 Don Russell, *The Lives and Legends of Buffalo Bill*, p. 320. In his *The Wild West or, A History of the Wild West Shows*, Don Russell calls our attention to Con Groner, known in the Buffalo Bill show as " 'the Cow-Boy Sheriff of the Platte.' One of his claims to fame was that of having rounded up Doc Middleton's gang of outlaws." (p. 19) This was undoubtedly Sheriff Groner's attempt to cash in on Doc's greater reputation, since we know that Groner did not participate directly in the capture of Middleton himself, though he was involved earlier in the apprehension of Doc's half-brother, William Riley, alias Charley Fugate.
4 James H. Cook, "Early Days in Ogalalla," *Nebraska History*, vol. 14, no. 2, pp. 91-92.
5 This story was told the author by Henry Chamberlain of Rushville, Nebraska, who in the 1880s trailed cattle from Texas to Nebraska. In the 1950s, when interviewed, he was in his eighties.
6 The newspapers cited here are the *Sioux City Weekly Journal*, March 26 and 27, 1891; and Dakota City's *North Nebraska Eagle*, March 26, April 2, and April 9, 1891. Nothing was found in the court records at Dakota City, the county seat. Two years after this fracas, Covington was consolidated with South Sioux City.

CHAPTER 15: CHADRON-CHICAGO COWBOY HORSE RACE

1 Much has been written about this race, but there are still enough

disagreements and puzzles left to preclude a simple summary of the event. And this is not the place to elaborate the issues of dispute and their possible resolution. Therefore, this chapter is not a definitive treatment of the race but primarily the story of Doc Middleton's participation. My own conclusions are based on a variety of sources. Many years ago I talked with Chadron oldtimers and recorded their tales of those days. I have also worked my way through all the archival material in Chadron, and of course I have read hundreds of old newspapers from Nebraska and elsewhere (the race was extensively covered by the contemporary press). For those unfamiliar with the secondary literature available, let me call attention to two articles which give careful treatment to the race. Harry T. Sly was for many years a respected newspaperman in Chadron. As a labor of love he collected all the material he could about the race and in 1931 wrote a five-page, single-spaced article summarizing his findings; this manuscript is now at the Chadron Public Library. More recently, William E. Deahl, Jr. published an impressive article on the race: "The Chadron-Chicago 1,000-Mile Cowboy Race," in *Nebraska History*, vol. 53 (1972), no. 2.

2 *Chadron Citizen*, June 1, 1893.

3 *Chadron Citizen*, June 15, 1893.

4 *Dawes County Journal*, May 12, 1893.

5 *St. Louis Post-Dispatch*, June 14, 1893.

6 *O'Neill Frontier*, June 22, 1893 (italics in original).

7 *Illinois State Journal*, June 14, 1893, as quoted in the William E. Deahl, Jr. article.

8 Revised Statutes, Illinois Criminal Code, Chap. 38, Div. 1, Sec. 78, ibid.

9 *Illinois State Journal*, June 14, 1893, ibid.

10 *Dawes County Journal*, May 19, 1893.

11 Registration rules called for payment of $10 of the entrance fee by May 1 and the remaining $15 by June 1 (*Chicago Daily Inter Ocean*, June 30, 1893). We can assume that in the flush of early excitement, many aspirants were willing to commit $10. However, enthusiasm may well have waned as the demands of the race became clearer—e.g., time and money. Two weeks or more of time could perhaps be come by, but expenses might be high, and financial backers were not likely to be found for as many as two dozen entrants.

12 *Chadron Citizen*, June 15, 1893; *O'Neill Frontier*, June 22, 1893. Other sources provide both additional information and discrepancies about the names of some horses, the ownership of some horses, and so forth. Suffice it to note here the following additions which seem rooted in good evidence: Campbell, Smith, and Stephens

(Rattlesnake Pete) were riding their own horses; Gillespie's horse
Billy Mack was owned by Charles Weller, and Gillespie himself
owned Billy Schafer; Middleton's horses were owned by William
Cooper, who traveled along the race route more or less with Doc
and was in Chicago with him.

13 *Chicago Herald*, June 28, 1893.
14 J. R. Johnson, *Representative Nebraskans*, p. 62.
15 Henry B. Sell and Victor Weybright, *Buffalo Bill and the Wild
West*, p. 199.
16 G. E. Lemmon, *Developing the West*, sec. 1, p. 6; this portion of
Lemmon's memoirs reads:

> These [western] men were raising horses and wanted to prove to
> the world the endurance of the western horse. Consequently five
> or six horsemen of western South Dakota met at Sturgis and de-
> cided to stage an endurance race starting at Chadron, Nebr., and
> ending at Chicago, a distance of exactly one thousand miles. The
> time allowed was thirteen days. This would necessitate an aver-
> age of seventy-seven miles per day.
>
> Until this time United States had not staged this kind of a
> race, but France had and its record was fifty miles per day.

17 *New York Times*, June 17, 1893, datelined "Valentine, Nebr.,
June 16."
18 *Chicago Daily Inter Ocean*, June 27, 1893, datelined "Seward, Ill.,
June 26."
19 *Dawes County Journal*, June 23, 1893.
20 *O'Neill Frontier*, June 22, 1893.
21 Ibid.
22 Ibid.
23 *Chicago Daily Inter Ocean*, June 26, 1893, datelined "Dubuque,
Iowa, June 25."
24 *Chicago Daily Inter Ocean*, June 27, 1893, datelined "Dubuque,
Iowa, June 26. Special Telegram." The *Chicago Herald* account on
June 27 said the same thing about his departure from Dubuque,
but its difference perhaps clarifies his arrival: "Middleton arrived
by train at 8 a.m. and took breakfast at the Julian. . . . He and his
horses left for Freeport on the Illinois Central at noon. 'Doc' says
he will ride from Freeport and will finish with the leaders."
25 *Chicago Tribune*, June 27, 1893; *Chicago Daily News*, June 26,
1893; both stories datelined Freeport.
26 *Chicago Herald*, June 27, 1893.
27 *Chicago Herald*, June 28, 1893.
28 *O'Neill Frontier*, June 22, 1893.
29 *Chicago Daily News*, June 26, 1893.
30 *Omaha Daily Bee*, June 28, 1893. The *Chicago Tribune* (June 28,

1893) calculated the final twenty-four-hour distance at 130 miles.
31 *Chicago Tribune,* June 28, 1893; *Chicago Daily Inter Ocean,* June 29, 1893.
32 *Chicago Herald,* July 2, 1893; *Chicago Tribune,* July 2, 1893.
33 *Chicago Daily Inter Ocean,* June 30, 1893.

CHAPTER 16:   FAMILY

1 C. H. Frady, "Fifty Years Gospel Giving on the Frontier," *Nebraska History,* vol. 10, no. 4, p. 274n; Sheldon, editor of *Nebraska History,* incorporated his comments in a note to Frady's autobiographical account.
2 *Valentine Pioneer Grip,* April 19, 1895; *Seward Weekly Reporter,* April 18, 1895.
3 *Long Pine Republican Journal,* September 15, 1899.
4 Gillespie County records and General Land Office records.
5 Gillespie County court records.
6 Interview by author with Mrs. Jessie M. Bryant, daughter of John Shepherd; at the time of the interview Mrs. Bryant was living at Clinton, Oklahoma, but she has since died.
7 The Will of Mary Cherry, Blanco County records, Johnson City, Texas.
8 Fredericksburg was settled in 1846 by German families. The landmark Vereins Kirche was completed the following year. It was a striking round (octagonal) building constructed of logs and stones; it had a conical roof with a watchtower and bell at the peak. The structure served as combination church, school, town hall, and fort. Fredericksburg held a gala 50th anniversary celebration in 1896, but shortly afterward the Vereins Kirche was torn down because of decay, crumbling walls, and lack or interest and funds to restore it. In 1934 a replica of the original Vereins Kirche was built, about 200 yards from the old site; it is a museum.
9 Interview by author with Mrs. Geraldine Henson, Dallas, Texas.
10 National Archives, War Records Branch.
11 According to information supplied by Mrs. Henson, James' (Doc's) first wife (the "Lizzy" mentioned in his letters) and their child died some time after James' flight north. This is the belief in the family, but there is nothing more known about it. Many mysteries remain. Maybe the child did survive. If so, are there descendants? One of Middleton's sons was quoted in a newspaper as stating that the "old man" had at one time been married to two women at once. Would this have meant the Texas wife and Mary? How much did he confide to his sons? His daughter, with whom I talked on

various occasions, had heard no mention of family at all except the vague reference to a brother, and she could scarcely believe her father's name had ever been anything but Middleton. On the other hand, among the four branches of the Texas family that I located and interviewed, only Claude Riley, son of Joe, knew of the Middleton name. This certainly suggests that whatever communication existed between Doc Middleton and his Texas relatives in later years must have been small.

12 Interview by author with Claude Riley; also with Don McCormick, of Eldorado, Texas, who remembered the Riley family.

13 The records of the United States Pension Agency (National Archives) show that Nancy C. Riley was last paid at $8 a month to February 4, 1907 and was dropped because of death. The cemetary lot in Eldorado is known but the space is not. Whether there was contact between her and her son James during these last years we do not know. Middleton's daughter did not appear to have any knowledge of her grandmother, though she was thirteen at the time of Nancy Riley's death.

CHAPTER 17:   ARDMORE, SOUTH DAKOTA

1 I substituted the name "John" in this story in deference to family members still living; and in deference to the reader's sensibilities, I eliminated Tom Richardson's colorful description of just how badly Wesley beat up John.

2 Newspaper items, her obituary, and Fall River County probate records use the name Irene when referring to Mrs. D. C. Middleton; and it will be remembered that the Middletons named a daughter Ruth Irene. The Census of 1880 gave her name as Arrena. But she was known throughout most of her life as Rene (rhymes with keen).

3 Presumably "these four little houses" refers to Doc Middleton's property in Ardmore; see note #4.

4 Fall River County records, Hot Springs, South Dakota. Middleton was granted the letters of administration and bond was set at $1,000. About twenty documents were made and filed on January 12, 1912. Three Ardmore properties were listed—one vacant lot and two lots with frame buildings on them. In the initial estate proceedings the value of real estate was given as $1,850. Before the closing this was revised downward twice; the lots with houses on them were valued then at $375. Finally, the total price received for all real estate was $370; the total claims against said real estate were noted as $370. See Epilogue.

CHAPTER 18: DOUGLAS, WYOMING

1 Reprinted from the *Douglas Enterprise,* December 3, 1913 (italics added).

CHAPTER 19: OBITUARY

1 This is a great exaggeration. There is no absolute certainty that the killings enumerated in this book comprise the total, but they are probably close.
2 There is no evidence of Middleton's involvement in a cattle rustling operation, with the possible exception of the one on Holt Creek.
3 Error.
4 Here the Hoodoos or the Hoodoo gang are the outlaws whom the vigilantes are pursuing. In Texas the vigilantes were the Hoodoos. For the latter see C. L. Sonnichsen, *Ten Texas Feuds,* Chapter 5, "The Hoodoo War": Cattle rustling provoked a vigilante committee into action in Mason County, Texas in 1875, but things got out of hand and lawless terrorism reigned in the county for almost two years, focused largely around an ethnic feud between Germans and "Americans." Sonnichsen calls our attention to the fact that Southern Negroes used to call Ku Klux Klan members Hoodoos and that "Lee Hall's Texas Rangers down on the Rio Grande had earned the same title." (p. 89) The word was also used as a handle by a few colorful Westerners, most notably Dodge City's Hyman G. Neill, known as Hoodoo Brown (Nyle H. Miller and Joseph W. Snell, *Great Gunfighters of the Kansas Cowtowns, 1867-1886,* p. 322). Also known as Hoodoo Brown was the Kansas road rancher George W. Brown. (Harry E. Chrisman, *Lost Trails of the Cimarron, pp.* 22-26, 294). Also, we can recall the 1891 *Sioux City Journal* article about a local character of questionable reputation being "ostracised as a hoodoo" (supra, p. 172) and the O'Neill newspaper columnist in 1893 who concluded that "the world must be a hoodoo." (supra, p. 186) Running through all these uses there is a negative or jinxed or bad luck quality. For other examples of similar usage see Mitford M. Mathews, *A Dictionary of Americanisms* or William A. Craigie and James R. Hulbert, *A Dictionary of American English.*
5 Another tall tale.
6 Hazen was neither a captain nor a gun fighter of note.
7 There were no cases called against Middleton involving rustling of cattle and very few for theft of horses; the one in Wyoming for which he was sentenced and the single theft in Antelope County,

Nebraska are all I have found after years of exhaustive research.

8 This could well be true.

9 Kid Wade was guilty of plenty of thefts. Some of the vigilantes were not exactly a credit to the group, but some were excellent citizens. It is not true that the majority were rotten to the core.

10 This alleged occurrence has no resemblance to anything I have come across.

11 This is another tall story, probably suggested by the chase after the shooting of Joe Smith.

12 Almost certainly another tall tale.

13 This is perhaps a curious combination of snippets from Middleton's life. He *did* serve eight months in prison at Huntsville, Texas for theft, before he escaped. He *did* lose a finger in an accident at the Nebraska Penitentiary. And certainly he *was* involved in more than one saloon brawl.

14 Another exaggeration. Middleton killed only James Keefe.

15 If Middleton lived at any of these places it was for a short time only, and I have not discovered it.

EPILOGUE

1 This was John's second marriage, his first wife, Sarah, having died some years earlier. At the turn of the century he married Dora Bell McCumber, and in 1903 they had a daughter, Loreatha.

2 Information about the Shepherd pamphlet comes from family members, who say that he mailed out over a thousand copies of the pamphlet which argued his case about the naming of the Chisholm Trail. However, the family has no copy of the pamphlet and no record of its title or date of publication; nor does the Old Trail Drivers Association of Texas (letter to author from J. J. McConnell, secretary, July 12, 1961). With the help of librarians and booksellers I have searched for a copy but have found none. Inasmuch as J. Frank Dobie interviewed Shepherd (supra, pp. 19-20) in 1938 and wrote an article about him and other articles about old trail driving days and about the Chisholm Trail, it seems reasonable to assume that Dobie would have had a copy of Shepherd's pamphlet; however, a search by the curator of the Dobie Collection at the University of Texas failed to turn up a copy. Of course, the pamphlet was likely small, and this ephemera could well be lost to us. On the other hand, the family might be wrong. On July 8, 1932 John Shepherd wrote a letter about the Chisholm Trail to George Saunders of the Old Trail Drivers Association (Wayne Gard, *The Chisholm Trail,* p. 266). Perhaps during the years, in

the telling of stories about grandfather, etc., this letter got inadvertently transformed into a pamphlet. I just do not know for sure. The Shepherd letter is as elusive as the pamphlet. Gard is not certain where he originally researched the document, but he says: "I must have seen either the original letter or an exact copy of it or I wouldn't have listed it in my bibliography." (letter, July 3, 1973) The letter cannot be found in the Dobie Collection or elsewhere at the University of Texas, at the Texas State Library, or among archives of the Old Trail Drivers Association in San Antonio.

APPENDIX B: DOC MIDDLETON'S ANCESTORS

1 Spanish Archives, General Land Office, Austin, Texas.
2 Crockett Riley, Riley letters, author's collection.
3 This is a family legend among the Riley descendants. It could be true, but I have found no other authentication. The story was originally related in a letter to me from Mrs. Nannie Riley Streigler of Fredericksburg, Texas. Mrs. Streigler is a daughter of George Riley, a son of James Riley, Sr. Riley letters, author's collection.
4 General Land Office, Austin, Texas.
5 Cherry family Bible and letter to author from Mrs. Geraldine Henson, Dallas. See note #10 for Chapter 2.
6 Letter to author from Mrs. Streigler, Fredericksburg. Doc's stepfather, J. B. Riley, had a brother and sister named David Crockett and Louisa Jane, and also children with these same names.
7 Riley's claim for the last of his pay for services rendered to the Republic is in the Public Debt papers, Texas State Archives, Austin.
8 War Records Branch, National Archives.

APPENDIX C: DOC MIDDLETON DEFENDS HIS NAME

1 "Two Remarkable Men" (Doc Middleton and W. H. H. Llewellyn), *Illustrated Police News,* November 8, 1884, p. 7. The only known copy of this issue is in the Rare Book Room, Library of Congress. Frank L. Mott says that while the *"National Police Gazette . . .* was to be found in nearly all barbershops and barrooms throughout the length and breadth of the country[, t]he Boston *Illustrated Police News* was similar to its New York contemporary, but had only a sectional circulation." (*A History of American Magazines,* vol. IV, p. 372) Obviously in Doc's case the *Police News* got outside its section, or else he read a reprint of the article somewhere, perhaps in a Nebraska newspaper.

Bibliography

BOOKS

Books offer little direct aid in researching Doc Middleton (for discussion of this point see Appendix A, which the publisher asked me to write). The items below are helpful primarily for setting the context or for only brief mentions of Middleton.

Bartlett, I. S. *History of Wyoming.* Chicago: S. J. Clarke Publishing Co., 1918.

Bratt, John. *Trails of Yesterday.* Lincoln: University Publishing Co., 1921.

Bronson, Edgar Beecher. *Cowboy Life on the Western Plains: The Reminiscences of a Ranchman.* New York: Grosset & Dunlap, 1910.

————. *The Red-Blooded.* Chicago: A. C. McClurg & Co., 1910.

Brown, Jesse and A. M. Willard. *The Black Hills Trails.* Rapid City: Rapid City Journal Co., 1924.

Butcher, S. D. *Pioneer History of Custer County.* Chicago: Sage Books, 1965.

Chaffin, Lorah B. *Sons of the West.* Caldwell: Caxton Printers, 1941.

Chrisman, Harry E. *The Ladder of Rivers: The Story of I. P. (Print) Olive.* Chicago: Sage Books, 1965.

————. *Lost Trails of the Cimarron.* Chicago: Sage Books, 1964.

Crawford, Lewis F. *Rekindling Camp Fires: The Exploits of Ben Arnold (Connor).* Bismarck: Capital Book Co., 1926.

Cook, James H. *Fifty Years on the Old Frontier as Cowboy, Hunter, Guide, Scout, and Ranchman.* Norman: University of Oklahoma Press, 1954.

Danker, Donald F. (ed.). *Man of the Plains: Recollections of Luther North, 1856-1882.* Lincoln: University of Nebraska Press, 1961.

Dewhurst, Henry S. *The Railroad Police.* Springfield, Illinois: Charles C. Thomas, 1955.

Duval, John C. *The Adventures of Big-foot Wallace, the Texas Ranger and Hunter.* Macon, Georgia: J. W. Burke & Co., 1885.

Erskine, Gladys Shaw. *Broncho Charlie.* New York: Thomas Y. Crowell, 1934.

Frink, Maurice. *Cow Country Cavalcade: Eighty Years of the Wyoming Stock Growers Association.* Denver: Old West Publishing Co., 1954.

Fulton, Frances Sims. *To and Through Nebraska.* Lincoln: Journal Co., 1884.

Greer, James Kimmins. *Colonel Jack Hays: Texas Frontier Leader and California Builder.* New York: E. P. Dutton, 1952.

Hicks, John Edward. *Adventures of a Tramp Printer, 1880-1890.* Kansas City: Midamericana Press, 1950.

Hunt, Frazier. *The Long Trail from Texas.* New York: Doubleday, Doran & Co., 1940.

Hunter, J. Marvin (ed.) *Trail Drivers of Texas.* (n.p.) 1920.

Huntington, Bill. *Good Men and Salty Cusses.* Billings: Western Livestock Reporter Press, 1952.

Jackson, Donald. *Custer's Gold: The United States Cavalry of 1874.* New Haven: Yale University Press, 1966.

Jennings, Napoleon A. *A Texas Ranger.* New York: Charles Scribner's Sons, 1899.

Johnson, J. R. *Representative Nebraskans.* Lincoln: Johnsen Publishing Co., 1954.

Kelsey, D. M. *History of Our Wild West*. Chicago: Charles C. Thompson Co., 1901.

Larson, T. A. *History of Wyoming*. Lincoln: University of Nebraska Press, 1965.

Leach, A. J. *A History of Antelope County Nebraska from Its First Settlement in 1868 to the Close of the Year 1883*. Chicago: R. R. Donnelley & Sons, 1909.

Lemmon, G. E. *Developing the West* [reprints from *Belle Fourche Bee*] (n.p., n.d.)

Lichty, Kathryne L. *A History of the Settlement of Nebraska Sandhills* [unpublished MA thesis]. Cheyenne: University of Wyoming, 1960.

Leonard, Elizabeth Jane and Julia Cody Goodman. *Buffalo Bill, King of the Old West: Biography of William F. Cody, Pony Express Rider, Buffalo Hunter, Plains Scout & Guide, Master Showman*. New York: Library Publishers, 1955.

Miller, Nyle H. and Joseph W. Snell. *Great Gunfighters of the Kansas Cowtowns, 1867-1886*. Lincoln University of Nebraska Press, 1963.

O'Reilly, Harrington. *Fifty Years on the Trail*. London: Chatto & Windus, 1889.

Parker, Watson. *Gold in the Black Hills*. Norman: University of Oklahoma Press, 1966.

Prassel, Frank R. *The Western Peace Officer: A Legacy of Law and Order*. Norman: University of Oklahoma Press, 1972.

Russell, Don. *The Lives and Legends of Buffalo Bill*. Norman: University of Oklahoma Press, 1960.

————. *The Wild West or, A History of the Wild West Shows. . . .* Fort Worth: Amon Carter Museum, 1970.

Sell, Henry Blackman and Victor Weybright. *Buffalo Bill and the Wild West*. New York: Oxford University Press, 1955.

Sheldon, Addison Erwin. *Nebraska Old and New*. Lincoln: University Publishing Co., 1937.

Sonnichsen, C. L. *I'll Die Before I'll Run: The Story of the Great Feuds of Texas*. New York: Harper & Bros., 1951.

————. *Ten Texas Feuds*. Albuquerque: University of New Mexico Press, 1957.

Spindler, Will Henry. *Rim of the Sandhills.* Mitchell, S.D.; Educator Supply Co., 1941.

Spring, Agnes Wright. *The Cheyenne and Black Hills Stage and Express Routes.* Glendale: Arthur H. Clark Co., 1949.

Tibbles, Thomas Henry. *Buckskin and Blanket Days.* Garden City: Doubleday & Co., 1957.

Walsh, Richard John. *The Making of Buffalo Bill.* Indianapolis: Bobbs-Merrill, 1928.

Webb, Walter Prescott. *The Texas Rangers: A Century of Frontier Defense.* Boston: Houghton Mifflin, 1935.

Westermeier, Clifford Peter. *Trailing the Cowboy: His Life and Lore As Told by Frontier Journalists.* Caldwell: Caxton Printers, 1955.

Wheeler, Homer Webster. *Buffalo Days: Forty Years in the Old West.* Indianapolis: Bobbs-Merrill, 1925.

———. *The Frontier Trail or, From Cowboy to Colonel.* Los Angeles: Times-Mirror Press, 1923.

Yost, Nellie Snyder (ed.). *Boss Cowman: The Recollections of Ed Lemmon, 1857-1946.* Lincoln: University of Nebraska Press, 1969.

DIARY, MANUSCRIPTS, TYPESCRIPT, AND MAGAZINE ARTICLES

Cook, James H. "Early Days in Ogalalla [sic]." *Nebraska History,* vol. 14, no. 2.

Deahl, William E., Jr. "The Chadron-Chicago 1,000-Mile Cowboy Race." *Nebraska History,* vol. 53, no. 2.

Dobie, J. Frank. "On the Trail in '66." *Frontier Times,* Fall 1958.

"Early History of Cheyenne and Kimball Counties." *Nebraska History,* vol. 7, no. 1.

Frady, C. H. "Fifty Years Gospel Giving on the Frontier" (entitled in the table of contents for the magazine: "Forty Years Frontiering as a Nebraska Sunday School Missionary"). *Nebraska History,* vol. 10, no. 4.

Long diary; see note #9 for Chapter 7 for details.

Richardson interview typescript; see Appendix A for details.
Sly manuscript; see note #1 for Chapter 15 for details.
Tienken memoirs manuscript; see note #9 for Chapter 5 for details.

NEWSPAPERS

If a newspaper changed its name during the span of Doc Middleton's life, I chose for citation purposes one title for that paper and used it uniformly throughout the book, trying to settle on the title most appropriate for the period covered. For example, the *Oakdale Pen and Plow* began in April 1877 with that name which lasted for two years, at which time it was changed to *Elkhorn Pen and Plow;* in October 1883 it was changed to *Oakdale Journal,* between January 1887 and February 1891 it was *Oakdale Pen and Plow* again, and for the last two months of its life (March and April 1891) it was *Oakdale Journal* once more.

Alliance Times-Herald, Alliance, Nebraska
Bill Barlow's Budget, Douglas, Wyoming
Chadron Citizen, Chadron, Nebraska
Cheyenne Daily Leader, Cheyenne, Wyoming
Cheyenne Sun, Cheyenne, Wyoming
Chicago Daily Inter Ocean, Chicago, Illinois
Chicago Daily News, Chicago, Illinois
Chicago Herald, Chicago, Illinois
Chicago Times, Chicago, Illinois
Chicago Tribune, Chicago, Illinois
Crawford Tribune, Crawford, Nebraska
Dawes County Journal, Chadron, Nebraska
Douglas Enterprise, Douglas, Wyoming
Fort Worth Star-Telegram, Fort Worth, Texas
Fremont Herald, Fremont, Nebraska
Gordon Journal, Gordon, Nebraska
Gordon Press, Gordon, Nebraska
Hammon Advocate, Hammon, Oklahoma
Harrison Sun, Harrison, Nebraska

Long Pine Republican Journal, Long Pine, Nebraska
New York Times, New York, New York
Niobrara Pioneer, Niobrara, Nebraska
North Nebraska Eagle, Dakota City, Nebraska
Oakdale Pen and Plow, Oakdale, Nebraska
Omaha Daily Bee, Omaha, Nebraska
Omaha Daily Herald, Omaha, Nebraska
O'Neill Frontier, O'Neill, Nebraska
Rio Grande Republican, Las Cruces, New Mexico
St. Louis Post-Dispatch, St. Louis, Missouri
Seward Weekly Reporter, Seward, Nebraska
Sidney Telegraph, Sidney, Nebraska
Sioux City Weekly Journal, Sioux City, Iowa
Valentine Pioneer Grip, Valentine, Nebraska
West Point Progress, West Point, Nebraska
Wichita Falls Record-News, Wichita Falls, Texas
Yankton Press and Dakotian, Yankton, South Dakota

Index

Italic numeral indicates illustration following that page.

203-05

Daggett, Dr. M. H., 126, 128
Dakota County, Neb., 171, 173
Dahlman, James, *202*
Davis, Jim, 81
Davis, Mrs. Jim, 81
Davis Junction, Ill., 189
Dawes County, Neb., 175
Dawson County, Neb., 91
Deadwood, S. D., 2, 132, 195, 205, 220
De Kalb, Ill., 176
Denison, Tex., 14, 25
Denver, Colo., 180
Devens, Charles, 105
Dewey, Dr., 189
Dickerson, Will, 46, 82, 141
Dixon, Ill., 189
Dobie, J. Frank, 19
Dodd, Howard, 199
Dodge City, Ks., 21, 25-26, 29, 31
Donaldson, Jess, 154
Douglas, Dave, 180, 184-85
Douglas, John W., 53
Douglas, Wyo., 206-09, 210-11, 214, 220
Draper, George A. (Sheriff), 139-40, 143
Drennan, R. F., 222
Drexel, Fred, 45
Dubuque, Ia., 176, 188
Duff, Col. James, 10
Dufrand, Phil, 69-70
Duncan, Ariz., 197
Dutcher, Orlando, 53
Duval, Claude, 73
Dyersville, Ia., 188

Eagle Creek (Neb.), 42. *See* Little Platte
Earlville, Ia., 188
East Laughing Water (Neb.), 119. *See* Laughing Water
Edgemont, S. D., 204
Edwards, Mary E., 12. *See* Mrs. James M. Riley
Eisley, George, 132, 244-45, 254n5
Eldorado, Tex., 197-98, 225-27, 232

Elk City, Okla., 225
Elkhorn River (Neb.), 40-41, 45, 48-49, 76, 87, 107, 114-16, 121, 135-36
Elkhorn Valley (Neb.), 39, 42, 47, 76, 100, 108, 150, 160, 192
Ellsworth, Ks., 24
Elmore, Mike, 180, 185
Eppelt, Pvt., 93
Erlenmeyer, Mr., 37
Ewing, James, 82
Ewing, Neb., 82

Ferris, Bob, 98
Ferritor, Robert, 247n2
Ferry, Neb., 97. *See* Carns
Feuchs, William, 56-57
Fitch boys, 70-71
Foley, Justice, 171
Fontaine, Paul, 181, 185, 190-91
Fort Dodge, Ia., 176, 188
Fort Gibson, Tex., 10, 22
Fort Hartsuff, Neb., 50, 66, 89, 92, 121, 126, 132, 244
Fort Laramie, Wyo., 106, 251n2
Fort Madison, Ia., 28-29, 103
Fort McKavett, Tex., 197
Fort Niobrara, Neb., 56, 151
Fort Robinson, Neb., 7, 28, 92, 105, 212, 244
Fort Worth, Tex., 22
Fort Zarah, Ks., 23, 24, 226
Fox, Fred J., 100-01
Franklin, F. J. (alias Mr. Barto), 42, 46, 58-64, 77, 242
Franklin, Mrs. F. J., 64
Fredericksburg, Tex., 10-11, 197
Freeport, Ill., 176, 188-89
Frémont, John C., 21
Fremont, Elkhorn & Missouri Valley Railroad, 39, 165
Frenchtown, Neb., 114
Fugate, Charles (alias), 36, 62-63, 65-68, 136, 165, 199, 243. *See* Texas Charley (nickname), William Riley
Furay, Maj. John B., 216

Galva, Ia., 176

Mabry, Seth, 45
Mackey, Lydia Hill. *See*
  Mrs. Joseph Riley
Maher, John G., 175-76
Mallon, Jack, 32
Malloy, Judge William, 97
Manchester, Ia., 176, 188
Martin, John A. (Deputy Sheriff),
  139-40, 143
Martinsburg, Tex., 36-37, 231
Mason, A., 59, 61
Mason County, Tex., 150, 197, 231
Massachusetts Society for the
  Prevention of Cruelty to
  Animals, 177, 189, 191
Matagorda County, Tex., 12
Mattoon, Ill., 22
May, Eva, 157
May, Mattie, 157
McAlister, J. J., 171, 172, 174
McCann, M. F., 45, 56-7, 65, 92
McCumber, Dora Bell, 225, 270n1.
  See Mrs. John D. Shepherd
McFarling, James, 41, 63, 72, 77, 79
McGillycuddy, Dr. V. T., 92, 94
McMillan, Mr., 205
McMullen, James, 131
McNeil Island (Wash.), 224
Mead, H. D., 179
Means, George, 79
Means, Lauren (son of George
  Means), 252n3, 256n10
Mercer, Dr. Samuel D., 216
Mexican War, 232, 238
Middle Loup river (Neb.), 51, 66
Middleton, David C., 26; D. C.
  Middleton name used in marriage
  to Rene Richardson, 156; 205;
  210-11. *See* Doc Middleton
Middleton, David Wesley (Doc
  Middleton's son), 165, 194, *196,*
  201-02, *202,* 203-04, 207, 210-11,
  212, 223-25
Middleton, Mrs. David Wesley,
  202, 203, 224-25
Middleton, Mrs. D. C. (nee Mary
  Richardson, Doc Middleton's
  second wife, legal married name:
  Mrs. James M. Sheppard), *96,*
  97-99, 111, 113,

133-34, 135-37, 141, 147, 149,
  156, 159, 168, 244-45
Middleton, Mrs. D. C. (nee Rene
  Richardson, Doc Middleton's
  third wife), 155-59, *158,* 164,
  167-68, 193-94, 196, *196, 202,*
  203-05, 222
Middleton, Doc (alias), murder by,
  4-7; jailed, 28, 30, 139, 146;
  hideouts, 43-44; near captures or
  deaths, 52, 59, 71, 118ff;
  called a "Robin Hood
  type," 82; called a "Rob Roy of
  the Sand Hills," 86; second
  marriage (to Mary Richardson),
  96-98; last capture, 133-35; third
  marriage (to Rene Richardson),
  156; lived in: Stuart, Neb., 159;
  Blair, Neb., 161; Valentine, Neb.,
  161; Gordon, Neb., 161ff;
  Chadron, Neb., 175, 192;
  Crawford, Neb., 195-96;
  Oelrichs, S. D., 196; Ardmore,
  S. D., 196, 199ff; Douglas, Wyo.,
  206ff; other towns (?), 220;
  birth of: daughter (Lulu B.),
  163; son (David Wesley), 165;
  son (Joseph William), 165; *168;*
  190; rider in Chadron-Chicago
  horse race, 180, 183ff; daughter
  (Ruth Irene), 193; son (Henry
  Thomas), 196; *196; 202;* death,
  211. *See* James M. Riley
Middleton, Henry (Harry) Thomas
  (Doc Middleton's son), 196, *202,*
  211-12, 222-23
Middleton, Joseph William (Willie,
  Bill) (Doc Middleton's son),
  165, 194, *196,* 201, 202, *202,* 204,
  211-12, 223-25
Middleton, Lulu B. (Doc
  Middleton's daughter), 163-64,
  167
Middleton, Mr. (Tex.), 9
Middleton, Ruth Irene (Doc
  Middleton's daughter), 193-94,
  196, *196, 202,* 204-05, 211, 213,
  222
Middleton, Vera, *202*
Middleton, William (Uncle Bill,

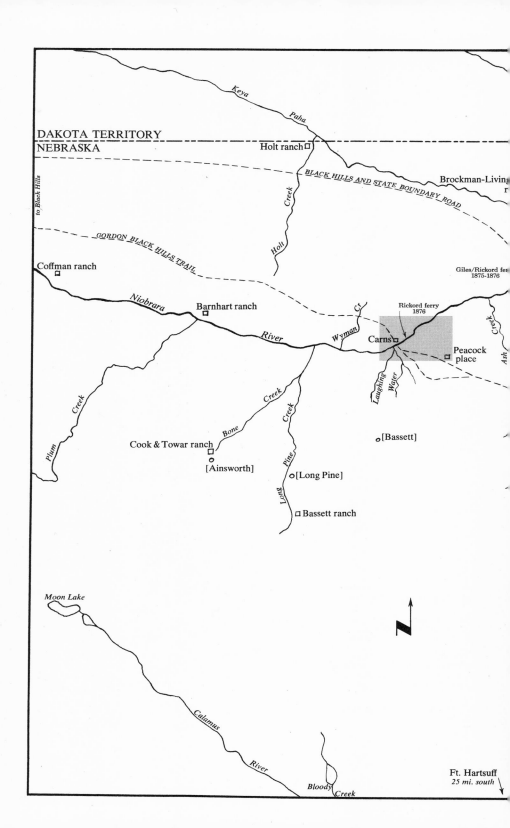